ABUNDANCE NOW

ABUNDANCE
NOW

Amplify Your Life and Achieve Prosperity Today

LISA NICHOLS
AND JANET SWITZER

Foreword by Steve Harvey

DEY ST.
AN IMPRINT OF WILLIAM MORROW *PUBLISHERS*

HarperCollins books may be purchased for educational, business, or sales promotional use. For information please e-mail the Special Markets Department at SPsales@harpercollins.com.

A hardcover edition of this book was published in 2016 by Dey Street Books, an imprint of William Morrow Publishers.

FIRST DEY STREET BOOKS PAPERBACK EDITION PUBLISHED 2016.

Designed by Shannon Nicole Plunkett

Library of Congress Cataloging-in-Publication Data has been applied for.

ISBN 978-0-06-241221-8

18 19 20 OV/RRD 10 9 8 7 6

I dedicate this book to my son, Jelani.
You've ridden this ever-eventful roller coaster with me.
You have selflessly shared me as I've pursued my outrageous
dream of infecting the planet with possibility. You've loved
me despite the endless long trips, the 19-hour workdays,
and the hundreds of thousands of people who've moved in
and out of our lives. You are one of the kindest people
I've ever been blessed to know.

I promised you at eight months old that I would
make our lives better. Thank you for always believing
in me and my promise to you. I'm honored to call you
my son and grateful to call you my friend.

CONTENTS

CHAPTER 4

The Third E: Engagement in Your Work for More Than Financial Reward 164

CHAPTER 5

The Fourth E: Endowment for a Beautiful Future   204

CHAPTER 6
Activating Future Abundance in the Present Moment   256

FOREWORD

"Why do people resist transformation?" That was a question I asked Lisa Nichols when she was a guest on my television show. I had been wondering how I might get my message through to people so they could benefit from it.

Several months earlier, I'd asked Lisa to coach me on building a self-development division of my company. Having used strategies for personal success to build my career in radio, comedy, and television, I wanted to help my audience and radio listeners with information that could change their lives, too.

Over the past year and a half, Lisa has helped me do just that.

When I listen to Lisa, I'm just in awe of her wisdom. When she lays out the system for achieving a rich and abundant life, I see the audience creep to the edge of their seats. When she explains how you should answer your unique calling, and then gives you a step-by-step process to implement it, I see people take massive notes. And when she inspires them to know that it's possible, things get explosive.

Man, her words just make *so much sense.*

And then when Lisa tells her own story of filling out paperwork at the government assistance office, I think, *Lots of us have something similar that threatens to stop us.* It might not be food stamps or public assistance for you, but it could be a crazy childhood, or lack of knowledge or direction, or one bad situation that threatens to take you out of the game for good.

You realize that you've got to *do something* to step out of lifelessness and step into greatness.

In my own life, I can pinpoint this realization to its exact date: October 8, 1985.

I was 27 years old and selling life insurance door-to-door. I was very good at making the sale, but I stunk at the follow-up. I didn't really like the product I was selling, and once it came in, I was embarrassed to deliver it to the buyer. But I had a young family. I had responsibilities at home.

I was also not in a good place personally. I wasn't happy because I hadn't discovered my purpose or my mission in life. I was sad all the time—primarily because I knew my life had to be more than this. I never felt fulfilled. I was always incomplete. Every day, I felt like I was trying to figure things out.

Then one day, I heard something that shook me to my core.

At the time, I happened to be writing jokes for a comedian friend of mine named A.J. Jamal. I had no idea what he was doing with the jokes, but over and over he would ask me to write some more. Eventually, he started paying me $10 per joke. Now keep in mind, I had no idea what he was doing with these jokes, until one day he told me he was performing at a private comedy club using the jokes I had written. Up until that point, I wasn't a professional comedian. I'd never been onstage as a stand-up comic or worked in a comedy club. I didn't even know they existed. But since A.J. appreciated the fact that I was his writer, this side gig of writing jokes went on for another year and a half.

Then, it just so happened I was at A.J.'s house and this woman came over named Gladys Jacobs. When she learned who I was, she said, "Oh, you're the guy that's been writing the jokes for A.J."

Frankly, I was surprised she knew who I was.

My chest puffed out a little and I was feeling pretty good about myself until she asked me the question that shook me to the core.

"Why don't you tell these jokes yourself?" she said.

I was frozen for a moment until the emotions began to rush in on me. I was excited. But I was also confused. *Tell the jokes where?* I thought. *Tell them to who? Why would anyone want to hear my jokes?*

It was my I-don't-know-what-I-don't-know moment.

You might have had one of these yourself in your own life. For instance, have you ever discovered that, even though *you* don't think much of what you're doing, it's incredibly impactful to somebody else?

The fact that my jokes were valuable and stage-worthy—and that I should be delivering them onstage *myself*—was a message that I didn't even know I needed.

It was like Gladys poured water on a dry seed, and that seed started to grow like crazy.

Maybe you, too, have had someone see something in you that you've never seen in yourself. Maybe you, too, have had someone try to show you your possibility, but you've got blinders on.

How many of us, when faced with our big break—our ticket to the abundant life—react the same exact way?

Just like I asked Lisa Nichols recently on my show: Why do some people resist transformation?

Maybe you know deep down what you want, but you're waiting for confirmation. Maybe you *do* have an inkling of what's ahead of you, but you're waiting for someone to validate you, help you claim your greatness, and give you permission to soar.

That's what Lisa Nichols will do for you in this powerful new book.

Now, you've got to know that my girl is candid, very transparent, and going to get in your face a bit. That's the way she rolls and shows us that she cares.

The thing is, you have abundance waiting inside of you, *right now*. You have the seed of greatness waiting for a little bit of water to rain down on you. All you need is a guiding hand, like Lisa's, to help you navigate through your start.

Don't resist the transformation that's on deck for your life. Don't limit yourself in any way. You *can* have the riches, you *can* have the lifestyle, you *can* have the community, you *can* have that love relationship, you *can* have abundance—you can have everything you want, *NOW*.

—Steve Harvey

INTRODUCTION

> Living a life that you love and loving the life that you are
> living is the truest demonstration of abundance.
> —Lisa Nichols

There hasn't been a day in the last three years that I haven't gasped a little or felt a tingle in my belly as I walk into the lobby of my corporate offices in Carlsbad, California. Today is a special day. I'm here—in town briefly between speaking engagements and media appearances—to sign my name to some documents that are the culmination of a 17-year dream.

As I step just inside the front entrance, I pause—still feeling a bit amazed by all that's happened over the last two decades. Our reception area, thankfully, is a restful, introspective place—graced with the soothing sound of a flowing fountain, the aroma of lavender candles, and the smooth melody of cool jazz playing low in the background. It's designed in the same color scheme as my living room at home—warm oranges, healing yellows, soft gold, and winter creams—all colors that I studied for their restorative properties and connecting feel. I feel comfortable here. And blessed. Especially when I pause and reflect on the monumental canvas before me—a gift from my staff of a soulful, reflective picture of me, praying after spending eight hours in Nelson Mandela's jail cell.

My life has been a journey.

Yet I wonder, *What else is before me?*, as I slowly make my way to my office, reflecting on the abundance that I've received so far. There, on my desk awaiting me, are the documents I've come to the office to sign: a stack of stock certificates imprinted at the top. *Motivating The Masses Inc.,* they say.

I've taken my company public.

At the same time, I've also become one of only two African American women founders to take her own company public. A part of me feels it's all a bit like Monopoly. There are thousands—millions—of shares that I'm signing my name to as CEO. But another part of me knows intimately the road I've traveled—and that it's been one filled with both huge wins and considerable losses.

This is very real, I think to myself.

It's time to get back to work.

FROM PUBLIC ASSISTANCE TO GOING PUBLIC

What does it take to overcome decades of confusion, pain, betrayal, and hardship—and step into clarity, passion, perseverance, and accomplishment?

Compared to my early years, my life today is barely recognizable. It includes sitting beside Oprah, laughing and talking with her during the commercial breaks—then, within weeks, sitting across from Larry King, watching his eyebrow lift at something I've said that (I believe) truly inspires him as a man and not just a host. It includes holding Steve Harvey's hands as we pray together backstage before stepping out onto the platform at the Essence Festival before more than 7,000 hungry, excited people.

Or getting that second phone call in a month to appear on the *Today* show as their Breakthrough Coach.

It's gratifying to experience the rock-star receptions and enormous love that I receive when I speak in Taipei, Bali, Thailand, Johannesburg, and Kazakhstan. I'm blown away that these audiences even know who I am or have even studied my work—since many don't even speak English. Each one of these experiences still feels new to me—even though I've been on this track since 2007 when the video and book *The Secret*—in which I was a featured teacher—became a worldwide phenomenon.

More dominant in my memory, regrettably, is the day in 1994 when I found myself standing in line at the government assistance office on Century Boulevard in Los Angeles—feeling humiliated and shamed as I filled out the application to get food stamps for me and my unborn baby. In the dark years to follow, I found myself broke—and broken—standing in the WIC (Women, Infants, and Children) line, embarrassed but grateful for the free cheese, milk, and pasta that allowed me to feed my young son, Jelani. I didn't have enough money in those days to make it through to the next month—so a pot of spaghetti or beanies-and-weenies, divided into six meals, had to last Jelani and me all week.

My brokenness only intensified when my son's father, for whom I had a special love, phoned one day in August and said, "Lisa, I'm in jail."

Jelani was just eight months old.

Soon, my "bad" went to worse as, year after year, I hoped he would be released from prison to at least father the son we had created. Even after I had given up on any chance of us being a couple again, three, five, ten years went by with no sign of parole. I secretly hoped, but publicly denounced, any affiliation with him, as 10, 15, 20 years went by—and counting.

Though I am finally at peace, my son is now dealing with the emotions surrounding a father who's imprisoned.

In those dark days, abundance and prosperity seemed very far away. But I discovered a resilience—and a perspective—that carried me through.

By 2009, I had been interviewed more than 150 times in just a five-month period when my book *No Matter What!* was released in stores. That book is a surprisingly transparent story of my personal journey, which led most of the interviewers to ask, "Lisa, how did you do it? How did you go from being on government assistance to building a multimillion-dollar business?"

For the sake of time, I often answered in a speedy way—trivializing the journey in two- to four-minute sound bites. "Well, it's focus," I would answer generically. Or "It comes from being passionate about my life."

Frankly, the rich and rewarding life I now enjoy—and the story of how it came to be—got somewhat lost in the book's emphasis on overcoming the obstacles in my past. And after the book tour was over, I knew inside that I had never really—I mean *really*—shared what it took to transform my life into something breathtaking, prosperous, and compelling. I simply hadn't recounted the process, shared the wisdom I had learned, or inspired the actions of others to easily achieve prosperity by following the same formula that I did.

What I have yet to share is the story of how I broke through from scarcity to abundance. And that is where this book begins.

MINDSET, APPLICATION, AND INTENTION IS THE SECRET CODE

Abundance is not a myth, nor is it mystical. There isn't some undisclosed, 007-style secret code to success that is keeping you from world-class achievement. Too many people have bought into the notion that achieving prosperity is difficult, time-consuming, or limited to special people.

But true abundance and a rich, rewarding lifestyle are simpler than you think.

In this book, I'd like to share what I've discovered about abundance—and reveal what I did, including the specific nuts and bolts of my journey. I'd like to give you the mindset, the application, and the intention—and share my journey unlike ever before, detailing what it took to rise above my own chaos and go from broke and broken to a place of prosperity and possibility that far exceeds anything I could have ever imagined.

What lessons did I learn? What practices did I have to master? What habits, behaviors, and beliefs did I have to develop in order to start living abundantly and prospering wildly?

You will discover those in this book.

CHAPTER BY CHAPTER, THE JOURNEY BEGINS

In Chapter 1, "Getting Ready for Transformation: Defining Abundance and Scarcity," you'll discover the new definition of abundance—and a new way of looking at your future. Through a short course on *personalized prosperity,* you'll look beyond what society, the media, your friends, and well-meaning family say prosperity is and begin to define it for yourself—perhaps for the first time *ever.* From rich and rewarding experiences, impressive financial assets, the joys of service, and the gratification of up-leveling your relationships, you will begin to sense you *can* create your own vision of the future and be happy.

With this forward-thinking new posture, you'll be primed to make plans for a breathtaking new future—getting crystal clear about what you truly want in every area of your life: abundant financial assets, a brilliant career, engaging friendships, powerful connections, compelling philanthropy, vibrant health, rich traditions, exciting pursuits, plus so much more.

You'll learn (as I have) to become non-negotiable about these new goals—while staying flexible about how you get there. You'll even learn to eliminate the toxic characteristics, procrastination, blame game, and victim mindset—*any* behavior that you've lived with and tolerated up until now—evicting these on behalf of your future. With this orientation in place, the next four chapters of the book will equip you with the process of creating abundance and show you how what I call "the 4 Es" are the key to making all the areas of your life (Self, Relationships, Work, and Money) work in concert to produce true prosperity.

The 4 Es start with "Enrichment"—of your whole Self—where we'll go to work enriching you with the skills and the mindset required to move from scarcity to abundance. In fact, abundance is your birthright. And together, we'll work on thinking bigger, uplifting your expectations, producing better outcomes, and expanding your vision of what's possible.

But don't worry if you feel you're not smart enough, connected enough, or "enough" in any other way. I never achieved any grade higher than a C+ in school and actually failed English in college. In the only public speaking class I ever took, I got a D– (and that was probably a gift from my teacher).

Advanced education required? No way. This only highlights the possibilities for you.

The second of the 4 Es is "Enchantment"—the feeling of delight and magic you get from your Relationships. I want you to become intentional about the quality of your relationships—not just the current ones, but the new ones you want to form. I want you to become deliberate about the caliber of people you spend time with, learning how to seek out those people who inspire you to do better, create more, play bigger, and win more often (especially in your family relationships and romantic relationships).

The third of the 4 Es is the "Engagement" you get from your Work. And in this chapter, you'll discover a unique approach to your right livelihood, treating your current job or career as a major investor in your future life. It's not difficult to move into a career you love—whether it's working for someone else or enjoying the freedom of owning your own business. I've done both.

Finally, the fourth of the 4 Es is taking an "Endowment" approach when it comes to your Money. In this chapter, we'll roll up our sleeves and start building your financial wealth. But first there's some work to do—eliminating those old "money mantras" you learned when you were younger. These are incompatible with the prosperous new path you've embarked on, and it's time you created a new relationship with money.

By the time we reach Chapter 6, "Activating Future Abundance in the Present Moment," you'll be ready to begin living abundantly *now*—enjoying the new prosperity mindset and breathtaking riches you've acquired over the last four chapters. Life is *not* short. You have time to build substantial financial wealth while enjoying a prosperous attitude and the joy of amassing non-monetary riches.

If only I had had—in my early years—the skills, techniques, mindset, and beliefs I want to share with you now, my journey would have been very different. I plan to share candidly my unexpected breakdowns and my ultimate breakthroughs.

One story, in fact, stands out in my mind. This was a tough lesson for me—it was even tougher on my dad—but it only served to galvanize my desire to be financially free. As a teenage girl growing up in a tough South Central Los Angeles neighborhood, I started running track when my dad decided it would keep me busy during the high-risk hours between 3:00 and 6:00—when gangs roamed the streets and girls got pregnant. For nine years, I enjoyed a successful career. I broke high school records in the 330 low hurdles and was a top city champion, and my team repeatedly won the state championship. I felt I'd accomplished everything with my sport that I'd wanted to; I was complete. But inevitably, colleges came courting with promises of tuition discounts—something my parents could not afford to ignore.

"Baby, if you run," my father said, "they'll give me a break on the bill."

Caving to the pressure, I agreed to run track for an out-of-state university for two years. In the first year, our team was undefeated, following two dry years where they hadn't won a single meet. I ran six events every Saturday, virtually nonstop. I was tired—burned out—finishing my first year of college with multiple injuries.

In my second year there, I was committed not to run. I was suffering from shin splints, injured tendons, a strained hamstring, and an agitated ankle. I knew that if I continued on this path, my body would be completely broken down by graduation. To add to my injuries, I had lost all enthusiasm for track and field. I wanted to do something more productive with my time after school. I was no longer willing to destroy my body for competition and rankings.

After missing the first week of preseason, I found myself in the athletic director's office, tallying up the back tuition I owed and the current year's tuition that had yet to be paid.

$10,500, he said.

It might as well have been $10 million. When I offered to work off the tuition—do anything but run track—he laughed and said I'd never earn enough money to pay the bill in full. When he slid a paper in front of me to sign, confirming that I had reneged on my agreement, I felt used. Sadly, what happened next is forever etched on my mind. To make certain I left campus, they changed the locks on my dorm room. The cafeteria canceled my meal plan. And my instructors forbade me from attending class.

With just $152 in my bank account plus $8 in cash my friends had put together for me, I flew home to Los Angeles, spending $150 of my precious reserve for the one-way airline ticket. With tears in my eyes, I begged a taxi driver to drive me home and accept the only $10 I had left in the world.

"I've been kicked out of school," I said, numb to whatever would happen next.

"Keep it," he replied, driving me 15 miles to my house for free.

Arriving home, I sat on the porch for eight hours until my landlord got home and let me in. I could not reach my dad, as this was long before the days of cellphones and he was away on business. When he returned home three days later, he was shocked to see me. While he called the school, I kept studying. I actually believed all would be resolved and I'd return to take my midterms. But as my dad asked the athletic director, "Isn't there anything you can do?" I could hear the defeat in his voice. I wasn't going back to school. With my brother in a vocational school and those expenses piling up, we just couldn't afford it.

In that moment, I made a decision. I promised myself that if I ever had a child, I would have the money to send him to college.

I never went back to school. I never graduated from college. But that experience created an even greater fire in me to succeed in becoming financially free.

If you've had experiences that left you desperate and broken, I want this book to become a bridge from that life to a breathtaking new future.

SHOUT OUT THE UNSPOKEN
DESIRES OF YOUR HEART

Whether it's moving yourself out of a place of discomfort—emotionally, physically, or financially—or simply stepping into the abundant and prosperous life you know deep down you deserve, *Abundance Now* will be your launchpad. The same will be true if you are using this book as your springboard into new possibilities, new results, and new outcomes. Whether it is to increase your income, improve your lifestyle, drive your business through the roof, or attract healthier relationships that fuel you, this book is where you start.

It will show you how to bring life to the unspoken desires of your heart and the unvoiced thoughts of your mind—using clear, practical steps for turning these thoughts and desires into a new reality.

You'll find that, with powerful intention, mindset management, and clear actionable steps, you'll experience accelerated growth and become wildly successful. And you'll discover that it's so much easier than you ever imagined. *Abundance Now* provides you with the fundamental techniques, ideas, and those necessary action steps to drastically transform your life into something unimaginable.

Come experience my journey and jump-start your own!

It's time to start living the life you imagined.
—Henry James, American novelist and playwright

CHAPTER 1

Getting Ready for Transformation: Defining Abundance and Scarcity

> Abundance is not something available for sale or
> purchase. It's something that we tap into, build, and grow.
> —Lisa Nichols

One of the most enduring myths in our culture today is that scarcity and deprivation early in life somehow ensures we'll experience struggle and hardship later. Because of mysterious and unkind forces outside our control (the economy, corporate greed, the job market), living a life of abundance seems beyond our reach—while scarcity seems to be readily available to everyone. In fact, sometimes it's even glamorized as the way "real" people live.

Of course the truth is that, no matter where you started out in life, *you have a choice* between scarcity and abundance. You have a choice between simply managing the struggle—or living a rich, rewarding life filled with unique experiences, exciting career options, nurturing relationships, and the comfort and ease that come with financial success.

Even better, this life of abundance is something you get to define for yourself.

Unfortunately, many people today—at times even me and perhaps you, too—let *others* define the trappings of a rich lifestyle. We see prosperous characters on television and think we know what prosperity is. We assume we have an accurate picture of the activities and luxuries that "rich people" enjoy. We listen to what our friends say, then strive to acquire those possessions *they* think are "necessary." We see reality TV shows flaunting expensive cars, monstrous homes, and megawatt jewelry—then call it "wealth." But we never stop to think about what *we ourselves* ultimately want from life.

What do abundance, prosperity, riches, and wealth mean to you?

Throughout this book, I'll be challenging you to define the ideal life for yourself, to go beyond what others think "abundance" means, and choose not only the lifestyle, relationships, career, philanthropic activities, and other hallmarks of your abundant life—but also the attitudes, behaviors, and habits you will live by every day.

THE NEW DEFINITION OF ABUNDANCE IS YOURS

Several months ago, a friend and I were reflecting on the many ways that people define abundance. And whether you use the word *abundance*—or interchange it with *prosperity, riches,* or *wealth* as I do throughout this book—the best definition of *abundance* I've seen by far is this one: *privileged circumstances.*

When you're living a life of privileged circumstances, you get to play a bigger game, connect with people who are making things happen, encounter more opportunities for advancement, and, along the way, take pleasure in a lifestyle that would be admired by many. It means you have the freedom to pursue those things you want to do, be, and have—including what your occupation will be, whom you'll share relationships with, the activities you'll enjoy, the possessions you'll own, and the ways in which you contribute to others and give back to society through philanthropic endeavors.

In the pursuit of these privileged circumstances, not only will your life become something that is compelling to you, but it will also serve as an inspiration to others.

When I was 25 years old, my definition of abundance was transformed abruptly—and the new mindset that came along with it literally gave me a new direction in life. Suddenly, I began to run toward my passion. My life was on fire. I felt an urgency to make sure my life would be amazing.

At the time, I was working at a computer software company doing customer service and training. It was just a job that paid the bills. It wasn't my future. Frankly, I didn't know what my future was. But I picked up a copy of Stephen Covey's classic success book, *The 7 Habits of Highly Effective People,** which had been recommended to me months earlier by a woman whom I admired immensely for her positive attitude and constant joy and the clarity she seemed to have in her life. Hoping that I could have the same, I began to read and came across Covey's advice to "begin with the end in mind."

He said, picture yourself at your own funeral *three years from now,* then listen as four speakers—a family member, a friend, a business acquaintance, and a community volunteer—describe your character and the difference you made in their lives.

What would they say about me? I wondered. *What would I* want *them to say about me?*

In that moment, I realized that my eulogy would not have been very compelling. I was kind, but I hadn't made a difference. I was motivated, but I lacked direction. I had never before *decided* upon the person I wanted to be—nor the accomplishments I wanted to achieve. One thing I did know, however, was that I wanted my eulogy to be powerful. I wanted to have lived "full

---

* *The 7 Habits of Highly Effective People: Powerful Lessons in Personal Change* by Stephen R. Covey, Free Press, 1989.

out" when my time came to go. Although I didn't know the exact path I would pursue, I made a start the only way I knew how. At 25, I stopped taking "just jobs" and instead pursued a position that elevated me and amplified my game. I began to travel for my employer, wore suits to work, mastered using a laptop and the latest technology—and focused all my energy on helping people. I volunteered for projects and assignments that no one else wanted to bother with. By the time the company decided to relocate to Spokane, Washington, not only was I doing the job of three or four people effortlessly, I was the only employee retained in a massive layoff as part of the move.

What would your eulogy say about you?

DOES YOUR CUP RUNNETH OVER?

When I work with clients and students to create their abundant life, I start by asking them to examine their spiritual life, relationships, finances, and health. What we're looking for is whether they feel fulfilled in those areas.

In just a moment, I'll ask you to examine these areas closely, but for now, think about whether you have reached a level of satisfaction in each area. Are you feeling connected in your spiritual walk, enjoying blissful relationships, satisfied with your finances, and experiencing vibrant good health? Do you feel whole and complete? Are you living your purpose or your current life assignment at this stage of life? Do you feel valued for your contribution—whether you're a stay-at-home parent, are running a multimillion-dollar corporation, or are somewhere in between?

Or do you constantly feel lack and frustration with your progress?

What I've discovered about abundance is that it's a *mindset* more than it's your actual circumstances. And this mindset doesn't require lots of money.

A perfect example of this mindset was my Grandma Bernice,

rest her soul—one of my first role models. Grandma Bernice was my dad's mother and, more than anyone I knew, Grandma Bernice seemed to have the most fulfilling life. She was a stately lady of small stature; we used to say she was 98 pounds soaking wet with weights in her pocket. But while she was tiny, she had a soft but stern voice and a heavy hand, and while that hand never tapped us, when she tapped the coffee table . . . well, we knew to be quiet.

As a former nurse, Grandma doubled up and was in overflow of love, admiration, and servanthood. She gave abundantly of her time and knowledge to family and community. She could make a pot of beans go in 50 different directions. She would feed her children, her grandchildren, and the neighbors; it was like that pot was never-ending because she just lived in abundance.

In her presence, I never felt scarcity—never heard her say the phrase "not enough." For example, she had this fireplace at her house that we rarely used. But later I found out that when the electricity was cut off, Grandma would build a fire and cook dinner in a cast-iron skillet over the open flame—never once complaining about lack.

At her funeral I sat enraptured, listening to friend after friend who revealed how Grandma Bernice hadn't just crossed a friend's path; she had changed the trajectory of that person's life. At 25 years old, I decided I wanted to be like her when I grew up. I wanted my funeral to be like hers.

And yet, Grandma Bernice didn't have a lot of money, she'd never started a company, and she didn't have lots of possessions. She simply lived in the overflow of spiritual wealth, rich relationships, and vibrant good health—with enough money to meet the basic needs of her family of seven children and with a small amount left over to share.

She was the most abundant woman I've ever known. And she taught me that abundance doesn't require becoming an entrepreneur or filling your bank account—it comes from living in the present and enjoying your "now." Grandma Bernice had *more than enough* to be happy. But just as important, she defined abundance *on her own terms*. She didn't let someone else measure her level of success.

What about you?

Do you have more than enough to be happy—in your spiritual life, your relationships, your finances, and your health? Does the person you show up to be in the world, both for yourself and others, play full out? Is your self-awareness and self-esteem—but also your humility—full? Have you defined what prosperity means to you, instead of adopting someone else's version of abundance?

To me, abundance is simple: it's having enough, being fulfilled, and feeling as though my cup is running over.

What does abundance look like to you?

CREATE A LIFE YOU LOVE . . . STARTING TODAY

If you and I were working privately on planning your abundant future, one of the first things I would ask you to do is assess your level of fulfillment and satisfaction in the key areas of your life.

Have you ever *really* examined your life? Do you know what is required for you to be happy?

To help you look at each of these key areas, I've put my entire Personal Prosperity Quiz online for you to access free of charge. It asks you to look at four areas: your spiritual life, your relationships, your career and finances, and finally, your health and wellness. And it steps you through determining how fulfilled you feel in these areas. Are you living in abundance? Is your cup running over? Or do you have work to do in order to achieve satisfaction in these areas? You'll find the Personal Prosperity Quiz at www.AbundanceNowOnline.com/resources.

Of course, although assessing your current prosperity through these questions is important as a starting point, to experience *future abundance* you have to embrace your current life. If you love your life now, then you'll be open to attracting and creating the more expanded future life you want.

Don't wait until you hit a specific money marker, have started your dream career, or have found your soul mate. Live abundantly *now* on your way to living an even better life. Love greatly *today* on the way to loving more openly in the future. And pursue health and wellness with vigor so you'll be ready for life's great adventures.

Living abundantly *now* doesn't require loads of cash.

When my son, Jelani, was small, many nights we ate beanies-and-weenies—a filling but mundane meal that became so repetitive, I created names for us as a way to add sparkle to our kitchen time together. Mustard Man was born, and I played Garlic Girl, Jelani's capable *sous-chef*. Night after night while in character, our creativity knew no bounds as we stirred up some of the most exciting, frightening, and filling meals imaginable. There were our famous teriyaki chicken wings that weren't "done" until they fell off the bone. Our Swedish meatballs could have doubled for tennis balls (except tennis balls probably would have tasted better). And our chocolate chip cookies—which were supposed to be soft and moist—ended up resembling the starship *Enterprise* and tasted like they were from outer space too. We even created brothless chicken noodle soup, a gluten-free pancake disaster, catastrophic key lime pie, and a tiramisu that oozed and sagged like cake left out in the rain.

Despite the disasters, cooking became the highlight of our day and a joyful time for both of us.

Years later, when my life expanded and our income grew with it, Jelani and I flew to both the British Virgin Islands and Italy as his graduation present before he started his studies at the world-famous culinary institute Le Cordon Bleu. When I surprised Jelani in Sicily with the first of thirty days of classes with various private chefs, the chef asked him, "What makes you want to become a chef, young man?"

Without looking up from the eggplant he was slicing, Jelani replied, "I've been head chef in our kitchen at home for a while and just wanna make it official." We both broke into laughter as we shared our stories of Mustard Man and Garlic Girl—and how cooking together made us feel abundant when scarcity was our reality. I could see in the chef's eyes the admiration he felt as we celebrated our new lives—now cooking classic fare in a professional kitchen with a private chef in one of the most incredible countries in the world.

Only the decision to focus on living abundantly *now* can make eventual prosperity—and prosperous activities like private cooking lessons in Italy—that meaningful.

Of course, this kind of focus on present prosperity extends to other areas of our life, as well—especially relationships. During a recent appearance on *The Steve Harvey Show,* I counseled a husband and wife who were struggling to bring love and affection back to their relationship after the husband had been involved in an online relationship. While I got the husband to own his part of the damage to their marriage, his wife had begun projecting into the future—anticipating the next time he would betray her in this way. She no longer trusted him because of what he *might do* in the future.

My coaching to the woman was that she was missing a thousand beautiful "now moments" by projecting and anticipating hurt into the future. Through further coaching, it became clear to her that she wasn't loving herself—and so she couldn't believe that her husband loved her either.

I gave her a nightly assignment—something known as The Mirror Exercise*—instructing her to verbally admire her own qualities and celebrate her own daily wins to the image she saw

---

* Just before bedtime, look into a mirror—gazing into your own eyes—and state out loud all the ways you appreciate yourself, especially for your accomplishments that day. You can find out more about The Mirror Exercise at my website: www.AbundanceNowOnline .com/resources.

before her . . . *herself.* By delivering these positive strokes to her subconscious mind nightly, she could begin to embrace and love herself in the present moment—and by extension give her husband permission to embrace and love her, too.

Whether you want loving supportive relationships—or are pursuing other areas of an abundant life—*never miss another now.* Acknowledge your bounty and brilliance today. After all, it's *this you*—the person you are in this moment—who will bring about the future you want. Unfortunately, far too many of us wait far too long to live abundantly. We think we need to achieve great wealth or accumulate important friends or somehow "become somebody" before we start pursuing our dreams. My advice is to stop planning and start *doing those things* that are part of an abundant life.

> You want to set a goal that is big enough
> that in the process of achieving it you become
> someone worth becoming.
>
> —Jim Rohn, self-made millionaire,
> success coach, and philosopher

My good friend Sandra Yancey was committed to pursuing success long before she had the means, connections, and expertise to do so. She'd been looking for an organization that provided a safe space for women entrepreneurs to network and create joint business opportunities. When she couldn't find one, she and her husband, Kym, founded eWomenNetwork—and literally created the company she was looking for.

Although today eWomenNetwork touches over 500,000 women entrepreneurs and generates millions of dollars annually, in its early growth years Sandra and Kym lived frugally. They worked 15 hours a day in a room over their garage. Sandra was the main speaker at the company's events. She ran the operations. She wore 13 other hats in the company—all while being a mother to two young children, a great wife, and a caring daughter to her aging mother. Kym also wore many hats—helping to shape the operations, overseeing marketing, handling the recruiting and the customer experience, and more. They took risks and they sacrificed. Sandra and Kym had to be fiscally tight. They stretched meals. They made vacations super special on a budget.

Today, Sandra and Kym have thousands of members in the eWomenNetwork organization, travel all over the world for business and play, and have raised millions of dollars for women and children in need. I watch them operate the company with grace and ease—and yet I also know the price they paid for the abundant life they lead now.

Just like Sandra and Kym Yancey, you too can pursue rich and rewarding experiences well before you have the finances, possessions, home, or career you desire. Make it your goal to accomplish at least two things every 90 days *that directly affect your bottom line*—that is, increase your income or business revenue.

At the same time, don't wait to start living inside your life. Start doing those things that bring you the most joy. Share your gifts and talents with the world. Fully express yourself, saying those things that need to be said and living a life of no regrets. Do *two more things* over the next 90 days that contribute to living the abundant life you want. If your dream is to travel to Paris and visit the Louvre, for example, schedule a day this month where you visit a local museum then enjoy a picnic lunch with elegant dishes and starched table linens you've packed. If you want to travel by private jet, grab three or four friends and jump on one of Jet Suite's last-minute Suite Deals flights for just $536. If you want to start a charity to save the world's oceans, start by volunteering with a group who is cleaning up the beaches in your own geographic area.

Focus *first* on the macro version of your life—the money— while you're also pursuing the micro version of your life—those fun activities that make your life enjoyable.

By "leaning in" and pursuing life in both areas, you'll find out whether you actually like those activities. You might change your mind or move in a slightly different direction. Plus, you'll find out how much money you really need to live your version of abundance.

Most important, you'll become unequivocal about what you ultimately want. You can't hit a moving target. It's time to make plans for your future.

YOU CAN'T HIT A MOVING TARGET: GET CRYSTAL CLEAR ABOUT WHAT YOU WANT

The Universe wants to deliver your fondest desires to you—at the time and in the manner you specify. But it can't hit a moving target. And the Universe doesn't recognize "someday" on the calendar. It needs *specific and compelling instructions from you* to bring about the self-transformation, career gains, beneficial relationships, and financial wealth you want to achieve.

It's time to get crystal clear about what you want.

> You cannot hit a moving target. Unclear goals make
> producing clear results impossible.
>
> —Lisa Nichols

When deciding what you want, the first step is to start with the end in mind. What would your life look like if you had already achieved your dreams? Strive to create a very clear picture in your mind.

See yourself in the house you would ultimately live in. Where is it located? What style is it? How is it decorated? What activities do you pursue there? Populate your images with colors, scents, sounds, and emotions of your ideal life in your dream home. Then go one step further and decide the exact date you'll move in.

Next, visualize your typical workday in the career of your dreams. What kind of work are you doing? What are the outcomes of your focused and productive day? What new business, new collaborations, and new value are you creating? Who else is in the picture? Assemble in your mind's eye the circle of employees, colleagues, mentors, and others who are the major support structure for your career.

Decide how much financial wealth you'll amass, then assign a specific date by which you will have accumulated that exact amount. What form will this wealth take—stock in your own company, mutual funds, art, real estate, or something else? What kind of person will you have become to capably manage this wealth?

Next, get clear on who you are spiritually. What are your daily spiritual practices? How do you inspire others through your own spiritual journey?

Finally, decide what kind of relationships you'll enjoy in your abundant future life. Have you met or do you plan to meet your soul mate? If so, by when? Are you aligned with top achievers and other persons of consequence? Are you surrounded by "Rocket Booster" friends—those people who love, encourage, and celebrate you? Is your community a supportive force for your career or business? Are you growing as a result of these alliances?

The key to visualizing your ideal life is to see it in pictures that are so real that you actually form an emotional relationship with what you want. What would you be *feeling* as you wake up in your dream home, spend a productive day in your dream career, enjoy your closest relationships, and reflect on the financial wealth you've accumulated?

The difference between remaining static and actually achieving is *feeling*. High achievers are passionate people. This passion extends to their visions of their best and highest future.

One story that illustrates why you should attach feelings and emotions to your pictures—causing the Universe to deliver unique opportunities for fulfilling your dreams—is a story of regret that I heard over fifteen years ago from a venture capitalist.

Back then, as I was growing my company, I held investor meetings every six to eight weeks. At one of those meetings, I met a gentleman who told me that, every day, he couldn't help kicking himself. When I asked why, he replied that over 25 years ago, he was approached by a long-haired, awkward technology geek who had a crazy idea to put a computer on every desk.

"When he asked me to invest $10,000," reflected the investor, "I didn't believe something so far-reaching, so different, would ever work. So I said no."

That awkward guy was Bill Gates. And by 2011, that original $10,000 investment in Microsoft—the company that Gates founded—would have been worth over $2.8 million.*

What would an investment like that have done for you and your family? If you had been that investor—someone who regularly visualized his or her future and attached strong feelings and emotions to your picture of future wealth—perhaps you would have been more likely to see an investment opportunity like that as a welcome opportunity the Universe had provided to fulfill your financial goals.

Your dreams—and the date by which you'll achieve your milestones—are the gas. The feelings and passion you tie to these future accomplishments are the turbo boost.

What emotional connection will you attach to each one of your goals?

AT THE SAME TIME YOU'RE DREAMING, SET GOALS THAT ARE BELIEVABLE AND ACHIEVABLE

I remember the first time I did this future-vision exercise. At the time, my goals seemed stunning in their breadth and magnitude. I wanted to build a financially stable and vibrant lifestyle for Jelani and me. I wanted to purchase an incredible home. I wanted to treat my family—including my grandmother and my

---

* Forbes.com reported that a $10,000 investment in Microsoft in 1986 would have been worth more than $2.8 million in 2011. http://www.forbes.com/forbes/2011/0523 /investing-john-reese-intrinsic-value-apples-oranges-microsoft.html

parents—to a luxury international trip at least once (if not several times). And I wanted to transform my body into a healthy, high-performance machine.

My goals seemed so exciting, they actually scared me. I was daunted by what I knew I'd have to accomplish in order to meet those goals.

Worse still, I realized that even small achievements—which by themselves were nearly impossible for me to accomplish at the time—would have been only incremental gains on the way to the major outcomes I wanted to create in my life. I wouldn't have been able to celebrate my own growth and triumph since none of these small goals would have been the major win I was looking for.

Here's the reality I discovered: most people unconsciously dream themselves out of their goals. They dream so far past their current reality—or what's currently possible—that they end up abandoning their goals and damaging their own self-esteem.

To prevent this scenario, don't engage in wishful thinking. Set believable and achievable goals for the season that you're in. As you grow and prosper, your goals (and your ability to achieve them) will expand. Don't kill your potential by believing that achievement only happens when you've reached a lofty, overwhelming goal.

MICRO WINS LEAD TO MACRO WINS

To further explain the point, most people want to jump from 1 to 1,000—when 1 to 10 might actually be a stunning accomplishment, and 10 to 20 might put them at the top of their field.

Because we live in a Google-download, microwavable, instant-gratification kind of world, too many people think success happens overnight. They say, *I want what you've accomplished without spending the 20 years that you worked to get it.*

Although you can cut 10–15 years off a learning curve

through good coaching and by accessing the right mentors, it still takes small, move-the-needle, incremental steps to achieve any large goal.

If you find yourself trying to skip past these necessary small achievements in the pursuit of unachievable goals, a better way to approach goal setting (and goal getting) is to establish clear deliverables and milestones. These are the micro wins that will produce your macro wins. These are the tiny goals that will lead to the big ones.

> You significantly enhance your chances of completing a
> goal if you actually get started. Breaking down your tasks
> into bite-sized, palatable, digestible pieces is what will
> actually help you get started.
>
> —Lisa Nichols

As you look over each area of life achievement in the next section, begin to set compelling goals for yourself—but also determine those incremental milestones you'll achieve on the way to accomplishing the breathtaking life changes you want.

12 LIFE-CHANGING AREAS WHERE YOU CAN ACHIEVE ASTOUNDING SUCCESS

To live a truly compelling life that is enjoyable for you and inspiring to others, you must set goals for your future and work daily to bring them about. These are goals beyond just wealth and material goods, goals that also include loving relationships, ample free time, hobbies, and other pursuits you enjoy—all of which are the hallmarks of an abundant life. In other words, who you become as a person should overshadow what you amass in your bank account.

What goals will you set in the 12 areas that follow?

Your Love Relationship

When you think about the person who commands your heart, the soul mate who knows you better than you know yourself, and the supportive partner who creates a safe space for you to achieve on a stunning level, what characteristics and qualities does he or she possess? What emotions do you feel when you visualize yourself with that person? If you're in that relationship already, what goal would you set to transform that relationship into something even more amazing that helps you achieve every other area of your life with grace and ease?

I'm reminded of a story one of my program participants shared with me.

When Alyse McConnell's marriage ended, she told herself she would never endanger her heart again. Not only did she get clear on other aspects of her life, but she also decided she wouldn't marry again, favoring serial monogamy over the risk of being trapped in a relationship that hurt.

Alyse had it all figured out.

Then one day, she started making a list—deciding that she would *consider* getting married again if she found someone who fit her exacting standards. She wrote the list at the back of her journal, and over the next several months added qualities and characteristics from physical traits to ways of being . . . even fashion choices. By the time she finished the list and put that journal on a shelf, she had written down 88 criteria a man would have to meet before she would marry again.

Two years passed.

Then when her doctor unexpectedly confirmed she was pregnant (which specialists had previously said was impossible), Alyse had to pause. The father of her unborn child was from another country, and the *only way* they could stay together and both be part of the baby's life was if they got married.

In a quiet moment, Alyse got out her journal.

And there, on the back page, was her original list of 88 must-haves. Reading them again two years after having put them on a shelf, she realized that her boyfriend, Klaas, met an astounding 85 of the criteria!

"There's no doubt I created him in my life," Alyse told me on the day they celebrated their 17th wedding anniversary.

What kind of love relationship are *you* looking for?

Your Family Relationships

At the end of your life, when you look at the quality of your life, it will likely be measured by the quality of your family relationships. It is by far the lion's share of where you measure your life's joy and fulfillment. Family relationships can be managed most effectively with clear communication and even, at times, positive "care-frontation"—the willingness to have difficult conversations for the sake of clarity and progress embraced in love and possibility.

To become crystal clear about what you want in your family relationships, you must first measure and take inventory. Think about each of your family members—your siblings, your parents, others who are close to you. If they were to transition tomorrow, would you have regret? Is there anything today that remains unsaid?

In my inner-circle workshops, I give attendees a scenario similar to one that I learned many years ago from my old friend Barry Spilchuk: If a nuclear bomb were to drop tomorrow, and you knew about it in advance, what would you want or need to say to be complete with each family member? What would the conversation sound like? In an emotion-fueled moment when people are reflecting on all of the unsaid things in each of their lives: I love you, I forgive you, I appreciate who you have been to me, I apologize. We then actually distribute cellphones so participants can telephone those family members they need to talk with. I urge them to say what they feel driven to say during this 15-minute exercise. Once the exercise is done, the room melts into healing forgiveness and admission of things the participants did years ago for which they failed to ask forgiveness, acknowledgment they have not given, or words unsaid.

Only when you've healed the past can you move forward and become uncompromising about what you want these relationships to look like—whether they should be supportive, loving, non-confrontational, acknowledging, or something else.

Who in your family do you need to reach out to?

Your Peers, Colleagues, and Social Circle

As you become crystal clear about those specific individuals you surround yourself with, can I make a suggestion? Surround yourself with people who inspire you to be a better woman or make you want to be a better man. They should call you to your greatness. They should stretch you and make you look forward to the person you will be five years from now. They should not only celebrate this future version, they should pour into you everything they can to help you achieve that goal.

They shouldn't be small-minded people inclined to drama and gossip. Your abundant life has no room for them. Your friends, peers, and colleagues should be people whom you can share your knowledge with, but who should also be sharing knowledge with you.

And if you find yourself pulling everyone else along? If you're the person who's ten steps ahead of everyone else, the inspiration, the focal point, and the end-all, be-all of these relationships, you have to ask yourself why you're in that social circle and whether you need to acquire new friends.

Are you in that friendship circle so you can be the savior? Or to be the best thing in town? Or have you outgrown your friendship circle entirely? This doesn't mean you need to abruptly drop your friends. But it does mean you need to acquire new people in your circle—others who can pour into you, while you're pouring into them.

What kind of friends, colleagues, peers, and social circle would amplify your life and bring you greater prosperity? Precisely define the qualities you want in the people who support you.

But be advised: it's common for people who are working on their own self-development and proactively creating their future to outgrow their friends. By the time you finish reading this book, you'll be ten steps ahead of most people in your social circle—because you will know now what it means to create intentional abundance.

One of the best gifts you can give your friends (and one of the best ways to help *them* support *you*) is to invite them to come along on your abundant journey. Give them their own copy of this book.

Giving books to friends is a long tradition with me. I've often purchased two or three copies of a book I like in order to distribute them to people who are growing with me. I want *all of us* to have expanded knowledge and skills.

Do you get what you need from your friend circle? Are you giving your friends what they need in return?

Your Mentors and Advisers

In the same way your friends, peers, and colleagues should nurture your future success, your mentors and advisers should also nourish you, too. And in fact, friends can grow into mentors and advisers—just as mentors can become lifelong friends. Some of my best mentoring relationships started as friendships, and it was inside of these friendships that I discovered they were brilliant in areas where I was still growing.

Therefore, a huge requirement in your friendships is to put your ego aside and—if your friends are capable of expanding your skill set—make it very clear, "I'd love for you to help me this way." Be quick to share their gift of knowledge with others, too.

Your Career or Business

To get crystal clear about what you want from your work life, you have to first decide what gives you joy. Do you enthusiastically jump into your day with a commitment to accomplish key objectives? Are you constantly suffused with ideas for expanding your area of influence or your ability to create more value? Do regular accomplishments bring you a sense of satisfaction, increased self-worth, and more confidence that drive you to create even greater achievements?

They should.

In fact, being joyful about your work—whether it's your own business or working for someone else—is the key indicator of whether you are on the right path for your career. If it feels right, if it's rewarding, if it brings you into relationship with people you want to spend time with, if it creates exciting opportunities for advancement, if it supports other professional activities you want to pursue in your work life—then you're in the right place.

If it doesn't provide these benefits, you have two choices: (1) take steps now to change careers, or (2) immediately reframe your relationship with your less-than-perfect career or business and start treating it as an investor in your breathtaking future. Determine what it *can do* to promote the life you want down the road—even if it's just the funding source of your abundant lifestyle.

Early in my work life, I determined that the dead-end job I was in would not create the life I wanted—except in one regard: it produced enough income for me to set aside money to start my dream business . . . the exciting, nonstop, breathtaking business I own today. Once I determined its usefulness to my future, I became more passionate about my job and the opportunity to work (and, in fact, passionately took on a second job to generate even more income). I even adjusted my expenses so these jobs would be able to "buy" my future. With this one decision—to become more passionate—my energy suddenly shifted toward my job because it was investing in the exciting, new Lisa Nichols that I was designing. I literally would not be where I am today without reframing my view of that original job.

If your key source of income, on the other hand, is your own business, realize that your business is a part of your life—but not your whole life. You're not defined by what you do. You're defined by who you choose to be *while doing what you do.* Your business should be designed to give you access to the lifestyle and personhood you choose—not tie you to something you hate or make you question whether you still love it.

So many times, I have to stop my clients from believing they're held hostage by their career or business. You've never been a victim. You've always had a choice. So run your business or work at your job as if you *do have* a choice. The most powerful action you can take every day is to *consciously choose* that business or job wholeheartedly while you're in it. The moment you choose to make a change, then powerfully make the change. But don't live as if you're held hostage to something that you're choosing on a daily basis. Be a big girl or big boy and realize that your life is in your hands.

Do you design your destiny?

Of course, the first step toward designing your ideal career or business is to get crystal clear about what you want. Determine those activities, skills, relationships, and accomplishments you would like to fill your day. Envision the perfect workday and jot down what you'd be doing, the kinds of people you would be interacting with, and the kinds of activities you would be involved in.

One way to be sure you fill your day with joyful, satisfying work is to focus on your *outstanding ability*—that one thing you do so well and that's so much fun for you, you can hardly believe that people pay you for it. You love doing it. It provides tremendous service to the planet. And it gives you the financial stability and abundant lifestyle you crave. Rearrange your business if you must (or work with management to re-create your job) so you can focus on it. But discover what your *outstanding ability* is and get crystal clear about how you can incorporate it into your job or business. Finally, resolve to take steps to do that.

Your Income or Business Revenue

In the same way you should be crystal clear about your job or business, you should also determine how big you'd like your weekly paycheck or business revenue to be.

Remember, you should begin with the end in mind.

Think about the abundant life you want to lead five years from now—or even three years out. How well do you want to live? What do you want to own? Do you want to grow your business? If so, how much revenue do you need to fund that growth and what exactly would you spend the money on? Design the lifestyle or business growth you want, and then back into that vision by calculating how much these activities will cost. Determine how much you'll need to earn from your wages, your business revenues, or the proceeds from your investments to pay for it all.

Of course, what I love about numbers is they don't ever live in gray. They're black and white. Either you hit your numbers or you don't. But don't plan your future life based on the money you're earning now—that will limit what you envision for yourself. Plan full out, then play full out. Research what you want to do, be, and have.

Not only does research give you actual numbers to work with, it helps you make plans based on knowledge—not longing. It helps you laser in on what *you* want versus what others say your dream life should include.

If you want to live in a breathtaking home, drive a luxury car, travel first class, or fund a philanthropic endeavor, research how much money that will take. If you want to send your children to college, pay down your mortgage, fund a sizable investment account, or start your own business, calculate those costs, too.

Then create a *strategy that earns that amount*—or more.

Allow your revenue to expand to the desire of your lifestyle, rather than limiting your lifestyle to your current revenues. In Chapter 5, I'll be giving you advice for earning more money. But here's some advice on what *not* to do: don't simply *hope* the extra money will show up. While many people say, *Dream and it will appear . . .* or *The Universe will provide the means for me to attain what I want . . .* or my favorite, *I've set the intention to win the lottery,* the reality is that honing your moneymaking skills by *taking action* on those activities that will meet your income goals will get you closer to your ideal lifestyle than simply dreaming.

Hope is not a strategy. A truly great life comes from having a plan.

What are your financial targets for creating the life you want?

Your Investments and Future Legacy

While your investment goals should align closely with your income goals, they should also go one step further and include the legacy you want to leave to your heirs and others. How do you want to extend your contribution to your family? What will you set aside for your children? What gift will you give to others from having been fiscally responsible?

To drill down on this area, you have to think beyond your own life. Ultimately, the result of your investments will be bigger than you and live long after you have passed.

What financial legacy do you want to leave behind?

Your Philanthropic Endeavors and Life of Service

To determine how you want to serve others, find out first what ignites your fire. Decide what makes your heart sing.

Sometimes this takes a little investigation. And often, this investigation reveals opportunities right in front of you. For instance, many of my clients and students say they want to work with children. Their dream is to travel to Mexico or Africa and build orphanages and schools.

My answer to them is always, "What about the children in your own backyard?"

What are their needs?

And if you want to help women refugees in Rwanda, I guarantee there's a battered women's shelter in your hometown that needs your help, too. Even simple acts of service, like attending a seminar and organizing participants to donate the unused shampoo and soap from their hotel rooms, can matter.

Find those acts of service that make you feel full just thinking about them. Then, take action. Small actions can ignite your service fire and help you formulate exactly what you ultimately want to do for others, and the world.

In a meeting recently with one of my top clients—a wealthy woman who's about 75% retired—we discussed her service idea, which originally focused on projects in Third World countries. I gave her the same advice I'm giving you. While you're researching projects outside your own country, why not pursue acts of service locally? Stick your toe in the water. Set up a visitation with a similar charity nearby. See how it's operated. Choose multiple locations and volunteer. Then, your true goals for paying it forward will come into focus.

What ignites your soul when it comes to service to others?

Your Physical Rewards

A physical reward should do several things. It should inspire you to stay laser focused on generating the means to acquire other tangible rewards. It should make you feel good about what you've accomplished so far. It should inspire those around you to emulate your focus without copying you. And it should be something that evokes a sense of gratitude in you—every time you walk into the home you purchased or start up your luxury automobile or wear that piece of designer jewelry.

Your physical rewards—that is, your home, car, possessions, the community where you live, and the trappings of your rich and rewarding lifestyle—should be used as an acknowledgment of your achievement. They *should not be used* to fabricate who you are or as a Band-Aid to mask your emotional pain.

When I first started working with Susie Carder, my executive coach (now my chief operating officer), she noticed that I was still driving an older-model Ford Explorer. Even though I had been in a position for years to upgrade my car, I simply didn't. But my car was no longer congruent with who I was as a person.

Immediately, I took Susie's advice and bought the new model year convertible. When I did, it felt like my own milestone reward. It felt good arriving at my appointments. It felt authentic that my outward life finally mirrored my message to others.

Of course, physical rewards should not give you future financial stress. You should never live outside your means and purchase things you can barely afford. Financial stress has no place in true abundance. Plus, at all times, flaunting expensive possessions is a fabricated conversation. Not only is it the myth of happiness, but it's also inauthentic—it's you telling the world a story you think they want to hear.

What tangible rewards are you striving for?

Your Playtime

Another area you'll want to be crystal clear about is how you play during your off-hours—including the importance of scheduling playtime by actually marking it on the calendar.

Playtime should allow you to completely disconnect from your responsibilities for the specified period of time—whether it's a one-hour respite, a two-week vacation, or a three-month sabbatical. Not only that, but playtime should also be spent in true enjoyment at an activity you love. It should never be spent merely catching up on your sleep, recovering from illness, or recuperating from a weeklong bout of overwork. Getting back on an even keel—for instance, going from a negative 4 to a zero—should never be the sole purpose of playtime.

How do you like to play? Playtime should be designed to create harmony in your life. Think about all the things you used to do ten years ago before you got busy.

When I'm off the clock, I like to go to the Caribbean. I swim in the ocean every single day. I wear different clothes, go dancing, and even turn off my cellphone so my mind knows I've unplugged.

Part of being devoted to creating playtime is that you also must carve out adequate time for it. Play days have to be scheduled. In my company, my team is required by the end of every January to allocate and schedule their playtime for the coming year. They don't have to know where they'll be going or what they'll be doing—but they must reserve time on their calendar. Scheduling in advance helps eliminate resentment for your work and requires you to be more productive during the days you *are* working. If you work for someone else and you're allotted vacation days, *take them*. You'll be refreshed and ready to perform at your peak when you get back. Plus, unplugging gives your mind the time and space to wander a little, solving problems and coming up with fresh ideas you can't muster when you're overworked.

Now that I'm older, I remember my play days with far more elation than I remember my workdays. The same little girl who grew up in South Central Los Angeles—who didn't have food to eat or money to pay her rent—has gone horseback riding in the primate (black monkey) sanctuaries of Puerto Rico, sailed off the coast of Croatia, gone swimming with horses in Montego Bay, Jamaica, played with dolphins in the British Virgin Islands, danced under the stars in St. Thomas, and reluctantly tasted buffalo, camel, and ostrich in Kenya with my father and son, among many other experiences. You can become deliberate about your play days, too.
When will your next playtime be?

Your Spiritual Awareness

I have worked hard at finding a rhythm inside my spiritual journey. By intentionally seeking and practicing peace of mind, grace, calm, and ease, I've created a greater spiritual awareness in my daily life.

You can, too.

When you find quiet time to listen to your GPS, your *God Placement System,* your intuition will always be talking to you—pointing you to those activities, people, and resources that will bring about your fondest desires. Often we're too busy or our self-talk is too loud to hear what our intuition is trying to tell us. We can't hear where it's trying to lead us.

So one of your most important activities should be to simply *be still.* If you need to create a new habit to help you be still, why not stay in bed an extra ten minutes every morning to practice gratitude or to meditate? It doesn't serve anyone to get out of bed running. During those ten minutes: (1) review the things you're grateful for, focusing primarily on what you're grateful for that has no cost attached to it; (2) create and delineate your intentions for the coming day or week—not to add to your to-do list, but simply to throw your wishes out to the Universe about those things you'd like to accomplish; and (3) just be still and feel your breath before you get started.

You'll find that the energy you greet the day with is the energy the day will give you back. Whatever face you show to the world is the same face the world will show you in return. For example, you *can* exhibit a face of grace and ease. It's found in your spiritual awareness—your ability to release what you cannot control and to commit to holding on to the things that matter most to you. This is the ability to expand and contract as needed—occupying all those spaces that allow us to be at one with our intentions, our gratitude, and our stillness.

When will you find the time to be "still"?

Your Physical Body

Do you love what you see in the mirror? We all have things that we tolerate about ourselves that we'd love to change, but what I'd like to laser in on for the sake of this conversation is if any physical feature is causing you to feel disempowered or depressed. If so, it's time to decide how you want to change your physical body. Whether it's your appearance, your weight, a specific feature, a health condition, or something else, you need to be focused on the "new you" and what you'll do to achieve that result.

To live an abundant life in every way, you need to love the skin you're in. When you do, you simply display a different energy, an inner smile, a contagious and sunny disposition that attracts people to you. I recently realized that I had spent 17 years without that inner smile—not wholeheartedly loving the skin I'm in. I compensated for the sense of powerlessness I felt toward my weight by building up my spiritual and intellectual muscles instead. Now I'm committed to holistic success more than ever, and in fact, I became resolute about achieving a healthy weight. I realized that I have always had the power to transform my physical body. By the time you read this book, I will have achieved what I once considered impossible: taking off the 75-pound jacket I used to wear. Day by day, it's easier than ever to say, "My hot is getting hotter."

Your appearance is important, but so is your stamina, agility, and physical resilience—and all these are required to accomplish your goals. Your body must have the ability to keep up with your life purpose. It must have the endurance to repeatedly show up and do what you need it to do.

What do you need to do to transform your body for your amazing journey toward abundance?

When you develop your goals in the 12 areas above, it's imperative to *be specific*. State how much and by when. Decide on the smaller, incremental targets you'll hit on your way to achieving bigger goals. Then, write down your goals and review them daily.

In Chapter 2, I'll reveal how to fast-track the attainment of these goals through daily affirmations and envisioning them as already complete.

JUST AS YOU DEFINE ABUNDANCE FOR YOURSELF, SCARCITY IS ALSO SOMETHING YOU DECIDE IN YOUR OWN MIND

Regardless of where you're starting today, abundance can be a part of your future—even if it has not been part of your past. Though I grew up in scarce circumstances, I realized as an adult that I have the power to change my future circumstances through planning, working hard, and surrendering to God's plan for me.

You have this power, too.

And whether your childhood experience was limited in terms of money, safety, love, or acknowledgment—you get to choose abundance on your own terms, starting today.

> We cannot change our last chapter, as it has already been written in ink. But we can change the way our next chapter will be written because we are still holding the pen in our hands.
>
> —Lisa Nichols

Susie Carder, my chief operating officer—and for many years my business coach—is today a brilliant and compassionate woman. But she often mentions how her childhood helped shape her current life of abundance, as well as her commitment to outwardly expressing love.

Because her mother could not provide the lifestyle Susie deserved, she left five-year-old Susie on Easter Day with her father—a committed family man, but a career soldier and ship welder with an eighth-grade education who was rigid, structured, and undemonstrative when it came to affection. With two stepsisters, three stepbrothers, one half-sister—plus Susie and her siblings—the family also suffered from lack of money, food, and resources. Susie's grandmother raised the children while her stepmom—a kind woman—worked as a seamstress. All they saw was the hard work and determination of an amazing man who raised nine kids with *no* debt, living paycheck to paycheck, and obtaining government rations like powdered milk and cheese to feed his family. Everything Susie wore was a hand-me-down. As the youngest child, she never had anything new. When Susie was sixteen and old enough to get a job at Kentucky Fried Chicken, her siblings would wait on the porch for her to come home, carrying a bucket of leftovers to feed the family that night. Susie learned to maximize leverage and be resourceful—something she still uses every day.

In this environment, it would have been easy for Susie to become a product of her childhood. But she had bigger plans.

She became a hairdresser and eventually created a system to upsell additional services and offer products to her customers. As one of the few hairdressers in America earning over $250,000 a year, she turned her expertise into a training and development company to teach business skills to other hairstylists—then sold it for millions of dollars after building it into the leading training company in her industry. Along the way, she amassed over ten million dollars in real estate.

Because she knew what *scarcity* looked like, she created just the opposite—an abundant and prosperous life. Not only that, but she also attributes her characteristics as a mother today—loving, generous, giving—to the love she did not get as a child. While Susie had every reason to continue in limitation and lack, today she is a classic example of how scarcity is a choice. She made a conscious choice as an adult to work for something better.

GRATITUDE HELPS YOU MOVE FORWARD INTO ABUNDANCE

How can *you* reframe scarcity and move forward into a life of abundance? One way that I've discovered is to express gratitude *for what you do have.*

When I first began to plan a life of abundance for myself, I made the conscious decision that my economic status does not equal my joy. In other words, my bank account balance doesn't get to determine how happy I choose to be every day. The bills I have to pay don't get to take the joy out of my life. My salary doesn't get to define how jubilant or peaceful I choose to be. In other words, none of my external economic circumstances have the power to define the person that I am in this or any moment. My economic status is a temporary situation, and my bank account is merely a financial tool that I manage.

Most important, my economic status is not an indicator of how much abundance I have in my life, because I think of abundance differently now.

Back when my transformation was starting, to confirm to myself just how much abundance *I already had* in my life, I spent ten minutes every morning in gratitude—choosing ten things to be grateful for that did not cost money. If you did the same Morning Gratitude Exercise, this abundant new mindset would go with you throughout your day, informing the Universe to deliver even more things, people, situations, and opportunities for which you could express gratitude.

Of course, the universal principle at work here is *Energy grows where energy goes.* If you want great things to come into your life, you have to *first* be overwhelmingly clear about the great things that *already exist* in your life. You have to give them your energy and attention.

As I mentioned, lately I've been working on my physical body. And one of the biggest lessons I've learned is that, if I want the next version of my body to emerge through my behavior, I first had to learn to love my existing body. Now *that* was a challenge! Not only was I frustrated about the body I was in, I had always felt that it was going to be impossible to achieve the shapely body I wanted. I put so much negative energy into thoughts about my body that it simply couldn't show up in return. It couldn't give me back something that looked beautiful to me.

It wasn't until I began to love my hips, love my thighs, love my arms—all at their current size—that I began to care enough to feed them better food, do my sit-ups and crunches, practice my lunges, get better rest to assist in my weight loss, and visit a holistic doctor to address my fatigue and burned-out adrenals.

Gratitude, I learned, pays homage and honor to what is. And it's a lesson I've tried to teach others.

When I first appeared on Oprah Winfrey's television show, I told her viewers to love themselves first before expecting others to love them.

"I'm the first example of how the world's supposed to love me," I said. "And I have to give them the best example ever."

When you pay homage and honor to what is, you open up a clear space to call forth what's to come. It's like planting beautiful seeds in soil that you've already tilled, watered, and nurtured. When you're not grateful, by contrast, your world is more like untilled soil—hardened, dry, and fallow. You wouldn't expect to plant new seeds and see them grow in ground like that. Gratitude is the cultivating you need to complete *first* so you can invite wonderful, beautiful things to grow.

ABUNDANCE USUALLY REQUIRES YOU TO MOVE TO A NEW MENTAL ZIP CODE

Over and over, changes that I've seen in the lives of my clients, participants, and students tell me that scarcity is more a mindset than a financial condition or physical condition. If you are stuck in scarcity physically, it's because you may be unconsciously committed to it mentally. I give you this truth with love—and a dose of cold water. If you are finding that life is hard, the problem may not exclusively be in your circumstances. It also has in large part to do with the choices that you've made.

The truth is we live in an abundant world. Now, that's not to say that there isn't real struggle and hurting people who have genuinely fallen on hard times. And the truth remains that there is enough for all of us. All that remains is for you to *choose* whether you'll be abundance-focused or consumed by the feeling of "impossible or lack."

And the moment you become non-negotiable about changing your mental ZIP code, pack your bags, and mentally move to a new zip code filled with prosperity instead of scarcity, you will begin to see your life change. The moment you begin to think like prosperous people think, study what prosperous people study, and be more intentional about attracting what you want to attract is the moment your life will begin to change.

The moment you change your mindset is the moment that your finances, relationships, and physical wellness will have to follow. And the good news is that thinking, studying, and acting like prosperous people do is easier than ever. There is more than enough information available today—enough role models, documentaries, books, websites, and training courses on how to achieve each of your specific goals—for you to easily determine a path to your abundant future. If you look, you will find many people who live in an abundant headspace and have the lives to prove it. Find them, model them, and start the actions that lead to living an abundant and prosperous life.

> If you want to be rich, you must not make
> a study of poverty.
>
> —Wallace D. Wattles, author of The Science of Getting Rich,
> first published in 1910

If more than enough information is available to us—on the Internet, through advisers, and in books—why do so many of us stay stuck in a scarcity mindset? Because it's simply human nature to remain more committed to a familiar discomfort than to an unfamiliar new possibility. The fear of the unknown often drives us to continue in an uncomfortable, unpleasant situation—whether it's financial difficulty, health concerns, relationship problems, or something else. We create the story that at least we know this chaos—and that it's easier to live with the chaos than to risk the unknown via some new possibility.

But the best way to get past being stuck is to acknowledge, *This is where I am. It's merely a mental barrier that I have to get past.* Too many people look for ways in which they are deficient or ways in which the outside world is somehow holding them back and then say, *See, I can't move forward into abundance because there are forces that always seem to be working against me.*

If you have a job and you blame your lack of financial wealth on your employer, realize that you've just surrendered your financial future to someone who did not even ask to take on that responsibility. Not only did you disempower yourself, but you also empowered someone else who's never asked to be your financial god.

To further the point, if you've ever said, *I would be happier if my job were . . . ,* you've also chosen to slide out of the driver's seat of your life and move into the passenger seat. Depending on the energy you put into that statement, you might move even further away—to the backseat and, in some cases, the trunk! It's now time for you to get back in the driver's seat of your life.

But what if you're already there—simply refusing to step on the gas because you're afraid you'll hit a curb, a wall, or the center divider? Realize that the only way you'll hit something *is if you're not steering.* Just like driving a real car, steering takes knowledge and practice—which you can't get when you're in the parking lot. So step on the gas, learn how to steer those parts of your life you need to control, and get into motion.

Another way that people keep themselves from moving forward is they hide behind ambiguity and lack of knowledge.

"I don't know what to do next," they say. "I am unclear."

If this describes you, simply lean into the uncertainty. Move forward, and if your first step doesn't feel right, then pick up your foot—scrape whatever you stepped in off the bottom of your shoe—then move in an alternative direction until you find success. Just keep moving.

Action beckons results, and results beckon clarity. Although you may want to see the entire path before you ever take a step, life just doesn't work that way.

> Take the first step in faith. You don't have to see the whole staircase. Just take the first step.
>
> —Martin Luther King Jr., legendary civil rights leader and Nobel Peace Prize recipient

One of the most immediate results I see happen when people decide to move forward is something I call *unconscious stagnation*. Because we fear other people's perception of us—and because we unconsciously suffer from our own fear of failure—we actually become more committed to looking good than to succeeding. We would rather stay stagnant and look good in mediocrity than risk making a fool of ourselves reaching for extraordinary.

Even worse, many of us spend lots of time, money, and energy being "busy" when what we're really doing is standing still. While we may be in motion, we're doing the wrong things. Our subconscious mind is silently keeping us from taking those actions that will truly help us meet our goals. There's no forward movement toward our future.

In my own life, I found myself experiencing unconscious stagnation around my weight. Knowing that I wanted (and needed) to release at least 70 pounds, I read about it, talked about it—even prayed about it. I went as far as buying healthy foods, protein shakes, and workout gear, yet I still seemed to only hover around the goal—far more than I was consistent in doing what was necessary. My fear of failing *myself* caused me to never really get started on achieving the weight loss that I so desperately desired.

To achieve an abundant life, however, you're going to have to take the position (as I did) that you would rather be in motion and possibly make a fool of yourself reaching for the extraordinary—than be complacent, ordinary, and living in mediocrity.

VISUALIZE YOUR ABUNDANT LIFE AS ALREADY ACHIEVED

When I hold weekend retreats for high achievers, I facilitate an intensive visualization process that helps participants bring about their future goals. As previously explained, visualization utilizes the demonstrable power of sight, sound, feeling, and emotion to stimulate the subconscious mind to find opportunities, connections, and other resources needed to achieve big goals.

Visualization also causes your body to have a visceral reaction to your goals by stimulating the brain's *reticular activating system* to notice opportunities, people, and lucky breaks that it previously would have ignored. According to Marilee B. Sprenger, international education neuroscience consultant and author of *The Leadership Brain for Dummies,* "The *reticular activating system* (RAS) is the portal through which nearly all information enters the brain. The RAS filters the incoming information and affects what you pay attention to."* Give your brain a directive to achieve a specific goal, and it will let in details from the millions of bits of information it receives daily.

---

* *The Leadership Brain for Dummies,* by Marilee Sprenger, Wiley Publishing, 2010.

This practice might cause you to remember a conversation you had eight months ago—including information you can just now use to your advantage. It could prompt you to call an old friend who might know of a specific resource you need. It might even suggest a strategic alliance with a company whose goals align with yours.

The more you visualize what you want, the more your mind can see it and your brain can go to work bringing it about. Set aside time every day to close your eyes and focus on your goals— creating vivid pictures in your mind's eye that incorporate color, sound, emotions, even scent. Visualize your goals as already complete by a specific date, even by a specific time of day. The more clear and compelling detail you can include, the more accelerated energy will be released.

But don't forget to follow part two of the visualization formula: once you visualize your goals as completed, take action on the instincts, prompts, insights, hunches, and other mental messages you receive.

Below you'll find a short script for a visualization process designed to focus you on abundance. To use it effectively, record it in your own voice (or have a friend record it), then replay the recording to guide you through the visualization session. Be sure to conduct your visualization sessions in a quiet and uninterrupted place. (It's not a process to do during gym time or while driving, for instance.) Give your daily visualizations the time and space *you* deserve.

RELAXING INTO THE VISUALIZATION PROCESS

Let's use the power of your mind to create your ideal life. Your future experiences will start in your mind first, so let's take a journey into your most creative, free, and powerful place ever— your imagination!

We become what we most think about. Your new possibilities and success can be created by you and only you. You will become what you think about every day.

Let's cut away all limiting thoughts, and rise above your fears to the place of freedom and creation.

Stand in your power! Success is your birthright! Move in this moment from optional to non-negotiable.

Every great leader, prophet, visionary, role model, and legend visualized their future *before* they took action.

Know that you have as much right to joy, love, happiness, and abundance as any other living creature on this planet, and it's yours for the asking and creating.

You have *nothing* to lose and *everything* to gain.

Now . . .

Choose a quiet place. Turn off your phone. Clear your mind. Everything you need to do will be there waiting for you on the other side of this journey. Let it all go for now. Relax and release any physical tension. Become more committed to your inner images than to your physical presence.

Now, take a deep cleansing breath, filling your abdominal area full of breath. And as you exhale, gently feel your body sinking into a relaxed state.

To help you go into a deep level of mind, I will gently guide you through a relaxation of your physical body.

Feel your scalp relax. Feel this gentle feeling of relaxation flow down your forehead. Now to your eyes . . . Feel your eyelids relax. Feel that sensation of relaxation on your eyelids. Feel that slowly flowing out throughout your body.

Move the soothing feeling to your face . . . and your throat . . . your neck . . . your shoulders. Feel them sink into deep relaxation.

Now your upper arms . . . your hands . . . your chest . . . your abdomen . . . your thighs . . . your knees . . . your calves . . . your feet.

And feel that feeling of relaxation flow all the way down to your toes.

VISUALIZATION SCRIPT FOR ABUNDANCE

Picture yourself in any lovely natural environment—perhaps by a green, open meadow with a lovely brook, or on white sand by the ocean . . .

Take some time to imagine all the beautiful details, and see yourself fully enjoying and appreciating your surroundings . . .

Now begin to walk, and soon find yourself in a different surrounding, perhaps exploring a waving field of golden grain, or swimming in a lake . . .

Continue to wander and explore—finding more and more exquisitely beautiful environments of great variety—mountains, forests, deserts, whatever suits your fantasy . . .

Take a little time to appreciate each one . . .

Now imagine returning home to a simple but comfortable environment, whatever would most suit you . . .

Imagine having loving family, friends, and community around you . . .

Visualize yourself doing work that you love, and expressing yourself creatively in ways that feel just right for you . . .

You are being amply rewarded for your efforts, in internal satisfaction, appreciation from others, and financial return . . .

Imagine yourself feeling fulfilled and thoroughly enjoying your life . . .

Step back, and see if you can imagine a world full of people living simply yet abundantly, in harmony with one another and the earth . . .

Say these affirmations in your mind:

- I find prosperity in simplicity.
- This is an abundant universe and there is plenty for all of us.
- Abundance is my true state of being. I am now ready to accept it fully and joyously.

- God is the unfailing, unlimited source of all my supply.
- I deserve to be prosperous and happy. I am now prosperous and happy!
- The more I prosper, the more I have to share with everyone else.
- I'm ready now to accept all the joy and prosperity life has to offer me.
- The world is now becoming an abundant place for everyone.
- Financial success is coming to me easily and effortlessly.
- I am now enjoying financial prosperity!
- Life is meant to be fun and I'm now willing to enjoy it!
- I am rich in consciousness and manifestation.
- I now have plenty of money for my own personal needs and the needs of my family.
- My good efforts to serve others will be rewarded.
- I feel deeply satisfied with my financial situation.
- I feel rich, well, and happy.
- I am open to receiving the blessings of this abundant universe.
- Everything good is coming to me easily and effortlessly.

CLOSING DOWN THE VISUALIZATION PROCESS

Slowly begin to feel your back against the chair. Feel your feet on the ground. Feel your breath again. Begin to come back into the room. When you are ready, very gradually bring yourself back into the now moment.

Now completely rejoin your physical body. Hear the sounds around you in your now environment. When you feel ready, you may open your eyes.

Welcome back! Go throughout your day thinking about and reciting positive affirmations that support and add great energy to your creative visualization.

Remember this in everything that you do: as was said in the Sermon on the Mount, "Ask and it will be given to you, seek and you will find, knock and the door will be opened to you. For everyone who asks receives, the one who seeks finds, and to the one who knocks the door will be opened."

Remember to be in bold radical *action* toward your goals. Ideas and visualizations are worthless without action.

Finally, accept that it is so! This is your future being shown to you like a motion picture with you as the star. All you need now is action, unwavering faith, and a purpose bigger than yourself.

I'm your sister in this journey and I believe in you.

———

When you visualize, try to incorporate as many stimulating elements and emotions as possible including: color, time of day, time of year, aromas, sounds, emotions felt within your body, and sensory feelings such as touch. When I experienced my very first visualization session, I envisioned my life five years out— traveling, teaching others, wearing business suits, being in front of an audience, and hearing the appreciation of those I had taught. I found myself crying tears of joy when I was actually able to "see" myself living the life of service and success that I had dreamt about for so many years. My chest was full, and my heart pounded rapidly with real excitement. That was my body responding as if success had already occurred—a visceral reaction to visualization.

KNOW THE "WHAT," THEN FIGURE OUT THE "HOW"

When you do visualize, don't worry about *how your goal will be accomplished*. Set the intention of what you want—then let the Universe provide the mechanism by which you'll achieve your goal.

Too many people get daunted by *how* they're going to make things happen. Don't merge the "what" and the "how" together.

When you do that, you overwhelm yourself with the *how* and don't allow the *what* to gain impact or traction.

Maintain 100% intention that your goal will be fulfilled. But, at the same time, have 0% concern about the *mechanism that will be used* to achieve it.

TeeJ Mercer, a participant in my yearlong Global Leadership Program, spent her entire career as a successful film editor—primarily for television shows in Hollywood's vast and unending production machine. She was good at her job, but her heart had always wanted to start a foundation to make people's dreams come true. Inspired by the Make-A-Wish Foundation, which fulfills unique requests for children with life-threatening illnesses, TeeJ pondered, *What about adults who have dreams, but who've simply forgotten them in the face of life's other priorities? What if I could "green-light" these dreams, assembling the necessary people, resources, and funding in the same way that television shows and movies get approved for production?*

With that single idea, Project DreamLight was born. But while TeeJ had 100% intention that her goal would be fulfilled, she had no idea how to make it work or even who she would approach for help with making the dream projects come to fruition. By her own admission, she was clueless. Yet for nearly three years, TeeJ kept broadcasting her intention to launch Project DreamLight. She talked about it incessantly. Soon people gravitated to her idea—enabling her to assemble a working board of directors with the financial means and knowledge to fulfill applicants' dreams.

And here's the best part: TeeJ doesn't require that applicants provide financial information or be disadvantaged in any way. She knows that everyone—even people with financial resources—have dreams. But too often they don't have the knowledge or connections to get their ideas off the ground. That's where Project DreamLight comes in. Plus, TeeJ puts *no boundaries* on the types of dreams that can be granted.

To date, Project DreamLight has facilitated everything from helping a screenwriter get software for properly formatting scripts, to developing a curriculum for homeless shelters to get people off the street, to dental work that's giving back the smile to a woman who was in a bicycle accident as a child—even mentoring inventors on patenting their inventions and bringing them to market.

On February 27, 2015, after green-lighting and funding her first 25 projects, TeeJ retired from her career as a television editor to work full-time on Project DreamLight along with the other dedicated people her 100% intention had brought about.

Just as TeeJ discovered, it's okay to be clueless. Know what you want to do, but don't overwhelm yourself before getting started with the uncertainties, financial needs, or other details of your goal. Just start down the path and watch the necessary resources, knowledge, people, and opportunities unfold before you.

Make a bold declaration of what you want to achieve. Make the declaration as if you have everything you need to move forward. And then, once you state what you want to achieve—and light your soul on fire about it—the Universe will conspire to line things up on your behalf. Of course, you still have to make an action plan. You still have to do the work. But first you have to get to this *how* by signing off on the *what*.

BECOME NON-NEGOTIABLE ABOUT YOUR GOALS

How many people do you know who want an exciting future but aren't willing to put the time and effort into achieving it? The reality is that merely *wanting* to achieve a goal isn't enough. You have to proceed as if the achievement of that goal is non-negotiable.

In other words, failure is not an option. It doesn't matter *how* the goal will be achieved. But you must maintain the conviction that achieving it is necessary and not open to compromise.

There's a reason for this conviction: not only do things happen when you move every other option off the table, but the intention, passion, and determination you broadcast to the Universe will help to bring forth the resources and opportunities you need to fulfill your goal. Suddenly, people, money, and other resources you need will appear. Roadblocks will magically disappear. Other projects that consume your time and focus will fade away in the face of achieving your all-important goal.

Being non-negotiable also means that "really wanting" your goal is not enough either. When you're not 100% committed, you still have an "out"—that is, the chance of stopping or becoming unfocused because you haven't taken other options off the table.

> Don't wait for the fear to stop before you leap.
> Be willing to leap afraid.
>
> —Lisa Nichols

Non-negotiable means you must also be willing to say the things you don't want to say—and do the things you don't want to do (or believe you could never do). You must also be willing to evict the toxic behaviors—and toxic people—from your life on behalf of your future.

Of course, while reaching your goal should be non-negotiable, *how you get there* should always remain flexible. Make sure your plans can be adjusted as needed whether it's changing strategy, partners, or other paths to your goal.

LOVE YOUR VISION, BUT DON'T EXPECT OTHERS TO APPLAUD IT

Something else you can expect when you become non-negotiable about your goals is for those around you to not share in your vision. Not only are we often surrounded by others who have a scarcity mindset, they may not see, or agree with, the importance or inevitability of our goals.

I realized that I have to stop sharing my million-dollar
dreams with hundred-dollar people.

—*Steve Harvey, Emmy Award–winning talk-show host
and author of* Act Like a Success, Think Like a Success

This truth was brought home to me the first time I embarked
on a major international speaking tour. I traveled to South Africa
at the invitation of a personal-empowerment group dedicated to
building a stronger, more effective South Africa. And while I
thought I was being hired for a standard multi-city motivational
tour, I discovered when I got there that my hosts were primarily
counting on me to bridge the great divide that existed between
the different racial groups who had suffered devastation, pain,
and divisiveness under South Africa's apartheid government.

They wanted and needed a message of healing. And I was supposed to deliver it for them.

Faced with the challenging duty to reframe their suffering,
make sense of their pain, and help them navigate to a new place
in the social landscape, I had to throw out everything I'd prepared. I completely rewrote my message, prayed 15 hours continuously for God's help, and let go of any "intended" experience
that I'd brought with me. I tapped into an as-yet-undiscovered
place in my soul and lived there for days as I spoke boldly and
compassionately—facilitating healing for the thousands of audience members that filled the rooms as I moved from town to town.

When I boarded the plane, utterly exhausted, for the return
flight to Los Angeles, it was one day before July 4th weekend—a
marathon of cooking, feasting, and camaraderie as 35 of my family members would assemble at my cousin's house for our yearly
celebration. With my soul-stirring work in South Africa still top-
of-mind, I made my way to the party. Just steps inside the front
door, my cousin yelled out, "We know you just came from doing
something really important in Africa 'cause we saw it all over

Facebook. But you're home now, and all we wanna know is . . . did you bring the peach cobbler?"

It was then that a truth hit me. My family is my family. What felt like a lack of interest in my work for many years has now proven to be my safe place to just "BE." With no need to produce anything but a peach cobbler with extra crust. This was truly my safe space. When I freed them to just be my family, I actually freed myself as well. They're not a part of what I do for a living. They're not inspired in the same way I am from my work.

As *you* move forward in your ideal life, don't blame others for not seeing your vision. God gave your vision to *you*. Don't try to convert your family to be your fans or supporters. Allow people to show up as they will. It's your job to give your vision life. Don't rely on anyone else to provide this momentum for you.

FORWARD DISRUPTION: EXPECT A SCARCITY MINDSET FROM OTHERS

The people who are closest to you will often experience mild to moderate disruption when you begin pursuing your goals in earnest. Why? It's because you're disrupting what's familiar to them—they're becoming uncomfortable with change. Unfortunately, those circumstances with which *you have become uncomfortable*—the modest income you earn, the unexceptional career you may have, or the ordinary lifestyle you lead—are familiar to the people closest to you.

As you move forward on creating an exceptional life experience, realize that you'll be creating something new and unknown for others.

But beware not to fall victim to this consequence yourself.

During a recent appearance on *The Steve Harvey Show,* Steve asked me, "What's something that makes transformation so difficult for some people?"

I responded, as I explained above, that people often become more committed to a *familiar discomfort* than they are to an *unfamiliar new possibility*.

If this describes you, realize that—once you break this cycle for yourself—it doesn't necessarily mean that everyone (or anyone) around you will also break it. As you redefine prosperity for yourself and begin to move forward on the road to a more abundant life, you might find family members, friends, and coworkers subconsciously sabotaging your efforts. It's not that they will consciously say, *Whoa, hold on there, you're becoming too prosperous.* But you'll likely find your new standards are simply outside their comfort zone.

Affectionately said, these time bandits, naysayers, and success saboteurs want you to stay where you are—mainly because they may be unconsciously afraid of the change or they don't want to risk what's required to grow along with you.

Stop doing what you're doing, they seem to say, *and stay where I am.*

Sometimes their conscious or unconscious sabotage is subtle. At other times, they'll use guilt, criticism, or manipulation. Even worse, they'll claim to know what's good for you—better than you know yourself. You might hear:

Trust me, I know. That idea will never work.

I can't trust people, and neither should you if you know what's good for you.

You work too hard. Let's go to the mall/movies/out for lunch this afternoon. You deserve a break.

I'm here if and when it doesn't work out for you, cuz you know I got your back.

I wouldn't pay down my mortgage early. You'll lose your tax write-off.

Why try again? You know you always gain the weight back.

It sounds too good to be true, so assume that it is too good to be true.

One thing you won't hear is, *Gosh, I'm so excited that my life is committed to scarcity.* But that's their ultimate message, isn't it? One of my favorite quotes is from Dr. Wayne Dyer, who says, "It's never crowded along the extra mile." The fear-based or limited thinkers in your life don't want to go the extra mile—even if you are doing just that every day. They don't want to step up, get better, do more, be uncomfortable, or get out of their comfort zone.

And they don't want you to, either. Not because they don't want you to win, but because they don't want to be left behind.

Unfortunately, in the past, as long as you were equals, you became a mirror for them. Your life looked like theirs. But now that you've started to grow, the image they see in the mirror no longer looks the same. Your forward momentum makes them take stock of their own current stagnation.

CREATE A NEW PATH, AND PEOPLE MAY REACT WITH EVEN GREATER RESISTANCE

Becoming a pathfinder and blazing new trails can create even more turbulence. Over the years, a number of my students have approached me and admitted they did not at first like me. Because *they* wanted to be an international transformational coach and bestselling author, they (erroneously) believed that I had taken up all available space for an African American woman to blaze that trail. Of course, this thinking assumed that there is space for only one such trailblazer—a notion that comes from a scarcity mindset.

Long before Nelson Mandela, Mother Teresa, Mahatma Gandhi, and Dr. Martin Luther King were

recognized as brilliant, people called them crazy.
If people think your ideas are strange, congratulations!
You're in great company.

—Lisa Nichols

In reality, I just smoothed the path. I made it possible for other African American women to become recognized and accepted in the role of transformational teacher and global change agent.

Even back in college—as tumultuous and dispiriting as that time was—one of my college counselors had a tremendous impact on my thinking. In fact, he told me I would be a "pacesetter." If I got bruises on my forehead, he said, it's because I'd be creating paths where they didn't exist before. Not only that, but I was a woman of color attending a small college in rural Oregon where—back in those days—there was still lingering racism among a lot of the student population. I refused to match their verbal insults because I knew—even at 19 years old—that there was a calling on my life to bridge the gap between cultures.

Day by day, this "knowing" became ever clearer to me. During my prayer time, I would remember my grandmother's instructions, "Baby, start every day that you're away from us by asking God how He wants to use you."

In my quiet time and through my query, I would hear in my heart that I am on this planet to inspire, heal, and serve others—to use my life, my energy, and my intention to create change and become an instrument for building bridges where only walls currently exist across cultural, geographical, economic, and religious boundaries. While there were so many things I was unclear about back then—the how, the when, the where, the who—I was *very clear,* even at 19 years old, about what I was supposed to do with my life.

Just like that college counselor did for me, perhaps in your life someone believed in you, too, whether it was someone close to you like a parent, grandparent, aunt, or friend, or just someone passing through your life like a short-term friendship, counselor, or even a brief acquaintance.

If that's the case, isn't it your responsibility to achieve great things—regardless of the disruption or discomfort you cause in others? And if these backers also put in hours of time to mentor you or put their faith in you—even when you didn't believe in yourself—wouldn't you be letting them down by *not doing everything possible* to achieve your dreams?

It's up to you to maintain the will and internal fortitude to succeed—regardless of toxic, scarcity-minded adversaries you might encounter.

Abundance is within your grasp. Let's get started on your path to embracing it!

THE 4 Es: YOUR PATH TO AN ABUNDANT FUTURE

Over the next four chapters, I'll introduce you to the formula for moving forward—leaving scarcity behind, and creating an exciting new life. An abundant life!

You'll experience **Enrichment** as you develop your whole Self into a focused and abundant thinker. I'll help you find **Enchantment**—connecting with others and developing Relationships that will support you in success. You'll discover the thrill of **Engagement** that comes from pursuing Work—either employment or your own business—that leads to exciting experiences (as my career has done) or ably bankrolls whatever you want to do.

Finally, we'll talk about a new approach to Money—seeing money as an **Endowment** that grows and continues to fund the kind of breathtaking lifestyle few can imagine. I'll teach you how to earn it, preserve it, nurture it, *and use it*—a tutorial you'll find encouraging regardless of the size of your bank account now.

CHAPTER 2

The First E: Enrichment of Your Whole Self

Self-development is a greater commitment and a greater
requirement than self-sacrifice.

—Lisa Nichols

What's the most critical ingredient to living an abundant life? It's your mindset—the "knowing" that enables you to push past limiting beliefs, take on new opportunities with confidence, and succeed in getting what you want.

This *knowing* precedes your ability to succeed and paves the way for you to enjoy abundance in every area of your life.

And it's this knowing that I want to help you develop now.

THE MINDSET REQUIRED FOR AN ABUNDANT, PROSPEROUS LIFE

To live an abundant life, you're going to have to take responsibility for your thoughts, your actions—and, most important, your *reactions* to what life throws at you. This isn't easy. In fact, while most people look outside themselves to place blame for what's wrong with their lives and for the reasons why they don't enjoy an abundant lifestyle, you have to take the position that *you have the power* to create the life of your dreams—regardless of your current circumstances.

You've always had this power.

Now it's time to add the requisite mindset to that power and begin living the life you deserve.

SHIFT YOUR LANGUAGE, SHIFT YOUR MIND

You—and you alone—are the creator of your abundant life. Once you recognize this fact, you can begin to do those things that will bring about the future you want.

And one of the very first to-do items is to begin *talking differently* about your plans, projects, relationships, and dreams. When you share them with others—using upbeat language about your intended outcomes and describing in vivid detail what success looks like to you (remember that visualization exercise?)—you create a picture in your mind of what you want in that area of your life.

This new language of abundance actually causes you—consciously and unconsciously—to overcome limiting beliefs and actually take those actions that will bring about the results you want.

How?

By setting up a state of *cognitive dissonance* in your mind. Cognitive dissonance is the feeling of discomfort that comes from a discrepancy between beliefs and behaviors. When you believe something strongly or you repeatedly behave a certain way—and then you suddenly add a new picture or belief or behavior to the mix—your brain will do everything in its power to resolve this discrepancy. It will strive to bring about the new behavior or pictured circumstances in order to get rid of the feelings of discomfort.

In his book *A Theory of Cognitive Dissonance,* psychologist Leon

Festinger likens this process to how your brain reacts when you're hungry. Whenever you feel hungry, the brain sends signals to your body to eat. In other words, it causes you to take those actions which will resolve your hunger. Similarly, when you begin speaking differently about your future and picturing it differently in your mind, your brain will also cause you to take those actions to bring about this exciting new future.

Just putting those abundant pictures in your mind through repeated visualization and verbalization will cause the brain to resolve the cognitive dissonance between your goals and your current circumstance.

I often tell my students that *what you think about you bring about.* To that I would add "what you *talk about* you bring about." You must begin to see the world as a wellspring of possibility. You must begin talking and thinking differently about your future.

When I was 15 years old, I competed on the swim team at the local community center. I loved everything about swimming, but I had one major challenge: I always came in dead last. If there were six lanes in the pool, I'd finish sixth. If there were ten, I'd finish tenth. I struggled so much with the embarrassment of what I came to believe was predestined failure that, one day, I vowed to quit swimming for good.

I was so committed to quitting, in fact, that I told my Grandmother Bernice. She was startled. And when she asked me to sit down next to her, I thought, *Here it comes. She's going to tell me I can fly.*

But she didn't.

She told me instead about my ancestors—my great-great-great-grandparents who came through the Middle Passage, surviving the voyage from Africa when so many thousands didn't. She told me how they worked in the fields under a broiling sun—from sunup to sundown—with blisters on their feet and aching bones from their labors. She reminded me that they weren't quitters. They didn't lay down their load. They lived and survived so that I could be here today. Even my parents did things I'll never know about—sacrificing and scraping by—to create a space for me to step into my greatness.

Quitters never win, she said, *and winners never quit.*

With Grandma Bernice's reproof in my mind, the next day I showed up at my swim meet—questioning whether I could win, but committed not to quit. When I realized I had missed the heat for 15- to 16-year-olds, it scared the bejeebies out of me. I'd now have to swim with the 17- to 18-year-olds instead. Having come in last in my own age group—at every competition—I knew the odds were completely stacked against me. And as the official told us to take our places, I prayed, *God, if there's anything left in me, give it to me now.*

When the starting gun went off, I hit the water cleanly. Chanting like my life depended on it—*quitters never win, winners never quit*—I neared the opposite wall and flipped for my return lap, swimming harder than ever. The chanting created a rhythm in my mind. In fact, every time I thought those words, a small part of me even began to believe I might win. Half a pool length from the finish, I even found a new burst of energy.

But as I hit the starting wall and finished the heat, I looked up—only to find myself *alone* at the end of the pool. *Had everyone else finished and left the pool?* I thought. No. My coach started shouting. People started pointing. And there—*behind me*—was the next closest competitor swimming forcefully toward the finish line.

Before that day, I'd been chanting, *I don't want to lose. Please don't let me come in last.* But just changing my language gave me an entirely different result. That day—at age 15—I broke the 17- to 18-year-old community record for the 400-meter freestyle and landed in the record books. Instead of going home with an Honorable Mention ribbon, I stepped into first place at the awards ceremony and received a huge trophy.

What could *you* accomplish simply by shifting your language about *your* future?

LIVE IN YOUR LIGHT BY FREEING YOURSELF
FROM OLD CONSTRAINTS

To step inside your greatness and begin using the genius that's been uniquely given to you—something I call "living in your light"—you're going to have to allow yourself to be free of old constraints and give yourself permission to stand in your power.

What does that look like?

Standing in your power is when you are committed to pushing past any negative self-talk, rising above your own fears, and evicting any disempowering thoughts or chatter that does not support your highest calling and greatest service.

You might be already doing that. But what would happen in your life if you took it to a whole new level? What must *you* do to begin *living in your light*?

1. *Strive to be at peace with all your choices, actions, and decisions*—including all your *past actions*. You must free yourself from any regret, shame, or blame of yourself and others. As well, you must forgive yourself for what you did in the past (or failed to do) and forgive others for their part in your past difficulties.

2. *Start looking for what's possible in your life.* Plan for what you want to create—not what you want to avoid. This is very important. When you speak in the language of possibility instead of the language of avoidance, you'll be constantly breathing life into every situation. You'll be moving away from negative, draining conversations that focus on "never enough," victimhood, or "why me"—powerless words that drain your energy and take your focus away from the good that can happen for you. Instead of comparing our journey to some ideal life (or someone else's journey), we can celebrate our own journey with all its highs and lows, celebration and woes, laughter and tears—knowing that our unique journey

has prepared us perfectly for greatness based on our personal history.

3. *Answer the question "why?"* Instead of constantly looking at life from the standpoint of victimhood—*Why did my father leave?, Why did my career take such a traumatic hit?, Why did that man touch me inappropriately?*—begin to reframe these questions and process the answers without you as the central figure. This immediately moves you from victimhood to a place of empowerment. Why did your father leave? *Because he wasn't ready to step up and be a father.* Why did your career take a traumatic hit? *Because jobs outgrow you if you're not growing— and you can also outgrow a job. Remember Man's rejection is God's protection. There is something better for you waiting on you.* There is always a better explanation to "why" questions than for you to be the cause or the victim.

STOP LYING TO YOURSELF ABOUT YOUR PAST EXPERIENCES

When you tell yourself that you aren't capable of accomplishing your goals or solving your problems—when you tell yourself that you're not rich enough, beautiful enough, smart enough, or "enough" in any other way that matters—you're drawing upon long-held beliefs in your mind that simply aren't true.

They're lies you're telling yourself—stories you've created around your past experiences that are now dictating what you believe about yourself.

It's time to stop and expose these lies so you can deal with them.

In my trainings, I walk participants through a powerful exercise that helps identify and resolve the lies they tell themselves. To begin, take out several sheets of lined paper and begin jotting down—in pencil—every lie you have told yourself that keeps you from being powerful, joyful, worthy, and proud. Look at the lies that you tell yourself around relationships, family, your body's physical abilities, money, and work. Your list might read:

I'm not good-looking enough to be considered attractive.

I am going to always be lonely even when I'm not alone.

I'm not brilliant enough to live my dreams.

I don't have enough money to start my own company.

I could never afford to live in the house I want.

I'm not talented enough to have my own television show.

I've been heavy for so long, I'll never lose this weight.

If people only knew how unprepared I am.

Take your time and take deep breaths as you write. Tears may flow as they did each of the six times that I have done this exercise for myself. You may be surprised with how many pages you fill up. The bigger you play in the world the more internal chatter you will have, so no worries. The most important thing is to dump it all out to disempower it, so don't feel ashamed of playing.

Leave three lines between each of the lies as you list them. Now take a red pen and write out what is *actually true* for each of the lies you've told yourself. Your list may look like this:

LIE: *I don't have enough money to start my own company.*

TRUTH: *There are multiple ways that I can fund my start-up company. Save aggressively from my day job, start small and grow, strengthen my business concept, and get investors.*

LIE: *I am going to always be lonely even when I'm not alone.*

TRUTH: *I can open up more and be more transparent in any moment and instantly increase my connection to others.*

Although writing down these lies—then investigating what's actually true—may be tough, it's necessary in order to break through those beliefs that are holding you back from living your light.

Before I went through this process and wrote my list, I told myself lies, too. Lots of them. When I was in my twenties, for instance, I told myself I was lonely. In fact, I used to look in the mirror and tell myself that. Pretty soon, I believed it. But I also genuinely wanted to be in a romantic relationship. So what did I do? I lowered the bar when it came to integrity. I let someone into my life who I very soon knew didn't deserve to be there.

Believing lies causes you to make these errors in judgment. You give yourself a story about why you don't deserve better, why you can't speak up for yourself, or why a bad relationship is better than nothing. The story you tell yourself isn't true—and it disempowers you—but because you've rehearsed the story repeatedly in your mind, it has now become a belief that produces undesirable outcomes.

By exposing each of your lies and writing down what's true instead (even if you can't believe it yet), you will begin to dissipate their power and influence over you.

BE DISCIPLINED AND FEARLESS IN PURSUING YOUR DREAMS

In Chapter 1, I asked you to get crystal clear about your future. What do you want? How will abundance manifest itself in your life? What will you have, be, and do as a result of your newfound prosperity?

While you've hopefully planned your life in the 12 areas I outlined, this instruction also comes with a caution: accidental success is a myth, so be methodical and disciplined in pursuing your dreams. What's the best way to do this? Break down your goals into milestones—baby steps that you can achieve in an hour, a day, or a week.

Let's say you've decided—as I did—to start your own business. And you've decided that you need $30,000 to do that. You might seek out a bank or investor to loan you all the money, or you could save that amount from your own earnings over time. Either path is workable—but each has a different set of baby steps that will bring you the $30,000. The money won't just show up overnight in your bank account. So research exactly how to obtain the money in the way that works best for you, and then create a plan around that strategy. For example, your list of baby steps might look like this:

$30,000 FROM A BANK OR INVESTOR	$30,000 FROM MY EARNINGS
Research types of private investors.	Open a special savings account.
Research banks and private lenders.	Research automatic payroll deductions.
Research methods of investment.	List household expenses to eliminate.
Decide whether to incorporate.	Set up biweekly transfers in online banking.
Determine how I'll spend the $30,000.	Determine how I'll spend the $30,000.
Write a business plan or PPM.*	Recruit side projects for extra pay.

---

* PPM stands for *private placement memorandum,* a legal document that informs investors about your business idea and the objectives, terms, and risks associated with investing in it.

Identifying your goal along with the 10 milestones or baby steps that will get you to that goal sets you up for victory as you are stretching yourself. Too often our goals are so lofty that, without milestones, we would constantly be focused on what remains to be done versus what we have accomplished already.

I recommend that you stop after every milestone and celebrate with at least one other person. Write yourself a check—even if it's only for $5. In the memo line, write the name of your dream. You can even set aside money from a specific source (such as earnings from a second job, an inheritance, or all the revenue from a single client) that you'll use to fund your dream. Or, achieve a milestone, get paid for it—then use those earnings to fund a physical reward such as a new car, a vacation home, a luxury trip, or a piece of jewelry.

The bottom line is that you have to plan to achieve your dreams. But you also need to build lifestyle stability and financial security into your life as you move forward. In my trainings, I caution my students to keep their PIS, or *Primary Income Stream,* until they achieve a replacement income that meets their needs. It's easier to dream from a place of abundance than from a place of lack.

When you *do have* your plan and a steady source of income in place, laser-focus on accomplishing one goal or aspect of your dream for the next 30 days. Once you get there, set the next goal for the next month. Be outcome-driven.

TRUST YOUR JUDGMENT AND INTUITION

You didn't get to this point in your life because you made a lot of mistakes. You got here because you experienced a combination of decisions, great decisions, and really great lessons.

When my son, Jelani, was small, he often made a game of touching the kitchen stove—just to see if it was hot. Of course, I'd warned him repeatedly about the dangers of doing this, but he was determined. One day, I started cooking dinner, and—as expected—he burned his little hand.

"Mommy, that's hot!" he cried, as I rubbed it with Neosporin and kissed away his tears.

"So did you get the lesson?" I asked in return, knowing that he'd only have to get burned once before disciplining himself to stay away.

Just like Jelani learned which situations caused pain, these kinds of life lessons also give us an incredible tool for achieving abundance: our own judgment and intuition. And trusting this discernment is a key requirement for living an abundant, prosperous life.

But what if you don't trust yourself?

I was one of those people who would ask nine different friends to get their opinion before moving forward. If five said yes, but four said no, I'd still be immobilized because I didn't trust my own opinion.

How can *you* begin to trust *your* intuition? First, give yourself the freedom to embrace the mistakes of the past. Recognize that each choice you made up until now has either given you a great outcome or a great lesson. Both are valuable. In fact, both are necessary. Second, begin to trust yourself more—first with small decisions, then with bigger life questions. Become quiet and listen to that intuition that's working inside of you (because it's working just fine). Listen to your heart and soul more than you listen to your head. Turn up the volume on your intuition and turn off the chatter in your mind. Your intuition has always been working; you just need to listen for it. And finally, remove any negative association you hold about having made the wrong decision in the past. All too often, we have a relationship to our decisions and outcomes. If a past decision brought us an outcome that was painful, we usually retain a negative association with both the decision—and our own decision-making ability.

Removing this negative association is essential for your breakthrough.

Remember that you are the creator of your own life experience, and if your past causes you grief, you can always transform your life experience into a more positive one. Reframe any past decisions that torment you by telling yourself that you may not have gotten a great outcome, but you certainly got one of the best lessons of your life.

With this knowledge, your intuition will tell you *what not to do* next time.

When you give yourself permission to have made mistakes in the past—when you begin to trust yourself about making new choices—that's when your intuition becomes reliable and trustworthy.

TAKE INSPIRED ACTION

Abundant, prosperous people have a tendency toward action. Instead of getting stuck in planning, analysis, and research, they move forward and listen for feedback about whether they are taking the right path along the way. In the process of being in action, new resources, opportunities, and information appear to help them move forward even faster—taking steps they never would have known about if they'd stayed on the sidelines.

Taking action is a critical element in the mindset required to live an abundant, prosperous life. But how do you know which steps to take and which steps to avoid? The key is to take what I call *inspired action*.

If you're reading this book, you're probably already busy looking for ways to amplify your life. *Action* is the act of movement, while *inspired action* is about calculating, strategizing, and forecasting what the optimal action should be for results.

Michael James is one of my students who took inspired action. Having fallen into a dark place emotionally and financially,

Michael knew he needed to do something drastic to change his circumstances. With no idea how he'd pay for the trip or be able to take the time off work, Michael decided to ride his bicycle across the United States—beginning on the West Coast—camping along the way and relying on himself to carry everything he needed.

Michael bought a one-way ticket to San Francisco, but he had no money to buy the supplies needed for the endeavor. He simply wanted to change his situation. So he began to look inward. He created a vision board detailing the perfect ride across the country—including a map of his starting point at the Pacific Ocean and his end point at the Atlantic shore. He taped it to his wall so he could look at it every day. He visualized himself arriving at the Atlantic seaboard at the end of the long trip. He began to train on weekends, riding 100 miles on Saturdays and another 100 on Sundays—plus anything he could squeeze in during the week.

Before long, other people heard about his plan. Someone donated a better bicycle. Someone else donated clothing. Even his cycling gear, GPS equipment, bike trailer, repair tools, tent, camping supplies—everything he needed to be self-supporting on the road—was offered to him at cost. He was so grateful. But while things were coming together, Michael still didn't think he could afford to take a month off work. He just kept believing and seeing himself finishing his trip at the Atlantic Ocean.

To keep himself from backing out, he flew to San Francisco, and started his trip—taking action when he didn't know the obstacles he'd still have to face. It would have been easy to give up had he known what lay ahead, but he didn't want to risk being broken yet again by failing to move forward on his goal.

As the trip unfolded, Michael suffered record-breaking 113-degree heat, flat tires, mechanical problems, even being run off the road and waking up to paramedics who were rescuing him—the list of the challenges he faced every hour of every day goes on and on.

On the second-to-last day, as Michael's trip was coming to an end, he broke down emotionally when he looked back at his ride and how he'd made it through every challenge. Even with his body physically tired, he still couldn't stop his ride. That day, he road more than 160 miles by setting little goals. He'd commit to riding just 10 miles, then another 10, then another.

On his 42nd day—3,500 miles from his original departure point—Michael made it to the Atlantic Ocean, where a crowd of people welcomed him, including his two children and his dad.

While he could have given up many times over the six months it took to prepare for his emotion-driven ride—or even during the 42 days of the ride itself—Michael James took action instead. And regained confidence in himself in the process.

What could *you* gain from taking inspired action?

BOUNCE BACK QUICKLY AFTER A FAILURE

When you do take action, sometimes (and even with the best planning) you will fail. You'll experience one of those life lessons I talked about earlier. You'll burn your hand.

So how do you find the strength to get back up? How do you summon the internal fortitude and sheer force of will to move ahead on your dreams? For one thing, stop focusing on what knocked you down in the first place. When you talk about it and think about it, your body will go through the pain again and again—just as if you were experiencing the episode *for real*.

It's true.

Scientists now know that the brain cannot tell the difference between a real experience and an imagined one. Neuroscientists at Harvard Medical School, for instance, gave two test groups a five-finger piano exercise to practice every day for five days. But while one test group actually played the piano every day, the other group *only imagined they were playing*. At the end of the test, scientists measured both groups' brain activity and discovered that *all*

test subjects—even those who merely imagined playing the piano—
had expanded function in the brain's motor cortex, the area that
controlled the piano-playing fingers.* This *neuroplasticity,* or the
power of the mind to change the brain, is one reason you should
be mindful of the stories you choose to keep reliving in your head.

How else can you find the strength to bounce back from a
failure? Recognize that you can't find something you already
have. Stop looking outside yourself for this strength and learn to
access, exercise, and utilize the strength that's already inside you.
Move past the lies, cut out the limiting beliefs, recognize them
when they pop up, deal with them, manage them, squash them,
and get back to expanding *you*—the authentic you that you've
been designed to be.

I'll never forget the day that I learned this lesson. I found
myself sitting at the Los Angeles County Welfare Office, completing forms to apply for government assistance. Though I'd been
working since I was 15 years old, that day I was desperate. I was
8 months pregnant with Jelani, and there was no money coming
in. I just needed some help to carry me over until I could generate an income again. I didn't have money for diapers. I was
reduced to eating canned vegetables, tons of pasta, or visiting
family often. A few weeks later, my food stamps booklet arrived
and—truly humbled for the first time in my life—I had to ask a
friend to explain how to use them. Later, at the grocery store,
I felt ashamed and humiliated. I was embarrassed to use these
food stamps until, suddenly, it hit me. Only a bigger person can
admit they need help—bigger than those who continually spiral
downward because their ego, arrogance, and pride stop them
from reaching out.

Resolutely, I drew my shoulders back. I picked up the baby
food, a bottle of juice, and other things I needed for my son,
then purposefully strode to the cash register to ask for help in

---

* As reported in *Time* magazine. "The Brain: How It Rewires Itself," by Sharon Begley.
January 19, 2007.

using the coupons from the food stamps booklet. By the time I received the next booklet in the mail, I had a decent-paying job. I even tried to return the coupons to the county and the surprised employee assured me that I had earned them through my hardship and insisted that I keep them.

I'll never forget those days. I'll always remember the moment I decided I deserved better. No one sprinkled fairy dust on me or showed up to fix my problems. I got creative. And I didn't just focus on getting out of debt—I focused on making money. By the time Jelani was three years old, I had three jobs and was making over $120,000 working long hours. Not only did I serve as a Healthy Start agency coordinator for the Los Angeles Unified School District, I was also a consultant for an urban philanthropic consortium—and I had begun doing paid speaking engagements. A friend would pick up Jelani from preschool and bring him to my office, where he sat with his coloring books and alphabet worksheets, then played until my work was done. I didn't spend money on my hair or nails. We never went out to dinner. I saved every dime possible. Now, you have to know that when I decided to save every penny and buy my breathtaking future, I was willing to be seen as bizarre, unstable and even a little cuckoo by my friends and family. I gave up the need to manage other people's perceptions of me.

I hope that, just like me, you too come to the realization that there is more money available to you than you ever thought possible. There are more resources than you could ever imagine. You are more gifted than you will ever know. If you simply tap into your gifts, put fear and ego aside, and find new ways to serve people, the revenue streams will follow.

Finally, to bounce back quickly after "failure," remind yourself of what you deserve and what you are worth. Get crystal clear on those points. Then, when anything that doesn't sit in alignment with that worth comes into your space, you can immediately make a decision. *Do I want to get involved in this? Do I want to buy into this other person's assessment of me? Do I want to be limited in this way?*

LOVE YOURSELF DEEPLY FOR WHO YOU ARE

As we grow up, we absorb from our parents and our guardians what happiness, joy, peace, and good living look like. Our parents, grandparents, or guardians are our first teachers. Some of what they teach us we really embrace—while other aspects give us pause. It's not *ours,* but we still hold on to it.

Then we begin to take on society's version of what life should look like. We strive for lifestyles and "things" others think are necessary. We take on careers that others think are acceptable. We strive for a body image based on what others say.

I fell into this trap. For years, I didn't go to the beach. Even though I love the water, for more than ten years I stayed away because I was ashamed of my body. If ever I did venture out, I looked like someone from Alaska in winter because I was so covered. Then in 2008 I said, *What can I do that will truly liberate me?* And the answer was, *Go to the beach, strip down to your swimsuit, and actually get in the water. Don't just look out at the water anymore. Get IN it.*

It was transformational for me.

Shortly thereafter, I was in Jamaica, where I used to go with my girlfriends to level set. One just happens to be a personal trainer and the other works undercover for the government. To say they have goddess-like bodies would be an understatement. But because I had stepped out of my negative self-talk and into my power—because I had stopped defining beauty by other people's standards—nothing could deter me. I stared at the water for a few hesitant moments, while everyone was chatting and sipping on Margaritas or lattes in their beautiful vibrant bikini tops with matching boy shorts. I chanted to myself repeatedly "I am uniquely beautiful in my own way" several times as I disrobed, then stood up and took off my cover-up. I took off my hat, I took off my shades, and I felt a big lump in my throat. But with every step toward the water I felt more and more liberated.

Of course, *your* what-am-I-waiting-for moment may be something different, but I'm here to tell you, I've never known water to feel that good. Why? Because it came with permission—from myself—allowing me to be exactly as I am. In that moment, I was standing in my light—I loved myself deeply for my courage. My belief in Lisa rose that day.

What does light look like to you? Identify it with your own definition rather than anyone else's.

When you do define it, celebrate it. Then take care of it. Too often today, we forget to love ourselves deeply in ways that matter. It's often said that we'll spend $150 on a new business gadget, but balk at spending that on a few hours at the spa. Guys will spend $150 getting their car detailed, but not $150 on an afternoon of pure enjoyment with their friends.

If I asked you to list all the ways you could love yourself deeply—lavishing care and heaping generosity on yourself— could you come up with anything that you'd actually do? Here's the list of what I'd recommend for you:

- Eat right and shop for the best food.
- Move your body in ways that make you feel energized and ways that you find fun.
- Keep your finances in order. Have enough in the bank, and then some.
- Draw boundaries for yourself with your family and friend circle. Exercise the word *No,* and recognize that it's a complete sentence.
- Open up and communicate more.
- Spend quiet time with yourself and with God.
- Be willing to ask others for what you need and receive what you deserve.

- Allow emotionally healthy people in your life to serve you.
- Love toxic people from a distance.

Of course, another part of loving yourself deeply is to practice self-care. But you also have to be laser-focused on your goals, right? The key to having both is grace, ease, and harmony.

Unfortunately, so many of us are servers—we're *in service* to others. We give until there isn't anything left to give—even to ourselves.

Have you ever said, *Don't worry about that, I'll take care of it?* Have you said it so many times that people have actually stopped asking if *you* need support? They know you. They know you're going to take care of it—and they know they might even be rebuffed in their offer to support you. Well, guess what? I have some sobering news for you.

You've trained people how to treat you. You may have even trained them to not show up for you.

By the time you realize the lie you've been broadcasting, you might really need help—but unfortunately, at that point you discover no one will give you that help. No one's checking on you. They might love you, but they expect you've got things handled. After all, your main statement may have been, "Don't worry about me, I'll be fine!"

Do you? Of course not. No one has things covered 100%. I've been with some of the most powerful and wealthy people on the planet, and guess what? They need support, too.

If you've gotten to the point where you've kept others from serving you, realize that *you* are the only one who can turn the tide. Start focusing on yourself before giving to others. Teach people how to treat you and start making it known that you need support—including suggesting ways others can help.

Focus on yourself first, so you'll have a full tank to give to others.

Second, make the distinction between self-care and indulgence. A massage, for example, used to be an indulgence for me. I thought, *Oh my gosh, I'm sneaking off to get a massage,* until I realized that I pass energy through my body. I touch people with my soul. If you've ever met me at a live event, you've seen that I work to be mentally, spiritually, and joyfully present to the very end; I work to give the people in the audience my energy. This requires self-care. In fact, caring for yourself so you can pour into others is not indulgence. *It's necessary.*

Self-care provides joy and energy in your soul, whether it's a massage or concert, play or dinner, weekend escape or a walk on the beach. Indulgence is the act that puts a strain on your future because of your choices in the now, such as overspending or poor time management.

And finally, be aware that good health is not optional. It's necessary, too. When you sing your song on the mountaintop, you've got to sing it boldly and loudly. No one can do what you can do. We're waiting on your greatness. Ensure that your energy levels and wellness are at their optimum so you can show up and give your all.

PRACTICE FORGIVENESS OF YOURSELF AND OTHERS

If you want to make more room in your heart for abundance, love, and goodness to come into your life, you must set yourself free with forgiveness. You have to create the space for new opportunities, new people, new adventures, and new love to enter in. When you hold on to anger or resentment toward someone who may have hurt you in the past, it's hard to be open and accepting of all good things now.

Believe me, I know.

At one point in my life, I'd decided I could never forgive the man who had been my fiancé. He had emotionally abused me. And then he physically abused me. I could forgive anyone for anything else, but I thought, *There has to be an exception clause that God allows for someone who's hurt me the way he did.*

I went through life with my personally invoked, non-forgiveness clause.

Though I was a motivational speaker—facilitating workshops all over the United States at the time—no matter how much energy I put out or how much I smiled, I secretly held on to that resentment in a corner of my heart.

I'll never forgive him, I had decided.

Then a colleague told me something so powerful it led me to nullify my exception clause. He said: "Staying angry at someone is like drinking poison and hoping the other person dies."

I had thought that if I forgave this man, I'd be letting him off the hook. I'd be freeing him from taking responsibility for his actions. But forgiveness wasn't about setting him free. It had everything to do with setting me free. Forgiveness was simply about freeing up that space in my heart so I could receive more love and goodness in MY life.

People are going to do exactly what they want and be exactly who they are, and you may not always agree with them. However, if they hurt you, forgiveness is always *your* option.

Is there an opportunity for you to forgive someone?

If you're holding on to anger, resentment, or hurt, I invite you now to let go of it so that something far more amazing, far more wonderful, and far more pleasing can fill that space in your heart.

How can you begin to forgive?

Recognize what you need to release, then compare it to *what you want to make space for* in your life. Which is worth more to you at this present moment . . . holding on to the hurt or letting the new feeling, opportunity, or relationship into your life?

Finally, work to forgive *yourself* for what you perceive as your failings, incompletes, errors, or lack of dedication. You did the best you could at the time with the skill set, knowledge, energy, and help you had. The past is the past. Stop holding on to it—

and holding at bay the glorious future that's trying desperately to show up for you.

GET COMFORTABLE WITH PLAYING BIG

When you move into the big league of life, you have to accept that some people will have opinions about what you are doing. *You're getting beyond your capabilities,* they might say. *That's never going to work. You're taking an awful risk. I wouldn't do that if I were you.*

How many times have you gotten so caught up in someone else's perception of you that you failed to focus on what you should have been doing? They gifted you with their opinion, and all of a sudden, you got so spun out that you moved off target. You stepped out of your power.

Here's what I know: other people's opinions of you are really none of your business.

Other people's opinions of you are just that—their opinions, their perceptions. But so often we make the mistake of allowing someone else's perception and opinion of us to become our truth.

You need to have faith in your own personal clarity and "self-awareness muscle" instead. Building your self-muscle lets you remain unconcerned about what other people think—not in an egotistical way or with an attitude, but with the energy that says, *I love you for who you are. However, I need to pursue who I'm destined to be. I'm exploring that person. I'm finding out who that is. I'm supposed to play big. I love you, but I don't have to listen to your opinions.*

No one around you should define you. If you give other people permission to define you, then please don't complain about their definition.

I am not advocating that you not seek counsel, garner advice from a friend or loved one, invest in a life coach, or seek out a mentor. All of these contributions are "valuable."

The first muscle you have to build in order to play big is getting over people's opinions of you.

The second muscle is thinking bigger about your future. When Janet Switzer and I separately do one-day consultations for business owners, we're often amazed (compassionate, but still amazed) at the number of clients who say, *You've blown my mind.* We give them a far bigger vision for their business future than they themselves were thinking. They didn't know what they didn't know.

Playing small often leaves you feeling trapped, resentful, and full of blame—it leaves you feeling anger, shame, and guilt. What does "playing small" look like? It's making excuses for not following through on your dreams; blaming others for where you are; surrendering your power to your husband, wife, or partner, or to being a mom or dad—and shrinking when an opportunity comes your way.

But when you play big, you're able to tap into compassion, forgiveness, self-love, gratitude, and appreciation. It means you step up to the plate and regularly operate outside of your comfort zone. You never hide behind what you "do," but instead, you're transparent to the world—you live who you are, authentically and openly. You forgive others (and yourself) freely—giving yourself a thousand second chances to get it right. And you love like you've never been betrayed.

Part of the mindset of an abundant, prosperous life is to simply get comfortable with playing big (even while your knees are knocking).

AMPLIFY YOUR GAME: START EXPANDING EVERY AREA OF YOUR LIFE

Once you master the mindset of an abundant, prosperous life, you can begin to amplify your game in earnest. To do that, you'll have to build a new infrastructure for your life. This isn't always easy. But with a strong foundation in place, you can begin to enrich yourself and grow into your destiny. What are the necessary pillars of this foundation?

PILLAR #1: GROW IN KNOWLEDGE

One of the biggest lessons I learned was that I couldn't transform my life based on the limited knowledge I had at the time. I had to find out what I didn't know. So amplifying your game is not just about doing more. It's about knowing more.

PILLAR #2: WORK FOR A GOAL THAT'S BIGGER THAN YOU

Beyond expanding your knowledge, amplifying your game also includes the willingness to work for something that's bigger and grander than you. It's that "woo-woo" conversation you've heard about leaving the world a better place than it was before you arrived.

When you subscribe to something greater than you, it causes you to become a better person. It causes you to want to put your ego (or, ladies, your "shego") aside. It causes you to want to expand your knowledge and your physical strength and deep-dive into your spiritual awareness to create something or to be a part of something that's greater than you.

PILLAR #3: RECOGNIZE THAT YOU'LL NEED HELP TO EXPAND YOUR IMPACT

Even leaders need help to take on the greatest tasks of our generation, so recognize that you need a team. Either get off your island or at least build a bridge so that people can get to you and work with you. Start identifying people who align with your dream and who can become enthusiastic about your goals alongside you.

PILLAR #4: PRACTICE SELF-ENRICHMENT IN ACTION

Oftentimes, self-development and personal growth can become static in people's minds. It becomes something they *do* versus something they *live*. They might journal at night by themselves or attend seminars on the weekend or even go away to a retreat. But self-enrichment has to be made into an active verb. You can't just study it—you have to live it.

This brings to mind what I've often heard from people I've worked with. They say, *You know what? I'm tired of planning. I'm tired of thinking. I'm tired of goal setting. I want to start doing. I want to start seeing my goals come to fruition.*

Self-enrichment lives in the action, not in the planning. Taking action—even little baby steps—moves you from constantly planning to actually doing those things that will get you to your goal. Self-enrichment is that act of creating a thousand micro wins, so you can have one macro win.

USE AFFIRMATIONS AND BEGIN LIVING THE "RICH LIFE" IN YOUR MIND

In my adult life, I've used a special tool for bringing about the abundance, prosperity, financial wealth, spiritual growth, and business opportunity I desire. The tool is called *affirmations*—brief, vividly clear word pictures written as statements I can recite over and over again that *affirm* my future desires *as if they're already so.*

Too often, we bombard ourselves with negative thoughts—even saying these thoughts out loud to ourselves and other people. We say things like: *That's not possible for me. There's no way they would say yes to me. I can't do that! I'll never find true love. Life's hard for someone like me, if you only knew what I've been through, then you'll know why it's so hard for a person like me.*

These are powerful messages. Unfortunately, our unconscious mind takes in these repeated messages, then causes us to take the actions that will deliver these results to us—over and over again. We actually re-create disappointing experiences in life by repeatedly thinking thoughts of failure, by holding harmful beliefs about ourselves, and by telling the same negative stories to ourselves and others.

But what if you changed your thoughts, beliefs, and stories to more positive statements that *also have the power to activate your unconscious mind*? And what if you repeated *those* positive statements over and over again?

Affirmations are positive statements I can repeat not only to affirm the person I am, but also to affirm the person I'm becoming. They're critical to cementing my "knowing" and sending my declarations out to the Universe. They're foundational to my future.

Affirmations begin with the words "I am"—the most powerful phrase you can use to trigger your unconscious mind to achieve your goals.

Whatever follows the words "I am" is true for your unconscious mind.

In the same way that guided visualizations trick the brain into "living" our abundant future life in our mind's eye, affirmations are another tool to focus the mind on our positive future. When we recite our affirmations several times a day, the mind cannot tell the difference between our real life and the imaginary life our affirmations describe—so long as the word pictures are compelling and emotionally charged enough. For instance, if you say, *I am brilliant,* that's true to your unconscious mind. If you say on the other hand, *I am lazy*—that's true, too. Whatever you speak using your conscious mind, your unconscious mind will absorb it and strive to make it come true.

We talked earlier about *cognitive dissonance* and how your mind will move heaven and earth to resolve the conflict between your actual circumstances and the exciting new pictures you introduce to your mind. Well, affirmations, or word pictures, are no different. Whether they are positive, compelling verbal statements—or damaging negative self-talk—your brain will work to bring these affirmations about in real life. Affirmations are just one more tool.

HOW TO WRITE AN AFFIRMATION

When you develop your goals in the 12 areas we discussed in Chapter 1, it's imperative as I mentioned to *be specific*. State how much and by when. Decide on the smaller, incremental targets you'll hit on your way to achieving bigger goals. Then, write down your goals and review them daily.

Why did I urge you to be specific? Because specific, compelling, and detailed goals can easily be turned into powerful, specific affirmations. When you add emotion to the wording of your goals—such as *I am joyfully opening the doors to my new business* or *I am proudly writing the check to pay off my mortgage,* then envision them as already complete, your unconscious mind will fast-track the attainment of these goals *by the date and in the manner you've written them.*

Be sure to speak to what you *want to create,* not what you're trying to avoid. An incorrect affirmation would be, *I am not going to fail the exam.* That's not affirming a positive outcome. A better affirmation would be, *I am confidently answering the questions on the certification exam and achieving a passing score with ease.*

Affirmations are not lengthy—three to five lines long at the most. They are clear, concise, and powerful.

You can write your own affirmations or look for the many collections available online. When I discover an affirmation I like, I often customize it for my own circumstances so that it has the opportunity to seep in at a cellular level. I'll rewrite others that I find useful. I customize them not because I'm a writer or because I'm a coach, but because I know what I want and where I'm aspiring to go. The value in writing your own affirmation is that it becomes even more powerful than the superbly written ones you find out there.

HOW TO USE AFFIRMATIONS

Aside from reciting your affirmations before you go to bed and the moment you wake up in the morning, you can post them in those physical spaces of your life so that, when your mind is in that particular zone, an affirmation there speaks to your future.

When I was in my self-restoration period—rescuing myself from depression, guilt, and blame after breaking off my engagement—I wrote affirmations that spoke to my value. I wrote affirmations that affirmed, *I am beautiful. I am worthy. I am loving.* I posted them on my bathroom mirror so these statements that reflected my inner beauty and outer beauty greeted me whenever I looked in the mirror. At that same time I was coming out of that abusive relationship, I posted on my headboard, *I deserve healthy love. I deserve to be honored and respected,* because that's the energy that I wanted in my bedroom. On my refrigerator, I posted, *My body is my temple given to me to live out my life's purpose,* to remind me that my body is a gift and I have a responsibility to it as I open the refrigerator. And on the back of the front door, I posted, *I am ready to serve the world. I hope the world is ready for me.*

Though it's been 17 years since I've used those affirmations, they still ring clear in my mind, because they were the affirmations that spoke life back into my soul. Just as I found benefit from affirmations, your personal affirmations will operate like a mantra in your life. They're designed to be something your mind naturally defaults to when the road gets rocky or you hit a speed bump.

Affirmations to Get You Started

In the area of your . . .

Love Relationship

I am designing and experiencing a loving, fulfilling relationship that WILL get better by the day.

I am open and ready to receiving and experiencing a loving, fulfilling relationship that WILL get better by the day.

Family Relationships

I am bringing value to my family. Within our imperfections, we share the perfect love.

Peers and Social Circle

I am accepted by my friends for who I am. Our love is unconditional, nurturing, and free of charge.

Mentors and Advisers

I am worth the investment that others place in me. I am a good teacher because I am a phenomenal student.

Career or Business

I am effortlessly growing my career/company as a result of my consistency, my determination, and my ability to bounce back from setbacks.

Income or Revenue

I am growing my income exponentially. Money loves me because I am a good steward of my earnings. I have an extremely healthy relationship to money, therefore it keeps flowing in my direction.

Investments and Legacy

My efforts and diligent work today create financial freedom for generations to come. I am able to shift the trajectory of my family's life through my decisions today.

Philanthropy and Service

My contributions help transform humanity. I am making a significant impact on the planet with my service. My life leaves an impression of service and responsibility.

Physical Rewards

I drive a beautiful car, live in a breathtaking sanctuary, travel the world, and live first-class because I've earned it.

Playtime

My life is full of mind-blowing explosive experiences that bring me immense joy and shape the best memories anyone could possibly have.

Spiritual Awareness	*I always remain connected to my Source. God uses me daily, hourly, minute by minute. I live in the grace and ease of following my ordered steps. I am always covered in love and protection.*
Physical Body	*I love my physical body, even as I continue to shape and strengthen it. I am grateful for the journey that it has taken me on. I honor where I am, and I honor where my body will take me.*

Once you've customized the above affirmations for your own life, you can move on to begin developing the personal skill set you'll need to think and affirm on a whole new level.

THE PERSONAL SKILL SET FOR TODAY'S ABUNDANT THINKER

What characteristics or skills do you need to be an abundant thinker—someone who constantly looks for opportunity, always attracts good things to yourself, and always thinks and acts abundantly? What's the personal skill set you need to develop in order to respond to life's opportunities and challenges like highly successful, financially prosperous, and spiritually evolved people do? Over the years, I've developed my own checklist:

✓ **Be creative.** Be willing to see opportunities that don't appear exactly as you had planned them—but that could be stunning opportunities when you add your own elements.

✓ **Be in alignment with your relationships.** The moment you achieve alignment in your relationship with yourself, with your money, with others, and with your business is the moment your abundant thinking will kick into high gear. What do you require of yourself—and what do you require from your money, peers, and business? Do you keep your commitments in these four areas? Do you complain? Do you say no for the same reasons in all four areas (and mean it) when you need to? Do your business, your link to peers, and your own actions allow for time off? Do you require your business to pay you a paycheck? Do you see money as a tool or an end goal? Do you have to work hard for your money and relationships or do they come effortlessly to you—in the same way that the other areas of your life are effortless? To be at the same place in these four areas means your life flows with harmony, grace, and ease.

✓ **Be willing to go beyond average.** Abundant thinkers don't stop when the five o'clock bell rings. They stop when the job is done. While average people are watching the clock, abundant thinkers are focused on what it will take to achieve the outcome they want—regardless of what's required. Abundant thinkers do things that are uncomfortable—learning new skills, calling powerful people, asking for help, making mistakes. They go above and beyond day after day after day, until it becomes a habit.

✓ **Be comfortable moving your "limit line."** In everyone's life, there's a limit to how far they will typically go outside of their normal routine or comfort zone. When you go past that line—such as negotiating an important business deal or writing a bestselling book or becoming a board member with your trade association—you've gone outside your limit line. Abundant thinkers, on the other hand, strive to move their limit lines forward. This allows them to make decisions based on an expanded field of opportunity and capability. By moving their limit lines, abundant thinkers have more money to work with, bigger opportunities to select from, and fewer either-or choices they have to make. They decide what kind of life they want, and then think three, five, even ten years ahead about the world they want to play in. They plan on operating with future limit lines that have become virtually limitless. Mediocre thinkers, on the other hand, stay safely behind their limit lines. While they may venture outside this continuum, they're fearful—and may even be punished for doing so.

✓ **Be focused on raising the top line, not preserving the bottom line.** Abundant thinkers are focused on expansion—expanding people, joy, abundance, revenue, and opportunity. Instead of constantly cutting expenses—which employs scarcity thinking—they use expansion thinking to constantly increase ways to earn, serve, love, and create. Scarcity thinkers, on the other hand, hold on tight.

✓ **Be aware of your spending, but focused on your earning.** Every week, I spend one hour with my CFO going over expenses—then spend another *thirty hours* working with the rest of my team to create bigger revenues. While I'm aware of what's being spent and how we're saving on costs (and, in fact, am responsible for it), I put my real energy into growing our top-line revenues. It's said that you get what you focus on. Energy grows where energy flows.

✓ **Fail forward.** Abundant thinkers look for the lesson in any situation where they didn't get the outcome they wanted. They fail, but they also move forward with greater clarity and better answers on how to maximize the next great idea.

✓ **Always make decisions in accordance with your highest values.** Even when a decision is costly, unpopular, or difficult, abundant thinkers always consider their highest values before deciding. What values are common among abundant thinkers? Integrity of action, quality of output, protection of people, and preservation of relationships, to name just a few.

VISUALIZE YOURSELF AS A SKILLED, ABUNDANT THINKER

In the last chapter, I introduced you to *guided visualization*—the process of seeing your future life and all the great things before you. As we work on enriching your Self, I have another visualization session that will help you find your limitless potential. As before, feel free to record this script in your own voice—or have a friend do it for you.

Visualization time should be reserved for a quiet place where you can meditate and reflect. Keep paper and pencil handy to jot down any impressions or messages you receive about ways to expand your abundant life.

RELAXING INTO THE VISUALIZATION PROCESS

I want to take you on a visualization journey to greatness. I want to help you find your limitless potential. I want you to find everything that's possible for you, everything that you deserve, everything that's waiting for you; I want it to be right there in front of you—great love, great health, great finances.

I want you to visualize yourself exactly where you call success, in the home, the family, the love, the openness; take a deep breath. Exhale; breathe in all that you need to make this real. Breathe it in, and when you exhale, release anything that doesn't serve you—release, exhale.

VISUALIZATION SCRIPT FOR ENRICHING YOUR SELF

I want you to see yourself standing in front of a room with everyone there celebrating you. Remember that moment. I want you to see yourself right where you say you want to be—your skin, your hair, your face, your heart, your soul, your home, your family, your car, your friends, your business, your spirituality—everything is right where you want it to be.

I want you to feel it; I want you to hear it; I want you to taste it—the most perfect meal. You're having dinner with the most perfect person and you have the most perfect life. Your most precious dreams have come true. Your most precious thoughts are real. Take a deep breath; breathe that in.

Feel it, enjoy it, smile; smile at all the faces that are smiling back at you. Who is coming up to you telling you how proud they are of you? Is it your mother, your father, your sister, your brother, your husband, your wife? Is it your friends, your children, colleagues, neighbors, people from your social circle? Look at their faces. *We're so proud of you; oh my God, you're such an inspiration.* Hear those words. Breathe that in and take a deep breath in and when you exhale, exhale anything that's holding you back from that, anything that doesn't serve you.

Release the fear, release the shame, release the guilt, release the worry—release it; you don't own it. It's not yours.

CLOSING DOWN THE VISUALIZATION PROCESS

Begin to feel yourself back in the room that you're in right now. Feel your feet on the floor, feel your back against the chair wherever you're sitting; feel yourself back in the room. Open your eyes slowly.

Now pick up your pen or your pencil and begin to write. What did you see? Who did you see? What messages were they telling you? Who was thanking you, acknowledging you? I want you to write that down. I want you to sit in silence, and be with your thoughts and your feelings. Write down every detail you can think of that came to you.

YOU DON'T HAVE TO MASTER EVERYTHING

When my company was a lot newer, I didn't think like a CEO. While lots of people were more talented than me in certain areas, and could do the tasks in those areas, I still tried to have a hand in every little detail of the company.

I'll never forget the week I spent hours creating a flyer for one of my speaking engagements—doing a terrible job, frankly, of writing it, designing it, and producing it. Not only did I feel I had to do everything in those days, I was convinced I had to be good at everything. For projects to end up the way I liked them, I felt I had to be the one responsible for every detail.

Perhaps you, too, have taken on the mindset that you have to be a master of the millions of tasks that go into building an abundant life.

You don't, of course. That's not possible.

In fact, abundant thinkers know they can easily find people who are not only better at certain tasks, but who will also joyfully complete those tasks in record time—producing a better outcome, too—because it's their passion. They've studied and refined and honed their skills year after year—while you've studied, refined, and honed what you are good at. Work together for the best possible outcome.

> Surround yourself with the best people you can find,
> delegate authority, and don't interfere as long as the
> policy you've decided upon is being carried out.
>
> —Ronald Reagan,
> 40th president of the United States of America

Another reason that successful people delegate to others who are more qualified is that they avoid spending their "dollar time" on "penny tasks." That doesn't minimize the value of the graphic designer who eventually created my flyers. But abundant thinkers recognize what *their own* highest revenue-generating activities are—and they focus their time on those activities that *only they can do.*

This is key.

I now spend my time solely on those activities that only I can do, and even then only on those activities that have the highest return. These are actions like providing content for this book, speaking onstage, coaching, meeting with clients for VIP days, appearing on television—things that literally only my name can be attached to in that particular way.

If five other talented people can do a task as well as you (or better), it's not the highest and best use of your time for you to do it. It doesn't deliver the highest return on your time spent. When I learned from Stephen Covey's book *The 7 Habits of Highly Effective People* that 80% of our time should be spent on our "Circle of Influence"—those things only we can do something about—my entire focus changed.

If you made a list of all the things the outcome of which *only you can influence,* then committed to spending 80% of your workweek in those areas, you would see your goals achieved in record time. Those of us who have an abundant way of thinking—who are committed to operating at a higher consciousness and a higher level of execution—spend 80% of our time on projects, initiatives, relationships, and revenue centers that we (and only we) can impact.

LIVE IN YOUR OWN LANE, NOT SOMEONE ELSE'S

A similar way to look at your life or business is to view it as a superhighway stretching across a dozen lanes or more. One lane might be marketing, another might be sales, while another might be accounting. You have a lane that no one else should be driving in, which frees you to speed along at 65 miles an hour. You get important work done with little distraction. And others experience the same freedom to produce and grow and expand because they, too, are safe in their own lanes.

But what if I decide to change lanes?

The minute I do that, it's like I've run over a nail. I'm outside my power place, now trying to operate at my maximum capacity in an area where I have less experience. Plus, there's already someone else in that lane, trying to drive too, whom I'm impacting and who is slowing me down.

I think one of the most powerful things I learned to do with my team was to get out of the way—to just stay in my lane. And I learned the same lesson at home with my son.

For years, I was the head chef in my kitchen. But once Jelani returned from culinary school, cooking became his main lane. Not only is he more experienced now, he's more passionate, too. So the best thing I could do was let him drive. On the rare occasion I forget this rule, we still get the meal done—but it takes twice as long and doesn't taste as good as if I had just stayed in my lane. The same issue came up when parenting him. When he was younger and found himself talking to someone new, he wouldn't say much. I often filled in the blanks for him in those days. But now he's a grown man. When I recently tried to answer for him, he respectfully pulled me aside later and said, "Respectfully, Mom, it feels like you just cut me off. And you didn't let me finish my thought. I know that you used to do that to assist me through a conversation, and you've taught me well. I'm good now."

Okay. I get it. That's no longer my lane.

When you're out of your own lane and in someone else's—calling the shots—you're actually disempowering them. A better approach is to stay in your lane and honor everyone else by letting them drive their cars.

THE IMPERATIVES: WHAT YOU ABSOLUTELY MUST GET GOOD AT

If it's best for all of us to stay in our own lanes, what then (if anything) must we absolutely get good at in addition to our *unique ability*? What intrinsic habits, wisdom, and intelligence must we have to "run our lane" as effectively as possible? I have a few suggestions:

1. *If you don't have a team yet, learn how to assemble the right group of people—whether or not you're a manager or own the business—and even if you're a stay-at-home parent.* If you're a solopreneur, the idea of delegating everything can be overwhelming if

there's no one to delegate to. You might try to assemble a group of vendors who can take on those parts of your work you simply shouldn't be doing. And a virtual assistant can make all the difference in the world. But another approach to consider is what I did: I recruited volunteer support. I found people whose expertise was much stronger than mine in those areas where I needed it. What might take me six hours to do because I wasn't skilled in that area took them ninety minutes or less. So I found people willing to donate a small amount of their time every month to my business.

When I first started my company, I went to lots of business conferences and would strike up fast friendships with other entrepreneurs. As is common at these functions, we would trade business cards. I always followed up, and with some people, I asked, "May I make a bold request of you? Would you be willing to volunteer in my company for the next six months, giving me ninety minutes of your time every month?"

"Could you look at my revenue forecast and give me some coaching?" I'd ask. "I'd be incredibly grateful."

Of course, in those days, I really meant ninety minutes and could easily stick to that request. My business was small and didn't require a whole lot of analysis of its products, customers, and cash flow. I'd pose the same question to product developers—asking for suggestions about curriculum and packaging. I even asked a recently retired corporate executive of IBM to draft some simple contracts for my business deals to come. Because I shared my vision with them of inspiring and transforming the lives of teens, these people gladly helped out for free.

Out of every ten people I asked for support, eight of them said yes, and let me tell you why: I put a time cap and end date on the volunteer commitment I was asking for. But what actually happened is that, when the six-month request expired, 100 percent of my volunteers stayed on and volunteered more time because they saw the growth and excitement in what I was doing. Unknowingly, I had assembled an entire "home team" of abundant thinkers who could help me grow my business—even though I didn't have a single employee at the time. And the retired contracts and compliance person? She volunteered for three years, giving up to fifteen hours a week in some cases. All because I put a cap on my "asks" and made them bite-sized, palatable, and doable for people. Now, over 14 years later I recently reached out to her to let her know that my company went public and that I was gifting her with shares because of her generosity and contribution to my beginning days. I know that she didn't volunteer for stock in my company, but what a pleasant surprise and acknowledgment of her service.

What's the key to making these requests work? For one thing, potential volunteers don't want to push your train out of the station; they want to jump on a moving train instead. So you have to show advancement of some kind—before you ask favors and while the volunteers are in support of you. Second, people want to be part of something exciting—show them that you've got a winning plan. Have a strategy. Excitement and a clear plan make people more willing to invest emotionally and mentally. Finally, don't request too much. People don't want to overcommit. This happens frequently in charitable organizations, most of which are wonderful. But volunteers want to be an added value—they don't want to feel as if they're your life-support system.

If you're a stay-at-home parent or the caregiver to an elderly family member—and you're trying to build your dream business or new career at the same time—it becomes even more imperative to get good at team building. Who is the babysitter, housekeeper, repairman, and pediatrician on your team? Which neighbors, friends, or fellow parents can you call on to help or volunteer? If you can't find people who can support you (or you don't have the resources to hire good help), why not check into local churches, charities, or city agencies who provide occasional help with home repairs, meal preparation, elder daycare, after-school tutoring, and more?

What else must you absolutely get good at while you're specializing in your lane?

2. *Become masterful at creating a clear vision, communicating it in compelling detail, and enrolling others to come along for the journey.* Your vision for the future of your business, project, initiative, or career *must be so clear* that it excites everyone—including you. Each time you talk about your vision, you are deliberately or unintentionally enrolling others in that vision. So be sure to enroll with integrity. Always speak the truth. Become a master visionary who can paint a picture so compelling that we have to stare.

If you're shy or lack confidence, but still know that you need to enroll people, you've got some homework to do. But here's what I know: if the desire to see your dream come to fruition is strong enough—if you're hungry enough—you'll strengthen your *communication muscle.* Two books I recommend that will help you become a better communicator of your vision are *Onward* by Howard Schultz and *Eleven Rings* by Phil Jackson.* Throughout the pages of these two books, I discovered great language for connecting with people. But more than that, I discovered two very powerful and influential men who were both committed to keeping their heart, integrity, and spiritual awareness at the center of every interaction in their business *and* personal lives. Even though these books are business related—Howard Schultz is the CEO of Starbucks and Phil Jackson is the president of the New York Knicks basketball team—their books made it crystal clear

---

* *Onward: How Starbucks Fought for Its Life without Losing Its Soul,* by Howard Schultz with Joanne Gordon, Rodale Books, 2012; *Eleven Rings: The Soul of Success,* by Phil Jackson and Hugh Delehanty, Penguin Books, 2014.

to me that success in any field is really about living in your passion, speaking your truth, and allowing your spirituality to be demonstrated through your words and actions. That's really exercising your communication muscle.

As your project or business grows, consider getting a partner. I love to see partnerships where you can tell, *Yeah, she's the brains and the infrastructure,* while *He's the visionary, the enroller, and the communicator.* Find someone whose strengths are different from yours.

3. *Get good at managing people.* At this point in my career, as the leader of a team, I'm clear that I am no longer doing project management and am 100% focused on people management. I actually have two customers—my company's clients and my valued employees. I have to listen to my individual team members, understand their needs, keep them aligned with one another, and keep them focused on our goals—all while constantly communicating the future vision that the company is working toward.

Remember that *your* team has also said yes to *your* vision. But, sometimes, in managing their day-to-day projects, goals, challenges, and tasks, they forget about the 30,000-foot vision and can only see the challenges in front of them. This is why I've learned the importance of being a WAM (walk-around manager).* Both my COO, Susie Carder, and I consistently do walk-around management. During this time, we are not only checking on the progress of the business, but more important, we ask the staff how their families are, how their lives are going—understanding that, if life at home is settled, then life at work is more likely to thrive. We eventually get to discussing

---

* A term that originated at Hewlett-Packard, *management by walking around* involves managers wandering through the workplace, in a random unstructured manner, to check with employees about the status of ongoing work. The expected benefit of these impromptu check-ins, versus prescheduled visits or meetings, is that a manager is more likely to improve morale, employees' sense of purpose, productivity, and total quality management.

current projects and nine times out of ten, they have a question in that moment that, when answered, will quantum-leap their results—clarity that they otherwise would have waited for an appointed time to discuss with me, hence slowing the process down. I also continuously work on my management skills by reading books authored by other great leaders. As I mentioned, I recommend *Eleven Rings* by Phil Jackson. In that book I learned of his profound spiritual practices and how he incorporated that into his coaching—even at the risk of being teased for his team's "weird" practices like meditation and breathing exercises before a game. Phil was confident that the more he served, inspired, and directed his players, the more successful the organization would be. Eleven NBA championships later, I'll bet more coaches are considering similar techniques. I also like Howard Schultz's book *Onward* and have to admit that I have a genuine CEO crush on Howard. His transparency, authenticity, and commitment to integrity-based leadership had me in tears when watching his interview with Oprah Winfrey. His book taught me to hold fast to my own integrity as a leader, even through the fire. Schultz urges leaders to invest in the people and strategy of the business, to never abandon your employees for the sake of the bottom line, and to know that in the end, all great decisions come back to you and all breakdowns are yours to claim, as well. Lead holistically. Even when it hurts, still lead. It's easy to be the leader on your best days when results and revenues are high. But great leaders start leading at new levels when they are confronted with what seems to be the worst days. You don't get to choose when you lead—just lead!

In my company, I have to lead even when a lack of follow-up produces an unhappy client or when incomplete communication creates an incorrect expectation with a strategic partner. I have to be willing to own mistakes made by my team, unfulfilled promises, or poorly worded commitments that get misinterpreted—even those situations when, as a company, we've flat-out dropped the ball. Even if I didn't individually make the error, I have to be willing to own these breakdowns.

4. *Learn to laser-focus on completing individual projects and meeting specific goals.* To really move quickly down your lane, take time now to put into place methods and boundaries that help you laser-focus on producing results. Allocate your time using a system, and create delivery benchmarks that keep you on track. If e-mail or phone calls or meetings distract you, set boundaries and answer your e-mail and phone calls only after 12 noon. If multiple meetings take your focus away from completing key tasks, ask to group them on a specific day of the week or— amazing, but possible—ask to be excused from these meetings altogether so that bigger milestones can be achieved.

When I first talked to Janet Switzer about coauthoring this book with me, she revealed that her system for writing books combines rigorous outlining with daily writing time and focused periods of research. Unlike other people who start their workday at 8:00 A.M., Janet writes from 5:30 to 12 noon, five days a week (*what?!*), then spends her afternoons running the many aspects of *her business.* She has a system that works for her and together, we produced this book in record time.

See? Laser focus.

5. *Finally, get good at carving out time to be still and to reflect.* As you step into your greatness and begin to lead an abundant life, you'll discover there will be more and more demands on your time—particularly if you own a business or lead people in any capacity. But part of an abundant life is quiet time to reflect, meditate, plan, and dream. It's imperative that, in addition to everything else, you get good at scheduling and protecting this

time on your calendar. Whether it's a daily hour before you go to work or a weekly ritual of a few hours, start carving out this sacred time and become non-negotiable about honoring it.

With these imperatives, and all the other self-enrichment work you'll be doing, you can pursue your goals in earnest. But be advised: not everything you do will work out perfectly. You have to be willing to move forward on your plans anyway—learning lessons and gaining feedback on better methods or easier alternatives, all of which will appear to you once you are in action.

BE WILLING TO FAIL, BUT NOT EXPECTING TO FAIL

To move forward on your goals, you're going to have to give yourself permission to do things wrong, to experience a bad result, to make a mess . . . to fail.

But giving yourself permission to fail *actually* gives you the go-ahead you need to succeed. When you give yourself permission to fail you actually say, *I'm gonna run to the edge and leap, regardless of the outcome. I'm going to get into motion regardless of what happens.* But if you don't give yourself this permission in the first place, you'll just run to the edge and look. No leaping, no risking, no forward movement of any kind will occur. You'll stop yourself from leaping—which also stops you before you've had *the chance to see yourself soar.*

If you think about how parachutists jump out of an airplane long before they open their chutes, you'd realize they fall a long way before achieving safety. They have to give themselves this permission to fall before they open their parachutes and soar.

Too often, we try to avoid that momentary fall or avoid the chance that we might hit the ground—not recognizing that failure is simply *not getting the outcome you hoped for.* Think of taking risks like buying a lottery ticket and failing to win the lottery. Your life hasn't changed. You didn't have millions in lottery winnings before you bought the ticket—and you don't have millions now. Your life hasn't gotten worse due to this "failure." It simply stayed the same.

As long as you're willing to "fail forward" like abundant thinkers do—meaning you learn lessons from your failures—then the potential of failure is not all that risky.

Two of the most valuable lessons I use today came from past failures. Early on in my business, I was horrible at hiring people. The criteria I used were just plain wrong. I hired if you hugged me well. I hired if you were a raving fan. I hired people who scared me because they used what my grandma calls "big fifteen-dollar words" and sounded smarter than me, and I'd think, *Wow, if only I had* that *really smart person on my team . . .*

I estimate that I've spent over $250,000 hiring incorrectly. And that's not to say these people were not good people. They just weren't the right people for my company. Now I have a system in place—a team of people and a company environment—that is a product of those errors I made back then. Highly qualified, abundant thinkers, servant leaders, integrity-centered and spiritually grounded.

Of course you should do everything in your power to make sure failure doesn't occur, including, *I'm gonna work overtime. I'm gonna ask for help. I'm gonna be coachable. I'm gonna do my due diligence.* But there's always that chance you will fail.

Leap anyway so you can learn.

A longtime student of mine, Cynthia James, gave herself permission to leap. An actress hoping to break into Hollywood, she entered the *Star Search* competition and advanced through seven grueling rounds of elimination before making it to the finals. At each exciting, scary, and momentous stage, there was a chance she'd be eliminated and return home having failed.

Then, on the night of the final round of competition, the producer of the show approached her and asked, "Do you know why you've won so many times? It's because people like *who* you are. Every character you've portrayed exhibits your charm and charisma. But the scene you've selected to do tonight is lacking YOU. Bring your authentic self back into the scene and you will be much happier in the end—win or lose."

Stunned by his revelation, Cynthia wanted to cry. Just at the point she was poised to soar, someone who knew the game reminded her of the potential for failure. Knocked off her center, when she heard them call her name to rehearse, she got up in a daze and moved to the stage. The rehearsal did not go well, and later, Cynthia sat in her dressing room in dismay. When her roommate offered to lift them both up in prayer, she affirmed that Cynthia would be her most authentic and inspiring self that night. At the end of the prayer, Cynthia declared she would go out there and soar.

As she stepped onstage, Cynthia felt the energy of the audience. Delivering her lines with humor and spontaneity, Cynthia knew when the scene was over that—win or lose—she had been amazing. With her heart beating madly and her body about to burst, Cynthia stepped back onstage to await the announcement of the winner. After what felt like forever, she heard the words, "and the winner of our *Star Search* competition is Cynthia James," and was handed her $100,000 check for winning the *Star Search* competition. Cynthia, stunned, in disbelief, joy, and a bit of shock, "I did it" bursting in her head "I really played full out and did it," experienced her moment of bliss and gave thanks for the producer who somehow had been sent to remind her never to let doubt convince her to dim her light. She vowed never again to hold back her true self for any reason. She faced potential failure and soared.

Don't *you* back away from the ledge either. Put yourself all the way out there so the world knows what you're up to. Make a bold declaration and get in the process of making your abundant life happen.

Just as Cynthia was willing to fail, you too have to face your fears and take action anyway.*

---

* Cynthia James eventually enjoyed a long career in Hollywood and was the first long-term "Lexie" on the television show *Days of Our Lives*. Today, she is one of our brightest

DO IT AFRAID: NAVIGATE YOUR WAY
THROUGH FEAR-STORMS

I've never been able to successfully outrun fear. I was afraid when I started my company. I was afraid when I negotiated to write *Chicken Soup for the African American Soul*. I was afraid when Rhonda Byrne asked to film me for *The Secret*.

When I went on *The Oprah Winfrey Show* and *Larry King Live*; served in South Africa, Kazakhstan, and Taipei; and when I filed with the SEC to take my company public—my job is to do it afraid.

The truth is you don't have to outrun fear. But you do have to look it in the face and take action anyway. If you're okay with being afraid, you won't want to move forward on your goals. The key is to navigate your way through these "fear-storms."

> It's real simple. If you never give yourself permission
> to fail, you've never really given yourself
> permission to succeed.
>
> —Lisa Nichols

What will reduce your fear as you're navigating through a storm? Information, knowledge, and advice. For anything that you want to do, someone else has accomplished something similar before you. Seek them out. Ask their advice. Search online for the stories, books, and courses from people who've successfully accomplished what you want to do.

When my business was about ten years old, I was doing okay, but things were never very far from a struggle. I was scared. After all, I'd put so much into my vision. I'd moved away from my family, and I was fearful about my future. Often in the midst of some fierce "fear-storms," I would call up my girlfriend Ann and ask

and best-loved inspirational teachers. She currently serves as associate minister at Mile Hi Church in Denver.

her out to lunch. While I always offered to pay, she never let me—bless her heart—because she knew how broke I was.

Ann and her husband had a wildly successful business and they were set for life. They lived in a stunning home in La Jolla, California, with spiral staircases and breathtaking views. Just being in their home inspired me.

Whenever I was down in the dumps, I would go to lunch with Ann and ask her to tell me the story of when she and her husband Richard lived in a three-bedroom house—nearly broke—before their business took off. As a way of inspiring me, she would share the story of those days when their lifestyle wasn't so lavish and things weren't so abundant. I would see two people who had been where I was—who had made it through and were living in a whole new paradigm. When the fear-storms came up, I'd ask Ann to take me back to their more challenging times when she had to have had some fears.

When you are going through a fear-storm, educate yourself as a way to calm your fears. Do your due diligence about the situation you're in. Ask more experienced people to explain what you don't know or don't understand.

Then give yourself permission to find a safe person to whom you can admit, *I'm scared*. Reach out to a Rocket Booster friend, who will see the best in you, calm your nerves, but still hold you accountable for your dreams. By the way, I still spend quality time with Ann as a way to relax and release and to calm the new fear-storms that rise because I'm committed to playing an even bigger game and it's often accompanied by knocking knees.

THE UNIVERSE CELEBRATES WHAT'S ALREADY BEING CELEBRATED

When you *do* make your way through the fear-storms and take action, celebrate those small accomplishments or "micro wins" that will lead to your new life. Celebrations are your way of saying, *I'm proud of myself for that accomplishment*.

And what gets celebrated gets repeated.

If you've ever seen a toddler in the midst of a celebration, you'd realize that this pride and repetition also rings true for adults. In fact, many of our actions are driven solely by the positive feedback we're given when we've done something good. When a toddler jumps and hears people clapping and shouting "Hooray!," you can expect to see that toddler jump again. When toddlers raise their little hands, open and close their palms, and say "Bye-bye"—only to see everyone in the room break into a smile—rest assured that, for the next week, one of their favorite words will be "Bye-bye" simply so they can be celebrated again. Energy grows where energy goes. And when you invest energy in celebrating yourself, you get inspired to produce even more results. Plus, when you celebrate your wins, you send out positive, emotionally charged energy to the Universe, which will reward you with other accomplishments that can also be celebrated.

The Universe rewards celebration.

But all too often, we wait until we've achieved a major macro win to celebrate. We wait until we've earned that advanced degree, landed a promotion at work, bought our first home, or gotten married when there are so many micro wins along the way.

How can you celebrate your micro wins? Here are some ideas:

- *Treat yourself to something special.* Buy yourself a special gift or give yourself an important pleasure. Whether that's sleeping in, a day at the spa, or a treat that warms your heart, this reward alerts your unconscious mind that achievement is desirable because there's celebration at the end of the achieving.
- *Invite a friend to celebrate with you.* Whether it's dinner, movie, or simply tea, make the occasion about celebrating your accomplishments.
- *Take yourself on a special vacation.*
- *Cook a special celebration dinner for you and your family.*

Whatever you do to celebrate, use it to focus on what you have accomplished, as well as on your courage to push through the challenges to hit your mark.

ENRICHING YOURSELF IS THE FIRST STEP TO SUCCESS

As you pursue your abundant life, realize that, unless you achieve the mindset and *personal* skills necessary—unless you work on the Enrichment of your Self that I've discussed in this chapter—all the other strategies you'll learn in this book will be less impactful. Take steps now to create the habits, schedule the time, process the past, lavish care on yourself, and celebrate your most recent wins. Then watch in awe as the achievement of your goals is accelerated.

CHAPTER 3

The Second E: Enchantment in Your Life Relationships

> When you sit down at the end of your life and reflect on
> its value, you will realize that your real treasures were in
> your relationships and not in your possessions.
>
> —*Lisa Nichols*

As you move forward on your path to abundance, you'll quickly discover that you're not alone on this journey. You've got family, friends, colleagues, co-workers, advisers, employees, love relationships, casual associates, and others who are on the bus with you. And whether they are abundant thinkers or not, whether they support you or criticize you, whether they challenge you or limit you, *how you relate to them* will determine the quality of your life.

But you might be thinking, *How do relationships fit into my life of abundance?*

Yeah, that's what I used to worry about. In fact, I thought (like most people) that abundance was, first and foremost, about achievement, societal status, money, possessions, and wealth creation—until I realized that every interaction I had, every decision I ever made, and virtually every experience I've ever been through in my life involved other people and would likely impact my future relationships too.

This gave me pause.

Of course, when I truly reflected on this idea, I realized that the quality of my life depends on the quality of my relationships. I began to look at the people in my life, becoming intentional about including mentally, emotionally, and spiritually evolved people who could amplify every area of *my* life—even if it meant simply giving me space to be my authentic, evolving, fearless self. People who stretched me to be a bigger better version of myself.

YOUR QUALITY OF LIFE IS DETERMINED BY THE QUALITY OF YOUR RELATIONSHIPS

What are the relationships we should all value the most? Those that inspire you to become the best possible version of yourself, those that call you to your greatness, and those that hold you accountable to the person that you are becoming, versus holding you hostage to the person that you have been.

Abundant relationships are those where you can take off your superhero cape and where you don't have to be everything to everybody. In fact, you can be nothing in that moment if necessary. Abundant relationships give you permission to be *not only* as brilliant, beautiful, and genius as you have always been—but also clueless, lost, and confused in that moment. There is no judgment in these kinds of relationships.

An abundant relationship holds you tight, but also gives you space to breathe.

When I sit with wildly successful people whom you and I would admire, 100% of the time they say that if they had it to do all over again, they would make changes in the area of their relationships. 100%!! They've discovered that their relationships are their greatest bank account—and the investment from which they make the highest return on investment, or ROI.

What could *you* do to become more heavily invested in relationships that matter the most to you?

COME TO TERMS WITH THE COMMUNITY
YOU WERE BORN INTO

The relationships that affected you the most growing up were those you were born with—parents, siblings, grandparents, and extended family. They're the ones who are there to greet you at every family reunion and every holiday with either great joy or great drama.

These are the links you're born into and, frankly, it's hard to get away from the influence they've had on your life.

I'm still close to my siblings and my parents. And although they don't guide my career or my business, I rely on them for the camaraderie and let-my-hair-down kind of family time that nurtures me and helps me inject playtime into my life.

The day after I met with my publishers on this book, I flew to Sacramento to go crab fishing with my brother, my dad, my son, and our friends who invited us. At the time, I had just come off a 21-day tour that included 17 events in multiple countries— followed by three days in New York meeting with my investment banking team and negotiating a major book deal with multiple publishing houses. To go from all that to the simplicity of seeing my dad laugh so hard it hurt, celebrating my brother who pulled up ten crabs at once, and watching Jelani prepare the most delicious crab bisque, crab cakes, and crab-and-cheese-stuffed mushrooms—man, it just showed me the roundness of life. It was as joyful as being onstage in front of 10,000 people. It was more joyful than sitting across a table and negotiating my next seven-figure business deal.

This trip was by no means diminished by its simplicity. I felt my feet on the ground. I thought, *Wow, this truly is what abundance means.* Abundance is being able to follow my professional calling and live *this life* at the same time.

DON'T DISRUPT THE OLD TRIBE TO CREATE A NEW ONE

Aside from your family, there's the community that you've selected—those friendships and professional relationships that you've surrounded yourself with over the years. Interestingly, as I counsel my students and clients on taking their game to the next level, these are typically the relationships that most people want to eliminate right away. Perhaps they're experiencing intolerance, pain, or discomfort in these relationships. Perhaps some relationships are broken while others cause too much drama. For whatever reason, the relationships just don't feel good anymore. When I teach program participants the tools for creating relationships that will enchant them, their very first inclination is to eliminate those relationships that are bringing pain.

But let me give you a word of caution here, before you start cutting ties.

Before breaking off multiple relationships at the same time, consider the disruption it will cause in your life—and the energy you will have to expend—energy that will keep you from focusing on your goals and daily micro wins.

Of course, I'm not advocating that you stay in relationships that suck the life out of you—relationships that are one-sided and no longer serve you. But what I *am recommending* is that you don't break out the Ginsu knives and chop off the heads of everyone in your tribe because you believe that is what will make you feel good. The fallout to this approach can potentially be more painful than a healthy, measured transition away from these relationships.

Of course, a "healthy transition" doesn't mean a long good-bye. It just means that you've thought through your exit—and you're not simply reacting to what you've read in this book. Don't be rigid. Keep these relationships for the time being while you form new relationships with people who are like-minded, who stir your soul, and who bring you the intellectual bond and pro-active support you need in your life.

When it comes to your romantic relationship, be especially prudent. If you feel it's not the relationship that will fulfill you long term, seek first to understand what's missing. If acknowledgment is something that's really important to you, for example, there are many places you can find integrity-based friendships where acknowledgment is part of the dynamic. When we conduct our workshops, for example, we make sure they are high in acknowledgment, love, and individual attention. Some people are uncomfortable with this level of touch. (But they're not the ones who attend our trainings!) But for everyone else, acknowledgment is exactly what they want. They come to get that need met.

Of course, ultimately, if a relationship is sucking the life out of you—if it's truly intolerable—my first question to you is, Have you tried everything possible to improve it? When I coach married couples in a state of breakdown—where one partner (or both) wants to divorce—I always start with the question, Have you tried everything?

Most often, the first few times we meet, they haven't.

I send them home to try everything again, giving them a list of what "everything" looks like. At the top of the list is simply having a truly transparent conversation that includes sentence starters like: *I'm angry that you . . . My biggest fear is that . . . I understand that . . . I take responsibility for . . . What I really want for us is . . . What I love about you is . . .* and *What I'm willing to do differently is . . .* Sentences that start with these honest and open statements are the first part of "trying everything."

The second thing to do is ask forgiveness for your short-falls in the relationship—for the part you have played in the breakdown—regardless of what your partner has done.

Finally, seek mutual support from the outside—via a coun-selor, therapist, or spiritual adviser—or attend a relationship workshop or another couples' activity that takes you both out of your day-to-day environment and makes evolving the rela-tionship its primary focus. These are all on my "have-you-tried-everything" checklist.

Why do I insist upon this? Because it's our job—all of us—to live a life of no regret. When we are in our final season of rest and reflection, my prayer for you and me both is that we have very few regrets. For that reason alone I say, in any relationship—sibling, friend, lover—if you feel that the relationship needs to end, make sure you've tried everything before giving up.

Most of us have not, and if we did, we might be surprised at what can be salvaged.

ACCESS ANOTHER LEVEL OF COMPASSION AND UNDERSTANDING WITHIN BROKEN RELATIONSHIPS

Sometimes, the pain can seem so all-consuming that you just want it to end. This goes not only for romantic relationships, but friend-ships, too. You're eager to cast off the entire relationship versus accessing another level of compassion and understanding within yourself. But often compassion and understanding will transform the other individual into the supportive, like-minded, and Rocket Booster friend (or romantic partner) we wish the person would be.

And it most certainly will transform us.

What's one way to take the high road, be more compassionate, and seek to understand? Begin *communicating* in ways you never have before. Because a breakdown in communication—not ask-ing for what you need, not setting healthy boundaries, the inability to say no, the inability to give a healthy yes—are all forms of *your* lack of good communication skills. Ouch. I told you I was going to lay the truth on you.

Similarly, when you withhold your frustrations until you become explosive and believe the only solution is to end the relationship, realize that *you* are very much a part of that breakdown. You didn't express how you really feel. You didn't say no in a healthy way. You didn't give your reasoning and ask for feedback. You just decided to give the other person a piece of your mind—which is simply another way of saying, "I'm gonna vomit all over you today."

Recognizing and owning that you need to build your own communication muscle in a relationship is one more way to be more compassionate and understanding. Strive to use the same authentic, transparent, and forthright communication guidelines in your friendships *and* your romantic relationships.

After all, a relationship is a relay. That's why it's called a *relay-tion-ship*. So often, we want to pass the baton and hope that no one runs with it. But it is impossible to run a relay race by yourself. When a friend or family member or romantic partner grabs the baton and runs with it—even when he or she becomes disruptive, argumentative, controlling, or defensive—you have to be mindful of how you will respond. I'm inviting you to consider how you'll respond *and* how you hand off that baton in the first place. Will it be with mature, considered, deliberate thought?

How you relay could breathe new life into your relationships.

LOVE TOXIC PEOPLE FROM A DISTANCE

While your job is to be intentional about your communications—and to pursue a high ROI with all your relationships—some of the people you spend time with now will never deliver a high ROI or give you the space to be intentional. On a scale of 1 to 10, they probably rate a 1 or 2. They're not supportive. Neither are they nurturing or even helpful. They bring down your energy. They limit your belief in your own future.

These are simply toxic relationships with toxic people. There's no getting around it.

But what if they're a boss, a coworker, or a family member? Someone you *have to deal with* and with whom you can't break things off as easily as you would like?

Love them from a distance.

Establish boundaries, healthy practices—but also uncompromising communication—to protect yourself as you grow and develop Rocket Booster relationships to replace them.

One boundary is to recognize actual abuse when it occurs. Communication that is belittling and degrading is abuse. Physical harm of any kind (or intent to harm) is not only abuse, it's your signal to take steps to protect yourself and loved ones in the future—whatever you have to do. If it's time to get out, get out!

Of course, the simplest healthy boundary is to course-correct the other person's communication any time they yell, curse at you, or become disrespectful in their language. You can even go as far as saying, "We can continue this conversation later when you're able to speak with me without cursing, yelling, or disrespecting me."

DETERMINE WHAT YOU CAN BE GRATEFUL FOR

Before you pull the plug on any relationship, check your level of gratitude. Often you can fall back in love, learn to appreciate again, deal with the situation for now, or even amplify the relationship into something spectacular—simply by considering what you can be grateful for in the other person.

A friend of mine who's going through a divorce helped me discover this truth.

Married to her high school sweetheart—who had cheated on

her multiple times—she was devastated. I gave her my book *No Matter What!* and extracted a promise that she would do the exercises I outlined every day.

"You'll want to stop," I told her, "because it's gonna require you to look at yourself."

The next time I saw her, my friend was like a different person! She attributed it to just one of my exercises, *Don't Supersize Me,* which asks readers to complete the four quadrants of this grid:

What I Love About You	*What I Choose to Embrace About You*
What I Would Miss About You	*What I Want You to Remember About Our Relationship*

By jotting down characteristics, memories, wisdom, and other attributes you can be grateful for in another person, you could either make significant strides in turning around a relationship (by sharing your notes and living your gratitude from that moment on) or—at the very least—complete the relationship in your own mind before moving on, and be grateful for what you've learned from the person, and the exercise.

Gratitude gives us a grace and ease with our circumstance that nothing else can provide.

In the case of my friend, who was ready to write down all the ways in which her husband had hurt her *and damaged the relationship,* the quadrant called "What I Choose to Embrace About You" caused her to look at all those things that were difficult to love about him *from the beginning*—and acknowledge that she chose to accept these when she accepted him. Her anger dissipated. She literally couldn't stay mad at him. She felt her energy return. Suddenly, she could breathe again for the first time in months.

Though they eventually decided to divorce, she began to see all that was possible for her despite the end of her marriage. Focusing on gratitude, she said, felt like tipping her chin up and aiming higher than ever before.

HAVE CLEARING CONVERSATIONS USING "CARE-FRONTATION"

In the same way you can practice gratitude in your relationships, you can also respond to upsets in a relationship by initiating clearing conversations that are "care-frontations"—a confrontation that doesn't make the other person wrong, but rather, uses grace, care, and compassion to work through challenges and understand the needs that lie behind someone else's hurt, fear, and anger. Here are some things to keep in mind for "care-frontations":

1. Don't wait to hold these conversations. Within twenty-four hours of a setback, approach the person you've had a challenge with and either talk with them, or schedule a time to talk with them. Go speak to *the one person* (only) who can make a difference. Don't gossip or involve others who can't make a difference to your outcome.

   Next, facilitate the conversation using the language of respect and grace. Use starting phrases like:

   What I love about you is . . .   *Where I need your support is . . .*
   What I admire about you is . . .   *What would work better for me is . . .*

What I appreciate about you is . . .   Here's how you can support me . . .
What I respect about you is . . .   Here's what feels better to me . . .

2. After the other party replies to your statements, respond with validating words including:
   I hear you.
   What I hear you saying is . . .
   I take responsibility for . . .

3. Ask permission to coach or offer feedback. Always give the other person the opportunity to say no. And always wait for a response before proceeding. To ask permission to coach or give feedback, use phrases such as:
   May I offer a new suggestion?
   May I coach you?
   May I give you feedback?
   May I share my opinion?

4. If you make a request, set up the other person to win. Always use the formula X by Y with a condition for fulfillment. Example: I request that you get back to me (X) by 5 P.M. today (Y), and give me the answer (condition for fulfillment).

5. Be responsible. Appropriate responses to a request from the other person include: acceptance, counteroffer, or a promise to respond by a specific time.

6. Listen carefully. Listen for the possibility or the unknown in what someone is saying.
   Listen for YOUR listening; what filter are you using?

   Be responsible for who you are being and how you are listening.

7. Honor your word if the person asks something of you or notify the other person immediately if you can't. If you must break your word, communicate specifically to the person to whom you gave your word. Use language like: I honor you. I see you. I acknowledge you.

Using the above "care-frontation" script, not only can you move a conversation forward instead of holding on to your emotions, you also avoid damaging the relationship beyond repair by internalizing your current hurt.

HIT THE RESET BUTTON: HOW TO RECONNECT AND HEAL WHAT YOU'RE RESPONSIBLE FOR

In the case of relationships that are beneficial or important to you, relationships that *could be* a tremendous alliance—but then something goes south—you need to reconnect, reset, and take ownership of any part you played in the breakdown. You also need to decide what you learned from an unpleasant circumstance and what you'll commit to doing differently as a result.

When teenagers participate in my "Motivating the Teen Spirit" program, they learn how to clean up any rifts they've personally caused—or breakdowns they've allowed to happen due to inaction. My Director of Teen Programs, Tia Ross, explains it this way: "When you raise the level of communication, self-expression, and self-disclosure between people, relationships are built, strengthened, or healed. When both people are sharing and taking risks, judgment gets replaced with acceptance."

What's so terrific in these programs is that our teen students actually learn to make agreements prior to having these reset conversations—agreements that require them to: (1) reserve judgment, (2) abstain from repercussions or comebacks, and (3) love each other unconditionally regardless of what's said. And while it might be awkward to make these agreements between professional colleagues, they should be a *requirement* prior to any crucial conversations between family members and romantic partners.

Here's my five-step process for healing breakdowns:

1. Start by acknowledging the impact of your hurtful words or actions. The truth is that our words have a long-lasting effect. You've probably experienced something that wounded you deeply—something that should now induce you to exercise care when speaking to others. So acknowledging any harsh words you've delivered, inaction you're accountable for, or deceitful activity you've engaged in will move you a long way toward taking ownership of your part of the breakdown. To begin the healing process, use these fill-in-the-blank sentences to communicate the fact that you affected another person in a hurtful way.

    Incomplete: *I know I affected _____ by _____.*

    Example: *I know I affected you by saying you can't do anything right.*

2. Take responsibility for the part you played in the breakdown. Our words, actions, and body language have a profound effect on the people around us—primarily on the people who love us and whom we love. To begin the healing process, use these fill-in-the-blank sentences to communicate the fact that you affected another person in a hurtful way.

    Incomplete: *I take responsibility for _____.*

    Example: *I take responsibility for starting arguments over trivial things.*

3. Honor the hurt feelings you caused. What lands on someone's heart usually stays on their mind. I once conducted a workshop for a police department where deputies were able to recount

profound memories of hurtful behavior that—in some cases—had occurred ten years earlier. One officer shared how sad he found himself after leaving a middle-school campus and hearing a student shout, "I hate all pigs!" Another officer sadly recalled the painful impact his words must have had when he told a young woman in his squad car, "If you don't end up dead, I wouldn't be surprised if you end up as a prostitute."

When honoring the hurt feelings you caused, it's critical that the other party recognizes that you understand him or her. Complete this fill-in-the-blank sentence using emotional words like *hurt, unloved, betrayed, disregarded, embarrassed,* and *fearful.*

> **Incomplete:** *I know it must have made you feel _____.*
>
> **Example:** *I know it must have made you fearful and frustrated that I seemed to be constantly unhappy in our marriage, when I actually feel happy and well cared for.*

4. Tell the other person that you have learned an important lesson. It's crucial that he or she knows you will now work to improve—and refrain from engaging in damaging behavior in the future. One fill-in-the-blank sentence you can try is:

> **Incomplete:** *What I learned is _____.*
>
> **Example:** *What I learned is that I'm projecting my destructive perfectionism onto you.*

5. Commit to approaching similar situations differently in the future. Healing cannot occur if the other party believes you'll engage in the same hurtful behavior in the future. And it's no use having the conversation in the first place unless you commit to change. One fill-in-the-blank sentence you can use to communicate your pledge is:

Incomplete: *What I commit to do differently is _____.*
Example: *What I commit to do differently is consider your feelings before speaking.*

While the strategies above work well to reset a broken relationship, luckily things aren't always so bad. There may not have been a breakdown—yet. But the relationship needs a serious pick-me-up to get it back on track.

Recently, for example, I realized I needed to invest in my relationship with my brother and my mother. We were always a tight-knit family growing up, and while I have always had immense love for both of them—and they for me—we simply drifted apart. For instance, at the same time that my brother left home in his twenties to celebrate his independence, I was away at college—then busy recalibrating my life when that ended. Time and distance grew greater and greater until, one day, he was in a serious motorcycle accident and I invited him to come live with me during his recuperation. That tragic experience presented a gift to both of us, as we rediscovered our close relationship.

My mom, on the other hand, was busy redefining her life after separating from my dad—and candidly, I had to mature in my assessment of her. Growing up, I thought that she was difficult, hard on me, and unfair in her treatment of me (versus the way she treated my brother). But as I matured, I realized that my mother was simply setting boundaries—the same ones I talk about today. Unfortunately, she and my dad separated just as I was maturing in my thinking. She was working to find her own oxygen in those days, when all I wanted was for her to be that oxygen mask for me. In short, we were two women struggling to find ourselves.

Through simply being overly busy (or maybe just using that as an excuse), I had neglected my relationships with them. Just like a houseplant that desperately needs water, fertilizer, and light, these relationships were going limp—as if they were saying, *I sure wish you'd give me some attention.*

Over the years, the same thing happened with my friends and cousins. There was never a serious breakdown. Nothing went wrong. The relationships simply withered away.

I realized that, while all my friends and cousins understood about my business obligations, at some point they stopped looking for my presence because they just assumed I was busy. I'd run into cousins at family barbecues and hear them talking about their girls' night out, their spa day, and their shopping spree—things they used to invite me to but stopped after hearing me say, "I'm busy. I'm busy. I'm busy."

They didn't have any negative energy around my lack of availability—they simply assumed I would say no.

Once I identified the problem and took responsibility for my own feelings being hurt, I made a bold request to them: "Listen, I don't want to miss another event with you all. Could I ask you to sit with me and my calendar, so I can share those dates when I'm free? This way, if it's convenient for everyone else, perhaps you could plan your girls' events around those dates so I can join you."

Rather than thinking I sounded like a prima donna, my cousins met my request with, "Of course!"

What seemed like a big request to me was an easy accommodation for them.

Do your relationships need a pick-me-up, too? If so, first identify what caused the connection to fade away. Second, take steps to put energy back into the relationship. Write a love note, pack a picnic, bake cookies together. It's going to require you to spend some time, because that's what these people need and deserve—what they're thirsting for—your time.

Too often, we try to throw money at limp relationships, such as a lavish dinner at an overpriced restaurant, which we drive to separately and leave from the minute the check arrives. But what we find instead is that our closest loved ones would much rather have three Thursdays, lounging in front of a great movie with homemade popcorn.

What could you do for your closest relationships by spending some quality time?

BECOME INTENTIONAL ABOUT CREATING "HIGH ROI" RELATIONSHIPS

In my life, I've achieved my goals, built my business, and improved my lifestyle faster than I would have been able to do with my own knowledge and skill set—simply by getting into relationships with people whose achievements, mindsets, and strategies I wanted to adopt. The return on my investment of time and attention to these relationships—the payoff in knowledge, growth, revenue, and lifestyle—has been astounding.

Which is why I call them *high ROI relationships*.

As part of your abundant life, I want you to seek out, develop, and maintain high ROI relationships of your own. I want you to create a diamond field of intellectually, spiritually, and emotionally fulfilling relationships that, when you need them, immediately give you something you didn't have before.

FIND EXPERTS WHOSE MINDSETS ARE WORTH ADOPTING

When I teach my program participants to seek out high ROI relationships, I tell them to start by finding multiple people who represent those things you want to be, do, or have. Not every person will be living the spiritual life, running the business, investing the kind of money, *and* pursuing the unique lifestyle that you want—and certainly no one person will do all these things. That's why you have to seek out multiple people and ask them to teach you how to do what they do—but most importantly how to adopt their mindsets.

For example, in seeking out someone who could be my spiritual teacher, I want to become as graceful, spiritual, and grounded as she is. I may not necessarily want to have her financial life, but I want her spiritual awareness. In the case of the gentleman who teaches me about money and finances, it's not so much that I want to have his wealth, but rather, I want his lifestyle freedom. When I look at my friend Ivan Misner, who's the founder of BNI International, I want to have Ivan's unique combination of business success and life harmony.

In every area where I want to grow, I know exactly who I admire and aspire to be.

When *you* are choosing your role models, choose people who are at least two steps—and ideally ten steps—ahead of you in that particular area, so there's room for you to grow into their level of success. There is space to grow in that direction—to the point that, if you grew to just 25% of who they are in that area, you might end up 50% to 100% beyond where you are now. Additionally, when you are looking for someone to help you amplify your life, look for people who will challenge you in an encouraging way. Not only should their presence challenge you to move out of your own way, but they should be generous with details on how they achieved their success and be able to break down the process of their success into smaller goals that you can adapt to your own goals.

Of course, when you find people to learn from, I recommend that you find out everything you can about them. Saturate yourself with who they are—not just how they do business, but what they eat for dinner, how they treat their family, how they conduct themselves in social settings, how they approach opportunity and crisis, how they deal with others, and so on. Really look at who they are as complete persons, because—guaranteed—who they are in one area crosses over into other areas, too. Their personality, attributes, and character will have multiple layers of influence on you.

One final caveat: don't think that your "mentor" needs to be a professional speaker or trainer.

Very early on in my life journey, I realized that valuable advice and mentorship doesn't always come from these professionals. There are people who are literally nearby right now who are teaching you grace and humility and servanthood. They are teaching you forgiveness. They are teaching resiliency and determination. They may be the people who are closest to you—people you're taking for granted. Look around and be aware.

Whose mindset and habits are you absorbing right now?

LOOK FOR PEOPLE WHO INSPIRE YOU

Where can *you* find people who are positive, empowering, and inspiring and who will challenge you? Everywhere. But a surprising fact to most people is that you don't ever have to meet your mentors in person. You don't have to score lunch with some bigwig or convince a Fortune 500 CEO to work with you on a regular basis. I've learned from many people who have helped to shape my character, but whom I've *never met in person*. So give yourself permission to access people who are both famous and not so famous.

For example, Nelson Mandela inspired me with his capacity to forgive—and his commitment to lead the largest forgiveness movement ever known, walking side by side with the men who guarded him in prison. He taught me that no act, violation, or betrayal is too big or too hurtful to be forgiven. Mother Teresa inspired me through her humility and service. She had a quiet voice, yet she worked with such commitment that she never had to market herself, shine a light on her mission, or advertise her good works. She inspired me to be the conversation that I want people to have about me, regardless of who might be watching. Stephen Covey inspired me with his prolific thinking—and with tools that helped me navigate toward new behaviors and eventually elevate my life.

To begin your search, look for people who inspire you. Use the Internet to read about them, sample their advice (if they write for a magazine or newsletter, for example), or watch YouTube videos of their speeches or TED talks. When you find individuals who have the expertise or mindset you want, investigate whether you can follow them and circulate in their world—either in person or through their literary works, audio programs, television or radio shows, videos, and more. Of course, the best part is that this immersion—which can often be on a par with a master's degree in their subject matter—is free of charge. I followed this path at first. It's how I developed my business acumen and the skills I needed to build my training company.

Today, I hear frequently that the Internet is how people find me and start circulating in my world. They see me on YouTube, on television, at a public event—I love to hear the stories of how people stumble upon my advice and distance-based mentorship.* In fact, some people say they start watching on YouTube—and are still watching three hours later when they finally look at the clock. Eventually, I get to meet them in one of my live train-ings. But by the time I finally *do* meet them in person—because they've so thoroughly immersed themselves in my advice—they know the stories I tell about Jelani, the story of my early years, the history of my financial journey, and the fact that I was on government assistance—they can literally can finish my stories exactly the same way I tell them *because they've immersed themselves so thoroughly in me and my worldview.*

A couple of years ago, at my Speak & Write to Make Millions program, Nadia Vincent from Belgium was able to finish almost every one of my stories—*as I was delivering them from the stage!* Almost before I said the words, she was silently mouthing them at her seat, almost as if she were cueing up my lines. While I had never met this woman before, I approached her at the break and asked how she knew my entire history.

---

* To find my free videos, reports, and short courses online, visit motivatingthemasses.com or my YouTube channel at www.youtube.com/user/motivatingthemasses.

"I watch you on YouTube every day!" she replied.

Nadia came all the way from Belgium to learn from me at that event, and eventually she started coaching with my team, too. What helped her gain traction so quickly is that she already felt she had a close relationship with me before we ever worked together. She had already adopted my mindset, skill set, and approaches long before we ever met in person.

You, too, can use the Internet to immerse *yourself* in a future mentor's world.

DO YOUR DUE DILIGENCE

Researching a potential adviser thoroughly is paramount in importance. But luckily, today, conducting *due diligence* (careful investigation done in advance) is easier than ever.

Unlike when I started out, which involved researching possible mentors using the Yellow Pages and referrals from dozens of people, now there are many different ways to research somebody, including: (1) social media and websites, (2) books, magazines, and newsletters, (3) subscribing to their blog, (4) searching out *other people* who have worked with them and had a positive experience, and (5) hearing them speak at business conferences and industry events.

Don't circumvent this due diligence process. I'm amazed at how lazy we can be—wanting results and information without putting in the research time. Our "Google society" has led us to expect everything instantly. We want to instantly walk away a success. We want to Google-download financial security. We want to instantly obtain a lifetime of industry knowledge. Life just doesn't work that way. As my grandmother used to say, "Baby, the best things in life are not created in a microwave."

Finding the best high ROI relationships for you is going to require mixing the ingredients, preheating the oven, letting it bake for a while, and waiting until it cools. Your success, your joy, and your abundance has got to have time to take shape. As my friend Ivan Misner told me recently, it took him 24 years to become an overnight success.

One final thing, just so we're clear: I don't believe that all critical information destined to transform my life needs to be free. If I have to invest in the due diligence process by buying a book, subscribing to a newsletter, or buying an hour of someone's time for a consultation, I consider it money well spent. After all, I'm about to put my future into this expert's hands by following his or her advice. That advice is something I want to check out in advance, too.

DETERMINE HOW YOU CAN CONTRIBUTE IN RETURN

As you do your research, look for ways that you can contribute to the advisory relationship. Be willing to invest in relationships where you don't just come with your hand out, seeing what you can get. Look for ways to approach the other person with your hand extended, offering what you can give.

Here's why.

Busy people are used to being asked for things. Successful people are always being pulled in a million different directions. Your request is one of many. So set yourself apart by envisioning how you can add value to *their* lives too.

When I decided I wanted to learn about corporate structure before I built my company, I sought to understand the process. Soon thereafter, I spoke at a business conference where Jim, a corporate attorney, was also a speaker. Everyone pulled on him. In fact, he was booked for 35 meetings over the multiday conference with people just asking questions—many of whom would not move forward and become clients. But Jim served anyway— and served and served and served.

At the time, I knew I needed a lot of help. I was clueless about how to start a company. In fact, I was so confused that I didn't even know the questions that I should have been asking. I was lost and yet, at the same time, I was one of the top speakers on that same stage at that same conference.

What did I do?

I swallowed my pride, became humble, and asked him if I could be his Girl Friday—just so I could sit in on those 35 meetings. Now remember, I was one of the top speakers at this conference, yet I was about to walk off the stage and become Jim's clerical help—getting him coffee, making his copies, stapling documents, getting signatures from newly signed clients, arranging lunch, and being his number one all-around gofer.

When Jim agreed to let me slog through the entire week for him, I was thrilled!

For the first few days, I sat, listened, and absorbed. I also got coffee, bought him lunch, tracked down new clients for their signed documents, and took massive notes. Jim, on the other hand, never took any. He would simply talk to people and say, "Lisa, make a note of that."

As I worked away in Jim's meetings, I could see the confusion in people's eyes. After all, here I was, one of the event's headline speakers who had delivered a powerhouse message that brought people to laughter and tears and closed with a standing ovation, yet during these meetings I was taking notes, getting coffee, and making copies. But I didn't care about people's perception of me. I was working for my breathtaking future and felt like this man knew something I needed to know.

I was clear that I wanted my dream to be bigger than me. I wanted to build a major training company. And I was willing to be the gofer for Jim because this man understood corporate structure.

Part of my due diligence ahead of the conference had been

research on what a PPM was, what ROI was, and how terms and conditions worked in an agreement. I had done the research, but I still did not understand any of what I had read.*

During the 33rd meeting, however, Jim asked me if any of it was starting to make sense.

"I got it!" I said.

When he verified that I understood what I needed, he said, "Yep, you've got it."

He even went on to present the financial component during my first few investor meetings. While investors didn't bite until I was able to present these numbers myself, what I learned from Jim helped me raise my first $532,000 in venture capital.

BE EQUALLY INTENTIONAL ABOUT THE QUALITY OF YOUR CLOSEST FRIENDSHIPS

The process of finding high ROI relationships can teach us a lot about developing high-quality friendships, too. While you may not proactively research and seek out friends the way you would a mentoring relationship, you can certainly hold high standards for friends' intelligence, opinions, and character—then approach them with ways to be in service. Become a Rocket Booster friend *yourself* before expecting that from others.

> Lots of people want to ride with you in the limo,
> but what you want is someone who will take the bus with
> you when the limo breaks down.
>
> —*Oprah Winfrey, legendary talk-show host
> and founder of Harpo Productions*

Along the way, building supportive, nurturing, challenging, and intellectually stimulating friendships with people who know

---

* PPM stands for *private placement memorandum,* ROI stands for *return on investment,* and terms and conditions feature prominently in all corporate contracts.

you well—and who will be there for the speed bumps, too—is one of the best investments you can make.

CREATE YOUR NEW COMMUNITY

When you look at the quality of your current relationships and don't quite like what you see—when you know that you need to make a change, but don't want to dump your friends wholesale, it's time to go to work proactively building a new community.

What do I mean by *community*?

It's a group of like-minded, forward-thinking, and evolved people who are *invested* in seeing you prosper—not so much financially invested, but psychically, energetically, and emotionally invested, for sure. Your wins (and those of others in the community) reassure everyone that they're aligned with winners—and your achievements help them feel more hopeful and joyous about their own future, too.

When you are living in abundance, your community is filled with supportive individuals who serve you—and whom you can serve in return. You learn from one another. You share wisdom and ideas. They're sounding boards for anything new you want to do.

Because you'll be spending time, talent, and treasures with these folks, it pays to be intentional about what you want. And be intentional about those personal attributes you're looking for.

For instance, my coauthor, Janet Switzer, and I tend to align ourselves with business owners or at least those who are investors or top executives in their companies. We speak the same language, experience similar challenges, and have a similar point of view when it comes to time off, travel, and family obligations. When we want to go to Europe for three weeks, for instance, we just plan that trip and go. When we need to urgently address a family crisis, we clear our calendar and handle it. We stay at each other's homes and show up at the same conferences. Everyone in our community is pursuing the same lifestyle—striving for harmony and the financial security that comes from our own effort.

Your community might be different. But there are a few hallmarks of every strong community—optimism, vitality, loyalty, family focus, creativity, compassion—and they're all important enough to your abundant future to focus on building a community around them.

BE A MAGNET FOR THE KIND OF PEOPLE YOU WANT TO ATTRACT

Unconsciously, we attract people who are like us. In a way, the manner in which we conduct our lives becomes a magnet for others who have the same values, outlook, and mindset we do. We attract those who have a similar level of achievement and goals. When we talk to one another, we are instantly understood. Not only that, but we're enchanted by one another—which means not only do we take great delight and enjoyment in the relationship, but we're charmed and want to spend time with each other, too. Who they are as people makes us want to circulate in their Universe, stay connected often, and do things together. We're excited by what they're up to. They are equally charmed by us—and when we get together or talk, the feeling of anticipation, possibility, enthusiasm, and "wow factor" is off the charts.

That's what a truly enchanting relationship looks like.

We have a sort of innate filter for attracting—and then allowing familiarity with—this type of person.

The problem occurs, however, when we turn that filter off for convenience. Our intuition is trying to talk to us, but we're not listening.

Some time ago, I was engaged to be married. Eventually, however, the relationship turned emotionally abusive, and later, physically abusive. I broke things off for my own safety (and Jelani's), and I would have loved to say that I didn't see it coming. As a matter of fact, I told the story for four whole years as if I'd been blindsided. I shared how romantic and loving he was, and how all my friends exclaimed, "Wow, does he have a brother?" When I told of how the abuse started suddenly, out of nowhere, that "story" became my truth.

But what was really happening in that relationship?

Day after day, I was ignoring my intuition in regard to this man. I had stepped away from my GPS—my God Placement System. I had closed my ears to the whisper that said, *Pause, slow down, this doesn't feel right.* I ignored the signs that told me he was prone to outbursts of bad temper. I was quiet when he used sharp words toward me.

You've probably experienced times in your own life when you didn't listen either. But when you don't listen, the whisper becomes a knock, then a firm knock, and then a scream—until eventually it does something drastic to make you pay attention.

While you don't want to be picky in attracting the kind of people you want to have around you—and you don't want to limit your flexibility—you *do need* to become firm and explicit about what are non-negotiable characteristics for you.

BE CLEAR ABOUT YOUR NON-NEGOTIABLES

In my life, the very first non-negotiable is that you have to be a person of high integrity. You can't play in "Shadyville"; you can't jump in and out of good character-integrity when it's convenient. If you see an iPhone lying in the street, you can't pick up that iPhone and slip it in your purse, saying, "It's their fault that they lost it."

Of course, you could do that. But you wouldn't be my friend.

Integrity means that, if you find an iPhone, you immediately look around to see if there's someone with a frantic expression who's lost it.

Similarly, if you're a parent, you can choose not to spend time with your children—making them eat dinner on their own or letting them stay out all night with friends and party—but if that's how you parent, you probably won't be a friend of mine.

So, although you can be flexible with who your friends are, you also need to have a core list of qualities, characteristics, values, and mindset that is non-negotiable. And even when every one of your boxes is ticked, you still need to listen to your GPS.

Dr. Judy Hinojosa-Sinks, one of my clients, is someone who listened to her intuition about her non-negotiables. As someone who had faced repeated illness—typhoid, meningitis, Bartonellosis, and other severe conditions involving her immune, endocrine, and neurological systems—she finally heard the calling to become a healer, not only for herself, but also to bring health to others.

Having faced days when the physical pain was so unbearable that Judy sobbed herself to sleep—asking God to either end her pain or end her life—Judy knew what it was like to live day by day not knowing if she would ever be well again. Eventually, her quest to find her own healing led her to become a holistic doctor. Her recovery after years of health challenges was the gift she wanted to give others. She committed herself 100% to this future, and—after arriving in the United States at age 17 unable to speak English fluently—Judy still graduated at the top of her class from medical school after a demanding and rigorous program.

In her first two years of medical practice, however, Judy worked for two different clinics and quickly realized that their ways did not align with her own beliefs about healing.

She found herself faced with a big decision—to continue working for other doctors or open her own healing center where she could offer a fully holistic approach to healing her patients.

Sitting in her car one day, with tears streaming down her face and her stomach in knots, Judy asked God to eliminate her anguish and fear—and give her the strength and wisdom to make the best decision. As a sense of peace came over her, Judy felt God's presence and knew then that she would open her own clinic. Her intuition spoke—telling her to merge her unique self-healing experience with her formal medical training to serve others in pain. She was at ease, despite having no business skills, no business plan, no funding—and not even the equipment to open with or the staff to help her.

None of this mattered. Opening her own wellness center had become non-negotiable for Judy—despite other people's opinions, fears, and judgments.

Now, five years later, Dr. Hinojosa's clinic has succeeded beyond even her own dreams of possibility. She owns a multimillion-dollar practice as a sole practitioner—one of the most successful naturopathic clinics in her city. She's received numerous awards and honors for excellent service and high deliverance of healing to the public.

Her commitment to listening to her intuition—and blazing her own path when her community's ideas did not align with hers—enabled Judy to honor her soul's calling and bring healing to others.

What do *you* need to become non-negotiable about when it comes to *your* community?

Here are a few more of my non-negotiables that you might consider.

I look for people who have spiritual awareness and consciousness in their lives, but also people who are servers. I learned the hard way that I need to be with people who love to serve because if someone is not a server, then they've got it made with me. I will serve and serve, and they will receive, but at some point my tank will run dry, leading to resentment and disenchantment. I need to allow myself to be loved in the same way I love others.

Another non-negotiable for me is that people in my community must be upwardly mobile. They are people who invest in themselves. They have a high sense of self-awareness. They're into both personal development and professional development in a big way. This goes for my close community of friends, but not necessarily for my family who are loved for the other things they bring to my life.

My colleagues, friends, and peers are also constant and never-ending learners. Even much later in life, they're still looking for new things to try, learn, and embrace and they're generous to share with me what they've learned—including business tactics that work.

They're interested in self-care; they're healthy; they schedule time off, eat nutritious foods, and exercise regularly. They live in healthy neighborhoods and drama-free environments. The towns they live in support their healthy lifestyle with quality restaurants, outdoor activities, and tranquil spaces. They invest in their health and well-being because they want their bodies to be able to live out their purpose.

These are just some of my non-negotiables—many of which I had to learn the hard way. Now I'm offering them to you as examples for creating your own list. I'm giving you my beliefs, my mindset, and my experiences—good, bad, and everything in between—so we can learn together as a community.

SEEK OUT LIKE-MINDED PEOPLE

If you want to get into relationship with like-minded people—people who exhibit specific qualities—there are many ways to find people who think like you. Aside from all the expected meeting grounds such as the workplace, professional organizations, and volunteer activities, if you're passionate about something, go to where other passionate people gather. I know a young woman—one of my Global Leadership participants—who met the love of her life at a CrossFit event. Both of them are CrossFit fanatics.

Another friend loves jazz festivals and met her boyfriend at one. If you're worried about visiting these places alone, consider the fact that a terrific new acquaintance, lifetime business contact, or your perfect soul mate might *also be visiting the same place, alone.* Don't be afraid to go where your passions are, even if you are the only one who has that passion.

But don't just go to these places to meet these possible connections. Go because you love that activity. Allow the Universe and God's Divine Plan to bring the right people to you. But also recognize that sharing a specific passion isn't necessarily where the commonalities end. Frequently, I will meet someone with whom I have one specific thing in common—usually a professional interest—but then, just like peeling an onion, I learn more and more about the individual *as a person.* I discover we both grew up in competitive sports or we both share an interest in travel or—seriously, it's happened—we're both at the same point in our romantic relationships, trying to answer the same exact questions and striving to attain the same desired bliss. That's a true and lasting friendship in the making.

Of course, it's this art of discovery that we should be exploring with every new relationship. Far from a "qualification process," it's an exploration with grace, ease, and acceptance. Once you've chosen someone as a friend, allow who the person is to unfold. One of the best books on this "art of discovery" for romantic relationships—a book I've recommended to more than 25 people—is *Intellectual Foreplay* by Eve Hogan.* After dating my sweetheart for nearly a year, I still keep this book with me to help me engage in great conversations with him. It allows us to deep-dive discover each other. What do we think about spirituality? How do we manage our finances? What are our philosophies on parenting, self-development, and personal responsibility—questions I'd never think to ask! In fact, I'd be nervous about asking these questions, but with *Intellectual Foreplay,* I get to blame the book! It's also helped me discover my relationship deal breakers—and ask those questions sooner. Now my significant other even picks questions to ask, too,

---

* *Intellectual Foreplay: A Book of Questions for Lovers and Lovers-to-Be,* by Eve Eschner Hogan, Hunter House, 2011.

and it literally has brought us so much closer emotionally and spiritually.

While this book is geared toward romantic relationships, it's convinced me that we've largely lost the art of conversation today—not just in romantic relationships, but in all our interactions. As our current culture moves more and more to mobiles, texting, e-mail, and social media, many people have simply lost the skill or desire for a really good chat. It helps to have some great conversation starters that will help *you* discover more about new people you've met.

ASK FOR WHAT YOU NEED IN A WAY THAT EMPOWERS PEOPLE IN YOUR COMMUNITY

Your community can help you on your journey toward abundance, but they can't help if they don't know what will serve you. Learn how to ask for what you need in a way that leaves your community feeling not only empowered to give you what you ask for, but inspired to do so. When you make requests using statements like those below, it allows the people who love you—and who want to make you happy—to understand what brings you joy versus what makes you angry.

What I'd love to experience is . . .   *Where I need your support is . . .*

It helps me when you . . .   *What would work better for me is . . .*

If you focus only on what makes you angry or what shuts you down, you're putting energy around feeling angry and shutting down. Compare this to positive language you can use with your community such as: *What makes me feel better is . . . What inspires me is . . . What feels good to me is . . .* Think of the change in response you will receive.

In your relationships, it's your responsibility to articulate your needs in a way that leaves your community, your lover, your spouse, your children, your colleagues, and your friends feeling inspired and encouraged to be connected to you. We wrongly put the responsibility on other people's shoulders to inspire us, yet it's 100% our responsibility to share with them what we need in order to be inspired. All too often, we expect people to know in advance what we need, as if they're mind readers. But, as my brilliant friend Ken Druck said to me recently, "Love and relationships are an open-book test." Don't make your community and loved ones guess what you need. It's not fair to them. Instead, proactively tell them—in an uplifting way—how to love you. If you love flowers, tell them: *One of the ways that I feel loved and acknowledged is to receive flowers. Is that okay for you?* Or similarly, *One of the ways I demonstrate love is cooking for you. Does that work for you?*

In the same way you should be an inspiration to your community, *let those you are connected to inspire you* with their stories, lives, and accomplishments. A few months ago, I was speaking at a training event for Wells Fargo Advisors where I met Stacey Schufford—a woman who's not only inspired me, she's inspired dozens of others with whom I've shared her story. As a longtime sufferer of multiple sclerosis, Stacey's body had deteriorated to the point where a wheelchair was necessary for daily activities. For five years, she couldn't get in or out of bed without assistance until, one day while lying in bed, her body began to tingle all over—as if it were talking to her. Though nothing medically caused the sensation, Stacey felt in her soul that she could stand up and begin walking on her own.

And she did.

Though she eventually had to regain her strength and muscle tone, Stacey began walking that day as if her body was simply ready to move again.

I heard Stacey's story for the first time at that speaking engagement. It resonated with me so much that I've gone on to share it with others. People are put into our lives to inspire us and to inform us of possibility. Let your community know how to inspire *you*.

START BENEFICIAL NEW RELATIONSHIPS THROUGH ACTS OF SERVICE

One way we can build our community is to start new relationships through acts of service. As you are getting to know someone new, ask them: *How can I serve you? What would help you meet your goals? What do you need to get from me?*

You can also proactively suggest contacts, resources, methods you employ, and other ways that you know would be helpful. This is one way that high achievers align with other achievers. This is a way for professionals to pour into each other, to strengthen and lengthen the relationship. This kind of sharing builds stronger bonds than just working on a project together or providing momentary input.

> When you reflect on your life journey, you'll clearly see that the moments when you were most alive are the moments when you loved the deepest, laughed the loudest, danced the hardest, and forgave the quickest.
>
> —Lisa Nichols

Plus, these acts of service also create a far greater bond than a mere monetary exchange can accomplish. When you take time to know people and understand them well enough to anticipate their needs—when you can assess any situation and instinctively know what will help them—their level of trust increases with you. They begin to think of you as a confidante, someone they can align themselves with long term, and someone they'll likely seek to include in future opportunities. That's what acts of service can do.

CHOOSE PEOPLE WHO MAKE YOU STAND
ON YOUR TIPPY-TOES

I've mentioned before that you should be very intentional about the people you decide to form new relationships with. Now, let me take things one step further.

These people should make you stand on your "tippy-toes."

Not only does this mean that they inspire you to stretch and grow, but it also means that *who they are* inspires you to be a bigger person, simply by who they are *being* in your presence.

When Jelani was eight years old, I booked a lengthy speaking tour that kept me on the road for 11 days. I had never been away from him that long and was really struggling with my conscience. During part of the tour, I spoke to an audience of about 700 people and had agreed to answer questions at the end of my presentation. During that Q&A time, a woman approached the microphone and, referring to the stories about Jelani that I'd told during my specch, she simply said, "Lisa, you're the most amazing mother."

Once my stage time was over, I returned to my hotel room— and cried and cried. I felt like a hypocrite, a fraud. Here I was, thousands of miles away from my baby—and had been for days. I didn't feel like an amazing mom. In fact, when I searched every fiber of my being, I couldn't find any motherly greatness in me at all. So I called my Rocket Booster friend Denise and asked her to tell me what she saw in me as a mother.

Without pausing to wonder why, Denise poured out ten minutes' worth of details. She didn't say merely that I was a wonderful mother. She described the way I woke up and cooked Jelani an omelet most mornings. The way we laughed until our stomachs hurt. Or the way we'd sing to each other in the car. Denise remembered—when I couldn't—all the little nuggets of happiness. It's like I was thirsty and she became my water.

In the same way Denise did for me, let someone else refresh

and encourage you. Allow someone to support you and have faith in you when you can't. Borrow their confidence when yours is low. They believe in you more than you can in certain moments. Just be crystal clear about what you need.

That day, Denise inspired me to be a bigger person simply by *her being a bigger person* in my presence. Tippy-toe friends will do that for you. Tippy-toe relationships are what happens when you get intentional about upgrading the people you attract and allow into your life.

THREE TYPES OF ROMANTIC RELATIONSHIPS: LIFETIME, LIFE-GIVING, AND PURPOSEFUL

When it comes to your romantic relationships, you'll also discover there are different levels of support, awareness, and growth in romantic partners—all of which affect you and your ability to grow into the abundant life you want.

I've been in romantic relationships where my mediocrity was welcomed, but my brilliance was not. In those moments when I was playing small, I was adored, loved, and celebrated. But in my genius moments, I was made to feel as if I was standing too tall and that to be "happy" in the relationship, to have peace of mind, I had to constantly dim my light.

I had to limit myself.

My belief at the time was that I did not want to outgrow the relationship, and I found myself constantly crouching down in order to stay in the relationship. I came into the relationship already too big for the relationship. I was running too fast, growing too much, and sowing too many seeds for my future. While my girlfriends lovingly pointed this out, what I really felt is that I was being forced to choose between my relationship and my life assignment.

Of course, none of it was done with malicious intent on the

part of my romantic partners at the time, with the consciousness of minimizing my greatness, or from a place of comparison
or competition. I think it was a decidedly *unconscious* response
fueled by a mindset of scarcity and lack that these men were
living in.

"Rein her in" was the unconscious response of these men in
my life.

I've come to realize now that romantic relationships are really
mirrors for how *we are showing up* in our lives. They will show us
our humanity toward others, our needs that must be met, and
our desire to serve and give back. For example, when I'm in a
relationship, I discover more about my level of trust in people (or
lack thereof). When I'm inside of a relationship, I see my willingness to release—or my desire to hold on tight. I see whether I am
a good leader or I'm better as a follower—or ideally whether I've
achieved a healthy balance between the two. Relationships are
here to build our muscle of compassion and understanding. But
they're also here to help us build our muscle of healthy boundaries. Do I say yes only when I want to say yes—and do I understand
what it means to say no?

Because relationships are dynamic and between two people,
they also help us see how we're currently showing up in the area
of communication. You can determine whether you're speaking
your mind or withholding your opinions—whether you're truly
listening to your partner or simply waiting for your next turn to
speak. Only then can you discover *why you communicate* in the way
you do and improve your communication skill set.

In addition to being a mirror that shows us how *we are showing up* in life, romantic relationships also provide specific and
necessary functions at different times in our lives. When I first
discovered these three types of romantic relationships from
my friend Iyanla Vanzant, they made so much sense to me. At
the time, I was going through a breakup. And because I had

thought he was The One, I was convinced my life was over. But when I stumbled across Iyanla's definitions, they changed everything for me.

What are these three types of relationships, and what do they look like?

Lifetime Relationship

No matter what you both do, this one is going to last forever. At different points in time, you might grow beyond each other, but you will always balance out. It might get rocky, and it may not be easy. But you were meant to be together . . . forever. Nothing you do will separate you. It's a done deal.

Life-Giving Relationships

Life-giving relationships, on the other hand, do not last very long. In fact, they typically range from a onetime meeting to a two-year relationship—but rarely more than that. They're designed to put a spark back into you and remind you that it's not over for you just yet. They put you back in the game and add a spring to your step. They remind you that you're still attractive, you're still sexy— you've still got it.

These short-term bonds remind you of your value, too, and remind you not to settle. They force you to get out of your head and start living in your body again. They're full of energy and excitement, and the giddiness that comes from being in love. But they can also be full of so much drama that you burn each other up. They're intense—either in fun, passion, or chaos.

They can also be a doorway to the eventual lifetime relationship you want. They get you ready to be a better partner to someone else. When they end, you'll understand why these relationships needed to come into your life—and why they needed to be over. Life-giving relationships will stay in your heart forever, but are necessary and finite.

Purposeful Relationships

The most prevalent type of relationship for most people today is the *purposeful relationship*. For a year or more—and sometimes decades—you and your romantic partner are tethered together, working side by side, for a specific purpose. Perhaps the relationship came about in order to raise children, build a business together, help each other grow up, get yourself out of a bad situation, get a good start in life, teach you to set healthy boundaries, or teach you how to love. It's not that you went into the relationship with this agenda, but that's the reality you're living anyway.

When its purpose is fulfilled, the relationship will likely end.

Unfortunately, turmoil happens when we try to turn a purposeful relationship into a lifetime one. For this reason, purposeful relationships cause the most turbulence and discord, the most frustration and hurt.

What we don't always recognize—but should because it's a constant feature of purposeful relationships—is that once the purpose is fulfilled, the relationship changes and never goes back to the way it was. Some people spend a lifetime trying to regain that former warmth, affection, and intimacy in a once-purposeful relationship.

When the kids go off to college, oftentimes a husband and wife will finally be able to stop and listen. They'll be hit with the epiphany that *Hey, I don't necessarily like being with this person. I don't want to be in this relationship.*

They're just now discovering that their bond was driven by purpose. Of course, this doesn't take anything away from the time they were together. It's simply time to move into a new season.

Your job—if you decide to move on—is to end the relationship with grace and ease, leaving your partner's dignity intact, so that when the story is told at the end of your days, your partner could be sitting in the audience and feel both honored and served.

It takes a big person to preserve their partner's dignity when separating—especially after 10, 20, or even 30 years together.

The *purposeful relationship* is just one of the three types you'll encounter. If you've never looked at your romantic relationships from this perspective, doing so now will give you much greater peace of mind. In fact, you could easily understand and complete every *past relationship* you've ever had by simply making a list of everyone you've ever dated—then deciding whether they were *lifetime, life-giving,* or *purposeful.*

When I did this exercise, I stopped asking why certain men had been in my life. I stopped obsessing over breakups and saw them instead as completions. I concluded that those relationships had run their cycle and provided me with exactly what they were supposed to provide at that time. I developed a much healthier mindset about why we came together in the first place.

This goes for friendships that fall into those three categories, too.

Of course, the beauty of knowing about these three categories is that you're released from trying to make everybody a lifetime friend or lifetime romantic partner. It removes much of the disappointment when relationships end. It keeps you focused on the present moment—without constantly obsessing over whether a connection will burn out or whether any *one thing* that you do might permanently damage the relationship. If it's meant to end, it will—because it was life-giving or purposeful to begin with.

Another comforting thought is that relationships are designed to occur within the seasons of our lives. Some seasons are 40 years, while others are 14 months. Your job is to determine what will be (or was) fulfilled in that season when you were involved with a specific person—and how the relationship supported that. What did you do that you couldn't have accomplished if you weren't in that relationship? Did you get the lessons, the moments, and the memories? Did you gather all your assets and your diamonds and walk away with the best things out of that relationship? Did you leave the relationship whole and complete?

From this day forward, I want you to never again say, "We broke up."

Say instead, "We're complete because we accomplished _____."

Using the word *complete* just feels better and reframes the end of the relationship in a way that reaffirms both of you. You're not broken. Your partner is not broken. There was no breakup—only completion.

Not only does this give you a level of tranquility about your past relationships, but it also lets you trust again—and not project your previous experience onto your next opportunity.

ASSEMBLE YOUR BREAKTHROUGH TEAM

Once you've mastered your personal relationships and built a community of people who support you, it's time to assemble the core team who will help you create major breakthroughs in your life, your career, and your business—even if your "business" is being a stay-at-home parent, a nonprofit volunteer, an upwardly mobile corporate employee, or a college student.

WHO SHOULD BE ON YOUR BREAKTHROUGH TEAM?

Your Breakthrough Team should consist of three to five people that I call your "foxhole friends"—people who are on the battlefield with you, in the foxhole, watching your back. They're willing to run when you run, walk when you get tired, and drag you when you want to quit. They're willing to hold you accountable to the person you say you want to become.

While these may be professional advisers—your lawyer, your accountant, your life coach—usually they're people who are willing to dream big with you. They're people you can speak your intentions to—they hold your vision. You can reach out to them in your S.O.S. moments. They have the emotional capacity, the physical capacity, and, in some cases, the financial capacity to handle your breakdowns. It's not uncommon for your Breakthrough Team to include at least one family member, such as a really supportive parent or a sibling, or even your spouse if your relationship is a lifetime relationship.

And if you're a business owner, your Breakthrough Team should include professionals who are in a position to advise you or protect you—but who are close and caring enough to allow you to break down in front of them—and won't hold it against you.

Your Breakthrough Team should have *no* agenda—other than to see you achieve your goals. They're not looking for anything from you. They're not expecting to build something off you. They're not going to color their advice with their own interests. They'll give it to you straight.

My Breakthrough Team includes my mentor, Pete Bissonette, and my executive manager, Margaret Packer—who holds me accountable for doing God's work. At my company, Margaret has her daytime title, but in my Breakthrough Team her role is to keep me focused on God's Divine Plan for me and putting it first according to my highest capacity. When I sit down or lie down or fall down on that job—when I crumble—she'll get in my face and remind me of who I was born to be. She won't stop until I stand up.

I've literally been on the floor—crumpled, tired, frustrated, hurt, and overwhelmed—and Margaret has gotten on the floor with me, two inches from my face, and talked me back up to standing.

"Who do you know yourself to be, Lisa?" she'll challenge. "What is your assignment?"

I can collapse down. But sooner or later, Margaret will prop me back up.

Other Breakthrough Team members are my dad—my

anchor—who's the comfort zone in my life where I don't have to be amazing. He'll constantly take things off my plate so I can serve the planet. He knows my assignment. My mom is on the team, too, for the very same reason—for comfort, safety, helpfulness, and understanding my calling.

If you're a stay-at-home parent, you need a Breakthrough Team, too. Not only do I recommend that you recruit 3–4 Rocket Booster friends, but I also recommend you recruit a seasoned, older parent to provide wisdom and help you forecast what's around the corner. If your child is 5 years old, that parent should be 35 years old. Make sure the parent you select has raised children through multiple seasons and has maintained a stable marriage. Be sure to choose your older parent(s) based on the relationship they have with *their children*. Many parents have the basic points down, but what if their adult children don't want to speak to them? That's a red flag.

As a stay-at-home parent, your Breakthrough Team should also include someone who has some type of entrepreneurial expertise. As your children become more independent and start school, not only could you start a small enterprise for extra household money, but keeping yourself busy with another activity will help you avoid becoming a "hovercraft parent"— micromanaging your children's every waking moment and robbing them of their natural inclination to stretch, explore, and develop independence.

If you're a 9-to-5 employee, your Breakthrough Team might include someone who's achieved corporate success—someone who's climbed the ladder at your own workplace or elsewhere—in addition to Rocket Booster friends. But also consider adding a "life mentor," since people who achieve significant corporate success aren't always the best advisers for creating a life of balance and harmony.

When I think back to the best mentors I've ever had—people who helped me shape my life and my business—they all were at least 10 to 20 levels above me in either spiritual awareness, relationship longevity, income, or business experience. My friend and spiritual teacher Pamela Loving would let me sit at her dining room table for hours sharing my fears of being a mother while traveling the world, my desire to find a safe romantic relationship to be in, and my immense fear of the life calling and leadership responsibility that seemed to be heading my way even back in 2004. Jelani was still very young. And I was questioning (almost daily) my ability to have a true impact on the lives of others.

One day, as I sat with Pam and her husband, may he rest in peace, at the Cracker Barrel restaurant in Flint, Michigan, I poured out my heart, saying, "Pam, I really want to pursue this idea of inspiring people, but what if I do it wrong and they all hate me? I'm so scared of what's in front of me, but I can't turn back now."

I burst into tears right there in the restaurant—in the middle of the dinner rush hour. Pam and William chuckled a bit as I broke down. Perplexed, I asked them why, and Pam's reply was one of a million pearls of wisdom I carry with me today.

"You're still trying to do it alone," she said calmly. "God gave you this gift and the desire in your heart. When you wake up every day, immediately die to yourself and your agenda—and live more in the Spirit while serving others."

At the time, I didn't understand what she meant, but I knew that someday I would need this wisdom. Wiping the tears that were streaming down my face, I tucked away that "pearl" and revisited it often until it made sense. Now, each day when I awake, my job is to dismiss my own ego, forfeit my selfish agenda, and raise my intentions to the calling on my life. My job is to walk through my day in complete and utter service to others.

I got it. I finally got it!

Pam has been more than just a friend. She's been my spiritual mother, reminding me that I'm perfect for the assignment that is placed on my life. Her guidance and wisdom have calmed many a storm in my world. These days, we can laugh (and cry) at the journey and recount each time when I thought I couldn't go on, but did.

Today, as the demands on my life have grown immensely, I don't get to sit with Pam at the Cracker Barrel or around her dinner table as often as I'd like, but I carry her lessons and blessings with me always. My wins are her wins.

In the same way, my chief operating officer, Susie Carder, lived a life that scared me. She traveled internationally. She'd built (then sold) an amazing company. She was the ideal mom. She had time to focus on her health. I made up the story in my mind that her life was perfect—that nothing was out of place. To play in her sandbox, I believed my life had to be perfect, too. I thought I'd never be able to live like she did, but I hitched myself to her as my coach—and eventually she became my business associate and friend. After 10 years of coaching me, Susie made a comment that indicated our relationship had changed. While on a train in Italy, she thought, *I'd love to travel here with a friend,* but she realized that none of her girlfriends could afford the trip. In that moment, she decided to change her circle. And when I got her call, asking me "So when are we going to Italy?," I knew I had achieved the lifestyle, the financial possibility, and the abundance that could make that trip possible. What a difference from the first day I sat with her for coaching.

VISUALIZE AMAZING RELATIONSHIPS

In previous chapters I've given you guided-visualization scripts to help you "see" your future life of abundance. Now, the script below will help you visualize ideal relationships—bonds that support you, nurture you, and amplify your life. You'll notice the opening and closing portions of this visualization are similar, but designed to be used as a complete script with all three parts. Again, you can audiorecord this script or have a friend do it.

RELAXING INTO THE VISUALIZATION PROCESS

Let's use the power of your mind to create your ideal life. Your future experiences will start in your mind first, so let's take a journey into your most creative, free, and powerful place—your imagination!

We become what we most think about. Your new possibilities and success can be created by you and only you. You will become what you think about every day.

Let's cut away all limiting thoughts, and rise above your fears to the place of freedom and creation. Stand in your power! Success is your birthright! Move in this moment from optional to non-negotiable. Every great leader, prophet, visionary, role model, and legend visualized their future *before* they took action.

Know that you have as much right to the joy, love, happiness, and abundance as any other living creature on this planet, and it's yours for the asking and creating.

You have *nothing* to lose and *everything* to gain.

Now . . .

Choose a quiet place. Turn off your phone. Clear your mind. Everything you need to do will be there waiting for you on the other side of this journey. Let it all go for now. Relax and release any physical tension. Become more committed to your inner images than to your physical presence.

Now, I want you to take a deep cleansing breath, filling your abdominal area full of breath. And as you exhale, gently feel your body sinking into a relaxed state.

To help you go into a deep level of mind, I will gently guide you through a relaxation of your physical body. Feel your scalp relax. Feel this gentle feeling of relaxation flow down your fore-head. Now to your eyes . . . Feel your eyelids relax. Feel that sen-sation of relaxation on your eyelids. Feel that slowly flowing out throughout your body. Move the soothing feeling to your face . . . and your throat . . . your neck . . . your shoulders. Feel them sink into deep relaxation. Now your upper arms . . . your hands . . . your chest . . . your abdomen . . . your thighs . . . your knees . . . your calves . . . your feet.

And feel that feeling of relaxation flow all the way down to your toes. There we go.

VISUALIZATION SCRIPT FOR MANIFESTING AMAZING RELATIONSHIPS

You have amazingly healthy relationships around you. You have created the type of relationships where you celebrate one anoth-er's victories, honor one another's imperfections, and commu-nicate to one another what you need. See yourself having social experiences with phenomenal friends, exquisite cuisine, soul-stirring music, belly-aching laughter, and fabulous pictures cre-ating great memories.

You have loving people around you who have watched you grow, learn, and come through difficult times, and they have stood by you. You have done the same for them. You may have walked through an illness together, supported one another through a difficult financial time, provided each a shoulder to lean on, held one or the other through a hurting heart. You have been there. You have put in your time, or you may have helped to pick one another back up again when your spirits were broken. You've chosen to show up for one another and today you get to live joyously within this safe community, together.

See yourself having learned how to ask for what you need, how to set healthy boundaries, and how to be more transparent and share your heart. Now see your friends or your family having learned the same skill set. Together you are growing, learning how to communicate with one another, how to be more committed to staying in harmony, and how to prioritize your love for one another. You no longer keep score of the negative or hurtful things done to you. You've learned to release and press "reset" more often. The quality of your life is not determined by how many people you know, but by the quality of your relationships, and you are committed to increasing the quality of your relationships every day. You no longer miss any opportunity to say *Thank you, I'm sorry, I love you, I miss you, I'm here for you,* or *I'm proud of you.*

You say what you need to say, and never hold in hurt. You never miss an opportunity to love your community and thank them for loving you.

CLOSING DOWN THE VISUALIZATION PROCESS

Slowly begin to feel your back against the chair again. Feel your feet on the ground. Feel your breath again. Begin to come back into the room. When you are ready, very gradually bring yourself back into the now moment.

Now completely rejoin your physical body. Hear the sounds around you in your now environment. When you feel ready, you may open your eyes.

Welcome back! Go throughout your day thinking about and reciting positive affirmations that support and add great energy to this creative visualization.

Remember this in everything that you do: as was said in the Sermon on the Mount, "Ask and it will be given to you, seek and you will find, knock and the door will be opened to you. For everyone who asks receives, the one who seeks finds, and to the one who knocks the door will be opened."

Remember to be in bold radical *action* toward your goals. Ideas and visualizations are worthless without action.

Finally, accept that this visualization is so! This is your future, being shown to you like a motion picture with you as the star. All you need now is action, unwavering faith, and a purpose bigger than yourself.

I'm your sister in this journey, and I believe in you.

ESTABLISH HEALTHY BOUNDARIES IN YOUR RELATIONSHIPS

Establishing healthy boundaries in your relationships is critical. These boundaries maintain peace, joy, love, and celebration as much as they prevent chaos, hurt, pain, disagreement, and disappointment.

I like to compare healthy boundaries to the bumper rails at a bowling alley. You put the bumper rails up just to make sure that, when you release the ball, it rolls down the lane and actually strikes the pins at the other end—rather than ending up in the gutter. The ball goes where you want it to go. And just like bumper rails, healthy boundaries communicate, *Let's stay within these lines. This lane feels the best.* They give you confidence.

Healthy boundaries feel more like agreements. They're not rules. What kinds of boundaries should you agree upon in your relationships?

Respectful Communication

When two people communicate in a mature and respectful way, they *speak* to each other. They don't yell. So one boundary—one agreement—should be that we will only speak to each other in voices that feel good. You may even decide, "We agree not to yell."

Acknowledgment of One Another's Feelings

Not everyone will display or discuss their feelings with you, but an important agreement is that we should acknowledge one another's feelings when presented.

Respectful of Time

You are busy. The people with whom you're in relationships are busy. You both will rarely have the same priorities and deadlines at the same time. So commanding respect for your schedule and deadlines is a healthy boundary you must guard carefully—especially if you are an entrepreneur with employees, partners, and family members all vying for your time. Someone who unerringly calls when you are on deadline and needs to aimlessly chat about their own needs for 30 minutes is not being respectful of your time.

Therefore, a good agreement is that you're allowed to state at the beginning of a call how much time you can allow, without the other person being offended—even if it's only two minutes. Another agreement governs how much time you'll spend together when traveling. I remember being in a relationship where we traveled together, but we liked to do different things during the day. So one of the healthy boundaries we agreed upon is that we could do whatever we wanted during the day, but that we reconnected by 10:30 P.M. so the other person didn't wonder at 3:00 A.M. what was happening. It worked very well because we would spend the first few minutes back together sharing the excitement of our day.

Workplace Boundaries

Healthy boundaries should exist in your workplace as well. And a big area of agreement must be the time frame in which you will accept phone calls. This is especially important for anyone who does detailed, focused work such as accounting, writing, graphic design, analysis, or strategic planning. They cannot stop what they're doing in order to serve you. I always check with my team about their phone call boundaries—and I honor those boundaries. Though these people are my employees, they're allowed to establish their own boundaries to ensure maximum productivity. They also have close-knit, active families. So whether it's "no business calls after 7:30 P.M." or "Sunday mornings are off-limits," we respect those healthy boundaries.

Healthy boundaries are designed to help you maintain a free-flowing relationship that feels good to both parties. But they also allow you to have a tranquil life outside of the relationship. On the other side of those boundaries is the time, focus, space, and permission you need to be present for other family members, pursue your hobbies, practice self-care, or be in *other* relationships—without hurt feelings, strong language, or guilt coming back at you.

Healthy boundaries are put in place to say, "This is what feels good." You don't have to expend energy focusing on what *doesn't* feel good—that just creates opportunity for dispute or argument. If you state what you want and what feels good to you, people will honor that by staying within those boundaries. Healthy boundaries are designed to keep relationships full, fulfilling, and flowing.

EVOLVE THOSE AROUND YOU: YOU'LL OUTGROW THOSE WHO DON'T GROW WITH YOU

Remember that, as you grow in abundance, not everyone will be growing at the same rate you are. They'll also be growing in different ways, possibly in ways that no longer align with your values, mindset, and goals. What was once acceptable to you in the past may no longer be acceptable in your future.

This phenomenon is not uncommon with high achievers. The reality is that those who don't grow with you, you will outgrow.

My advice is to recognize this tendency and find ways to inspire your community to grow—whether it's attending personal growth seminars or reading the same self-help books you read. It might be asking them to join you for coaching sessions or asking them to go through a training course with you. It might mean you'll need to work with them to help them plan their own breathtaking future. Whatever method you choose to inspire them, be intentional and proactive about inspiring them to grow.

PREVENT A PYRRHIC VICTORY: BRING YOUR FAMILY ALONG WITH YOU

In 279 B.C., King Pyrrhus defeated the Roman army, but sustained such severe casualties on his own side that his "victory" seemed more like a loss. Today, we use the term *Pyrrhic victory* to describe an achievement that is only accomplished with heavy losses.

Of course, we've seen lots of these Pyrrhic victories in the news over the years—millionaire businessmen whose children die of drug overdoses. Female entrepreneurs who've had three or four failed marriages. Media superstars who are estranged from their parents.

These are families who lost their anchor, while one of their kind blazed a new trail and soared into success. I want you to avoid the Pyrrhic victory of gaining an amazing life, but losing your family as you build a life of abundance and ultimate riches for yourself. The truth is you *can't enjoy an expanded life* if your family relationships haven't been nurtured. The ultimate success is creating a lifestyle you want and helping those you love in it.

Nurturing these foundational relationships is not something that happens by accident. It's intentional. You have to set aside time and focus to connect, support, and celebrate. Call to ask about their lives and find out what's new. Create ways to invent new memories and traditions. I go to the spa every other month with my grandmother, creating great memories for both of us in the process. I've done cooking sessions with my dad, shared movie time with Mom, and created countless special memories with Jelani.

Your family is a unique bank account into which you make deposits. And if your family history doesn't feel good to you, it's more important than ever to make new memories together.

If we all discovered that we had only five minutes left
to say all that we wanted to say, every telephone booth
would be occupied by people calling other people to tell
them that they loved them.

—*Christopher Morley, American journalist,
essayist, and author of more than 100 novels,
anthologies, and volumes of poetry*

One last idea: loving you should be simple. Regardless of whether you're the top dog in your field or the richest kid from your old neighborhood, don't require your family to know the intricacies of your accomplishments or how staggeringly difficult your goals were to achieve. They don't know what you know. So get past requiring them to have the same vision as you do, or to make them fans or business partners. Love them as your family. That is enough.

WITH YOUR RELATIONSHIPS SOLID, IT'S TIME TO GET ENGAGED

With your relationships on the upswing and Rocket Booster friends and loved ones bringing Enchantment to your abundant life, it's time to move on to the next of the 4 Es—Engagement with your work, career, or business. In the next chapter, I'll give you a reality check and reveal a whole new perspective about the different roles your "job" can fulfill in your abundant new life.

CHAPTER 4

The Third E: Engagement in Your Work for More Than Financial Reward

Success is not defined by your bank account balance,
your career title, or your impressive possessions.
Success is defined by how deeply you love and are loved,
how freely you give and receive from others, and
how continuously you live in your passion. That is the
new definition of success.

—Lisa Nichols

If you've ever worked the whole day through, being well paid to immerse yourself in something fun and exciting—where the day flew by and come the next morning, you wanted to get up and do it all over again—that was a day when you were in your right livelihood.

With our work consuming at least eight hours a day (if not ten or more), getting this part of our abundant life right is critical. But more than that, because our "work" defines us, contributes to our identity, and figures prominently in the social circle and professional relationships we choose, I want to help ensure that you are enthusiastically engaged in the "life assignment" that's been prepared for you through the Divine Plan.

YOU HAVE A LIFE ASSIGNMENT THAT COMMANDS YOUR TIME, TALENT, AND TREASURES

Our life happens in stages or *seasons*. This is especially true of our working years as we move from early jobs to professional advancement to possibly owning a business to working to build our legacy. At each stage, we're called—I believe by God's Divine Plan—to move with grace and ease into our next life assignment.

How can we know what our life assignment is at each stage?

You have to listen to your intuitive self. Your intuitive self is that pull in your belly that draws you toward a specific passion such as working with children, educating others, advocating for the environment, or helping seniors. It may pull you toward music or travel, art or writing. It may beckon you toward inventing new technologies, developing a new part of your business, or stepping into management at your workplace. It might call you to start a family, volunteer at a charity, or become active in your church's mission projects.

Whatever it is—whether career related or something outside of your professional life—your life assignment is something you naturally feel in your soul and, like a magnet, it will continue to draw you toward it whether you respond or not. Of course, you may intellectually justify why you can't pursue it. Or you may talk yourself out of it because you're fearful of what the assignment might entail. But you will feel the pull anyway, and your soul can't help but respond—whether or not your mind and body agrees.

YOUR LIFE ASSIGNMENT MAY NOT BE RELATED TO YOUR JOB OR BUSINESS

Lots of books tell us that we should strive to turn our hobby or passion into our career or business so we can "live our joy" every day. This has always struck me as unsound advice because, most of the time, it's the very fact that we *don't have* daily tasks, deadlines, and deliverables—or the need to make money from our hobby or passion—that makes it so enjoyable!

You *don't* have to pursue your passion as a business or career. In fact, it may be that your job or business will *not include* your passion or calling at all. Instead, your life assignment may be a labor of love you give to the world, to your family, to your local community, or to a specific group of like-minded people. Making your hobby or passionate pursuit a simple outlet simplifies things tremendously. This kind of life assignment (based on your passion) allows you to pursue—if you wish—a less than exciting career that becomes merely the steady, solid financial support you need. I think many people make the mistake of believing that if their business is technical, traditional, or dull, if it's not tied to a huge social cause or visible on the world stage—their work is somehow stifling them from pursuing their life calling.

But that's not true, at all.

Remember that your job or your business could be the major investor in your amazing future. It could provide the financial means for you to pursue your true life's work—and give you the freedom to pursue your calling without stress or regret. If your assignment requires traveling to Third World countries to work with women and children, great! Accumulate your vacation time and take three weeks off—letting your job finance the work that you plan to do.

Though we live in an *either-or* world, I want to invite you to consider the *and* possibility. Working at a job that serves the needs of your family, your lifestyle, your employer, *and* you—while giving you the opportunity to live your life assignment—is a mature and responsible thing to do.

WHAT DOES A BREATHTAKING LIFE ASSIGNMENT LOOK LIKE?

One of the reasons I can speak with such conviction on this subject is that I've been privileged to live my life's assignment for more than 20 years.

When I first started out in the early 1990s, I had a pull in my belly to work with teenagers. I wanted to inspire them as someone who had come through tumultuous teen years myself. While I had an amazing family, I still experienced all the self-doubt, the self-criticism, and the suicidal thoughts that are not uncommon with teens—in addition to a tough life lived raw in South Central Los Angeles. As a result of surviving some very dark years of my own, I believed I could have an impact on the lives of young adults in need of guidance.

When I first recognized my calling, I did little things that allowed me to lean into it, and test the waters. I volunteered at teen centers and that felt good. I expanded my reach to serve at local high schools, mentor athletic teams, and work with faith-based youth programs—and still the pull was there. Eventually, I founded Motivating the Teen Spirit and began to hold my own events—developing a curriculum, recruiting corporate sponsors, and implementing my teen programs in schools and the juvenile justice system.

It was so fulfilling.

In fact, I worked exclusively with teens for 10 years and lived *passionately* inside that assignment. In fact, I could have done that for the next 40 years and it would have been enough—teaching teens how to put words to their feelings, teaching them how to fall madly in love with themselves, teaching them to make integrity-based decisions, set healthy boundaries, and apologize when necessary. Those were some of the most fulfilling years of my life—and that division of my company is still fulfilling to me today. Since I founded those early programs more than 211,000 teens have graduated from our programs, more than 2,500 drop-outs have been inspired to return to school, and more than 3,800 teen suicides have been prevented—plus we've reunited thousands of teens with their families.

As I grew that business and began to speak on behalf of teens, I started to be invited to speak at adult events. My name began to float in circles where others wanted to do business with me. At the time, I was the "teen lady"—a label I was absolutely fine with carrying. Some fairly influential people in the self-development world were inspired by my work and introduced me to Jack Canfield, the originator of the *Chicken Soup for the Soul* book series—and now a good friend of mine.

Jack wanted me to coauthor *Chicken Soup for the African American Soul* with him, and I'm embarrassed to admit that my negative self-talk and mind chatter caused me to decline the invitation FIVE TIMES before I finally accepted this calling. What was I so afraid of? I was fearful that they'd find out I wasn't strong in grammar and that there was a reason I failed my freshman English class in college. Lo and behold, when Jack read my stories, he said they were some of the most powerful he had ever read. It was in that moment that I had to accept that someone else's perception of me (that of my college English teacher) was not my reality—unless I allowed it to be.

Once *Chicken Soup for the African American Soul* was released in bookstores, I went on a very aggressive book tour—knowing in my heart that this was my first chance to show the world who I was. I didn't know how long the door would be open—but I knew I had been called to step through that doorway and explore a life assignment that would take me beyond my work with teenagers.

I organized an aggressive 27-city tour—funding the vast majority of it myself. I lovingly called it the "The Chicken Soup Chitlin Circuit" tour since, to keep my travel budget manageable, the majority of the story contributors in the book hosted me in their homes and organized speaking engagements at their local churches.

Needless to say, I signed lots and lots of books.

I also spoke in front of thousands more people than I had previously. My brand began to grow tremendously.

All along, I was improving my skill set. In fact, I began to shift my focus from being a "technician"—a speaker, writer, and author—into a competent businessperson, learning how to grow my business as a CEO. I had to educate myself about things like scalability, brand extension, online databases, and personnel management. I no longer wanted to be just a speaker, because that was going to be just one line on my business plan—just one revenue stream, just one form of impact.

By 2005, I considered myself an "infopreneur"—responsible for delivering information, inspiration, and education on multiple platforms. Once I approached business from that perspective, my job totally changed. I had defined many new platforms—going from a single-lane highway to a multi-lane highway. My platforms broadened to speaking, writing, keynotes, trainings, workshops, and—with the birth of my first audio program, "Ladies Can We Talk?"—packaged courses.

This is when I had to start seeing myself as the CEO of a training and development company. No longer was I just a keynote speaker or a coach for teens. I was running a business whose product was education. I had two independent contractors, Amondra McClendon and Tia Ross, who served as teen facilitators—and no employees.

But I was tracking my business for *where it could go* instead of *where it is now.*

Once I ceased to sell the "speaking services" of Lisa Nichols and just workshops for teenagers, we experienced a huge growth trajectory.

As it turns out, it was just in the nick of time.

Within 18 months, a documentary filmmaker named Rhonda Byrne approached me to be a featured teacher in *The Secret*—a movie about The Law of Attraction. Rhonda had seen my work, thought my message was universal, and filmed several minutes of my insights for the original version of the film.

When *The Secret* and its companion book were released to worldwide acclaim, my work and I were introduced to more than 20 million people worldwide. My brand skyrocketed.

Of course, becoming famous doesn't necessarily translate into financial success or further growth in and of itself. But, because I had built a business infrastructure to capitalize on this opportunity, *The Secret* put my company on a whole new level. As "*The Secret* tsunami" picked up steam, I quickly developed a back-end system to capture newfound followers on my website, then further communicate with them about my products and programs. Not only did I add hundreds of thousands of people to my community, but I could regularly survey them—and then produce products and services they asked for. I went from working a 12-hour day to being willing to work a 20-hour day as I caught up with the demand.

Even when Rhonda Byrne asked me to play a larger role in the second version of *The Secret*, I still had no idea how big that phenomenon would really get. And, to be honest, I wasn't completely prepared. But I went for it and found ways to leverage the major media appearances I soon found myself doing—including *The Oprah Winfrey Show, Larry King Live, Extra!,* and others—into growth for my company.

The Secret was my launching pad to the next big thing.

YOU'LL GET INDICATORS ALONG THE WAY THAT YOU'RE ON THE RIGHT PATH

How did I know I was on the right path? And how can you know that *you* are living your life assignment? Some days, I would end my work feeling like I had spent the day living in bliss—doing exactly what I was born to do. In fact, I've said in more than 100 speeches and webinars that if God chose to take me tonight, I had spent today doing exactly what I was born to do.

This kind of bliss should be your indicator, too.

Another indicator that I was on the right path was that I was having astounding success at things that had nothing to do with my own talents. Oftentimes, I didn't have anywhere near the skill set to get through a particular experience, yet—because I was on the right path—I would achieve success where, admittedly, I probably had no right to do so. I had the passion, the heart, and the intention—but not the skill set. I had 100% intention, but 0% concern about the mechanism. It was always an indicator that I was on the right path when the mechanism showed up.

But I had to be in action first. The resources, the people, the money, the opportunities—all showed up whenever I was in action. As long as the idea was only percolating in my head, the resources would not appear. But the minute I moved into action—no matter how big the step (or baby the step)—the right people, financial resources, talent, tools, clients, customers . . . they just showed up. It wasn't magic. I was willing to put my neck out too and ask for things—ask for the help, ask for the partnership, ask for the deal.

STEPPING INTO YOUR LIFE ASSIGNMENT
FORCES YOU TO GROW

Sometimes your life assignment will push you into new areas, make you a little uncomfortable, and require you to rapidly gain new skills you didn't have before. Sometimes, like me, you'll make mistakes as you learn and mature.

As the media firestorm around *The Secret* grew, my company grew, too. Sometimes things were easy, but at other times, I lurched my way through and called it progress. For example, I hired people—badly—spending $222,000 on consultants, employees, and contractors who were raving fans, hugged really well, had intimidating credentials, or were just interested in my cause for personal reasons. I hired people who were skilled but who lacked personality—I didn't hire holistically. With each one, I soon learned that I had hired them for all the wrong reasons. By the time the craziness was over, I had spent nearly a quarter million dollars learning how *not to hire* people. At the same time, I was doing a lot of things right. From 2005 to 2011, I worked with a business coach and a life coach—constantly reinvesting in myself to build my skill set as a CEO.

> The secret to my success is that I grabbed my fears by the hand, then leaped off the ledge.
>
> —Lisa Nichols

Little by little, day by day, I built my business using bubble gum, Band-Aids, shoestring, and duct tape. Eventually my business coach, Susie Carder, became my chief operating officer—and both of us recognized how much I wanted to grow the business to a whole new level. But we knew that to do that, we'd have to infuse the business with growth capital (outside money), and not use our operating capital to fund new activity. I had to grow again—learning the distinction between the two kinds of money. Luckily, we had the people, sales infrastructure, and operational infrastructure in place. The accounting was solid, and we were already running the business like a much bigger company.

Could going public and attracting investors be possible for a company like mine?

Taking the company public, we felt, would not only bring us the growth capital we needed—but in my quieter moments I also thought, *What an inspiration it would be to my community and others who are living the reality I was 20 years ago.* If I could overcome the desperation of standing in the welfare line—transforming my life from public assistance to going public—anyone could do the same.

The decision was made. We took steps in 2013 to kick off an S-1 filing and launch Motivating the Masses, Inc. as a publicly traded company.

DON'T WORRY IF OTHER PEOPLE JUDGE YOU OR YOUR LIFE ASSIGNMENT

What a process it all turned out to be! And I had to grow personally as a result. For one thing, I had to get over the fear of exposing my business, my financials, and my growth plans to outside scrutiny. *Would people judge me?* I worried. *It's like people going through my lingerie drawer.*

"They may be looking at our underwear," Susie quipped, "but luckily everything's clean and everything's folded!".

Finally, instead of running the business on duct tape and a dream, we'd be able to secure a strong financial infusion that would help us replace our guerrilla-style solutions with real systems, superqualified people, and structured business development activity. It was the culmination of a 17-year dream to have the kind of company that would attract the attention of consumers, partners, and investors.

But one of the most inspiring aspects of the tedious and tumultuous journey was the great energy that my students, audiences, and partners gave me, jumping in with full-on belief as we went through a process that was three times longer than anyone expected. To prove that the company was attractive to prospective investors, we were advised—pre-filing—to go to the market and raise our first $250,000 on our own.

We raised $1.8 million instead.

And who were the people who put up $10,000 . . . $100,000 . . . and in some cases, as much as $250,000 to build this dream even bigger? They were mothers and fathers, young entrepreneurs, seasoned businesspeople, my students, and others from my community. To see them with tears of gratitude at just the idea of getting involved in the early stages of the company's growth kept me going.

In fact, years from now, when the company has thousands of nameless investors trading our stock, those *initial 97 investors* who believed in me will still occupy a sacred place in my heart. Even though they saw my knees knocking and my teeth chattering, they still jumped in when Motivating the Masses was just an idea. It wasn't our P&L, it wasn't our forecast—it was their faith in me and the possibility of what we were going to co-create that inspired them to come on board.

I know that eventually, when we're actively trading on Wall Street—when things get overwhelming and all I want to do is sit down—it's their faces I see that will keep me going.

They are all special to me.

THERE'S A SPIRITUAL ELEMENT TO YOUR LIFE ASSIGNMENT

When your spirit calls you to seek and acknowledge God's plan for you, to dismiss it is unacceptable. God's Divine Plan for my life is something that I have had to become very aware of and very committed to.

What does your soul call you to do? What is your soul saying is necessary? What brings you joy? What contribution do you know you should be making to this planet? Are you sharing your gifts or hoarding your gifts because you're nervous about how you might look?

One thing most people don't realize is that just the gifts of listening, nurturing, humor, and compassion are desperately needed—even though they don't make sense or don't seem "big" enough. But the reality is that you're supposed to share your gift even if you don't understand its value. Our God-given talents aren't *always* the business skills or scientific knowledge or technical expertise we get compensated for. Sometimes our talent is plain old everyday people skills that have been lost in our fast-paced society—listening, compassion, a sense of humor, and a positive outlook.

What I like so much about my business today is that it's now a conduit for distributing an awareness that there's a calling on everyone's life. Isn't this another great reason for my business to exist? I think so.

The minute you accept your calling, insignificant though *you may think* it is, your life will become indescribable, unrecognizable—breathtaking!—in ways you never imagined.

That's what happened to me.

I'm a very human and very ordinary woman who chose to allow God and the Divine to work through me so I can make an extraordinary impact on the world. Once I made that choice, once I surrendered, the impact happened.

DON'T LIVE SOMEONE ELSE'S LIFE ASSIGNMENT

As I cautioned before, to dismiss God's Divine Plan for our life is misguided. But isn't that what many people do and then justify it as a smart move?

We go to medical school because our parents want that. We give up our dream career in the arts because, somehow, it's not a "real job." We take over the family business, though we're not suited for it and feel uninspired by the daily routine.

These are all examples of someone imposing *their idea* of a life assignment on you. And while I know I've said that our daily job—even one we dislike—can be the investor in our great calling, sometimes you just have to face facts that you're in the wrong place.

Nicole Roberts Jones came to this conclusion. Growing

up, like me, in a tough neighborhood near Los Angeles, she decided early on that the only way to have a better life was to go to college. It wasn't easy, but she got herself in and she got herself out, and even landed a "dream job" in Hollywood after graduation. What she soon realized, however, is that living the charmed life working in Hollywood was a dream that *everyone else said she should pursue.*

"Go into the entertainment field," they said.

So that's what Nicole did.

She had the look, she had the style, she had the expertise. So she listened to everyone but herself.

But she soon realized that going to all the hot Hollywood parties and rubbing elbows with celebrities—even dating a few—was really someone else's dream. As a matter of fact, she felt empty. What she really wanted was to make a difference in the world.

Then one night, Nicole found herself speaking at a youth program at her church, confronted by 300 teenagers with the same glimmer in their eye that Nicole had had just years before. They thrilled at the possibility for their future, but feared the unknown, too. And as Nicole took up her workweek in Hollywood the next day, she remembered those eyes.

Nicole also realized that to escape the crime-ridden streets of her childhood, she had followed a path recommended by others. She simply hadn't known any other way at the time. She'd allowed other people to dictate her future like a remote control and, as a result, not only was she living someone else's version of success—but in taking her "dream job," Nicole had lost herself.

What was Nicole truly inspired to do? She wanted to educate and inspire and shepherd those who found themselves at a crossroads. But there was no Hollywood glamour in that—and there was surely no paycheck in it either.

That night after work, Nicole made a decision. Though she was recognized in Hollywood circles, she decided she was willing to become unrecognizable in order to step into a better future. Today, Nicole Roberts Jones is one of my team of in-demand executive coaches for entrepreneurs who are at a crossroads in their careers, and who need to identify the catalyst that will sky-rocket their new business.

Just like Nicole, your life's calling doesn't have to be Hollywood-big or televised worldwide. It could be working with children at a local youth center or starting a fund to clean up nearby parks. Take the word *grand* out of *your* life assignment and insert the words *fulfillment* and *contribution* instead.

YOUR LIFE ASSIGNMENT WILL CHANGE THROUGHOUT THE SEASONS OF YOUR LIFE

We look at the idea of a life calling as if we have one chance to get it right—that there's just one life assignment for us on this earth. But the reality is that God has you on redial. You can be called at one point in your life for one thing but called again later for something else. And He'll keep calling you with whatever the world needs (and wherever you're needed). As your life evolves and you have more experience, your life assignment will evolve with you.

While it may become more expansive or it may contract—while it may become more laser focused and move you into a smaller niche—you have to be open-minded and ask the right questions: *What am I supposed to be doing in* this *season? What's my contribution in* this *moment?*

The truth is the contribution and service you're supposed to be living will change. Twenty years ago, the contribution you were making was very different from the contribution you're making now. But a lot of the discord, discomfort, and disruption we experience happens when we try to force that dated, 20-year-old assignment into our "now" reality.

Why not be in your now, instead?

Comparison is the thief of joy.

—*Theodore Roosevelt, author, naturalist, explorer,
and 26th president of the United States of America*

Of course, sometimes the transition from one season to another is filled with drama, upheaval, and uncertainty. Kate McKay had built a multimillion-dollar company without ever taking a business class. She had an indescribable desire to succeed and knew in her gut that her future, as well as her children's, depended on it. But as her business grew, her marriage crumbled. She'd been an at-home working mom following an old lifestyle model that no longer served her.

Her life assignment was about to change.

Torn between the "accepted norm" she'd been living and the uncertainty that was to come, Kate was frozen in fear, self-doubt, and feelings of unworthiness. Sitting in her car outside her accountant's office reflecting on the shame of her impending divorce (and the guilt of putting her three kids through the ordeal), pride, shame, excitement, and terror converged as Kate glanced at her paperwork and read the bottom line.

Holy cow! she thought.

The number was astounding. She wiped away her tears, took a deep breath, and picked up the phone.

"Hello, Dad," Kate said, "I have some really exciting news . . ."

Financial independence shifted her into a new life assignment that inspires Kate daily to help others experience the same. By following her intuition and accepting her calling courageously, Kate McKay found her way through.

YOUR JOB IS AN INVESTOR IN YOUR BREATHTAKING FUTURE

Back in Chapter 1, I talked about reframing the way you view your employment. If you have a less-than-perfect job or unexciting career, one way to regain that excitement is to start treating your job as an investor in your breathtaking future.

When I was in my 20s, I did just that. I recognized that, though my job wasn't the life assignment I would ultimately pursue, it *could become the catalyst* for stepping into the amazing life I wanted.

Your career could be the same for you.

But first you need to have an inkling of what you want to do, be, have, or create—and how much it will cost. You need a financial goal. Whether you're in a $40,000-a-year job or a six-figure career, decide what you can set aside toward that goal. Alternatively, decide what activity or life assignment your income will support now. You could even designate a specific amount or percentage each week that would fund a specific activity.

Let's say that your calling is to work with landlords, residents, and local agencies to clean up public housing. You have an idea that if someone like you spearheaded the effort, you could help residents gain job skills, obtain employment, and bring pride (and a paycheck) back to their homes. Well, what is needed to make that happen and how much does that cost?

Similarly, if you work for a large consulting firm, but are inspired to help bring music education back to public schools, could you designate consulting fees from a new client you just signed to fund such a program with a local orchestra who would play at area schools?

Whatever you decide to fund, you must be diligent and disciplined about setting money aside from your current job.

WHAT LIFESTYLE IS YOUR INVESTOR HELPING TO CREATE?

One thing I recommend is to make decisions about the lifestyle and living standards your paycheck should be helping to create in your life. Jot down two or three lifestyle choices in each area, then decide how much it will cost and how you will designate that money from your regular paycheck.

Experiences	Cost	Amount to Be Deducted	Deduct Weekly	Deduct Monthly
_____	$ _____	$ _____	☐	☐
_____	$ _____	$ _____	☐	☐
_____	$ _____	$ _____	☐	☐
Financial Goals				
_____	$ _____	$ _____	☐	☐
_____	$ _____	$ _____	☐	☐
_____	$ _____	$ _____	☐	☐
Physical Rewards				
_____	$ _____	$ _____	☐	☐
_____	$ _____	$ _____	☐	☐
_____	$ _____	$ _____	☐	☐

IF YOU'RE WONDERING WHETHER TO QUIT YOUR JOB . . .

Be aware that it's negligent to run out and quit your job today. It's irresponsible in your relationship with your current investor to quit until you have another investor that can satisfy your livelihood and basic needs.

You cannot be creative wondering if your bills are going to be paid, or worrying that you have only limited savings to live on.

When people excitedly approach me at public events and say, "I'm so happy. I quit my job," I reply, "I wish you would have talked to me first."

ONE MORE REASON TO REMAIN ENTHUSIASTIC
ABOUT YOUR CURRENT JOB

Lee Reimann had a good-paying job, but it didn't excite her to go to work. As an attorney, she prepared legal documents for clients, but something was missing. Her heart just wasn't engaged.

Then one day, Lee thought about what she was really meant to do. Wasn't she already helping others with passion—working with families to ensure that the wishes of older adults were communicated and respected? Today, Lee sees her job as a laboratory for developing her platform for teaching families. While she still creates legal documents, she now sees the bigger picture— and the missing link—that speaks to her heart. Not only has Lee promoted a retreat where families can hold mediated, crucial conversations in a "safe" environment, she's developed a seven-step approach to conducting family meetings that supports the discussion of difficult topics. Lee also speaks frequently at events in her local community and, during this outreach, stresses the importance of communicating decisions made by older family members so that, ultimately, their wishes can be honored.

What do you do every day at your workplace that you can reframe and become more enthusiastic about? Is your job *already providing the mechanism* for something you're called to do?

Another program participant of mine, Marie Mbouni, discovered that answer for herself. As an anesthesiologist, Marie had reached the point where she was starting to ask deeper questions such as, *What is my purpose? What is my unique gift? What did I come here to share with the world?*

This was scary for her because being a doctor is a giving profession. Doctors "do good" in the world every day, yet Marie knew there was something more she could offer. After praying repeatedly and telling God, "I'm ready," Marie got a terrifying answer.

Her life assignment was spiritual work!

This threw her into a tailspin. How could she do that when

she'd been trained for something else? Who would even listen to her?

Marie wasn't even a regular churchgoer. And even more pressing was the question of *how she would support herself.* She had a house she loved—but with a mortgage and financial obligations. She felt trapped, scared, filled with anxiety, and guilt-ridden, too.

She had asked God repeatedly to reveal her calling, and now, all she was finding were roadblocks. She wasn't feeling good about the situation or herself. Crying herself to sleep night after night from pure nervous exhaustion, Marie only knew that she had to fulfill her purpose, now that it had been revealed to her.

Soon after, Marie came across one of my recordings. Committed to meeting me, she attended one of my events and struck up a conversation. When she told me she wanted to quit her job to pursue her dream, I stopped her.

"Baby, your job is your investor," I said.

Almost immediately, Marie felt such a huge release that she started screaming with tears streaming down her face.

Today, whenever Marie has a patient who is difficult or if she gets tired, she just thinks about her new mantra, *My job is my investor,* and smiles with happiness and gratitude. She's on her way to her true calling.

VISUALIZE YOURSELF LIVING YOUR LIFE ASSIGNMENT

Throughout this book, I've introduced you to *visualization*—a tool that helps you "see" your future life *as if* you've already accomplished it. Now I want to help you *act as if* you're already living your life assignment in this season by giving you a visualization script that will put those pictures into your mind. As always, to use this script effectively, record it in your own voice (or have a friend record it), then replay the recording to guide you through the visualization session.

RELAXING INTO THE VISUALIZATION PROCESS

Let's use the power of your mind to create your ideal life. Your future experiences will start in your mind first, so let's take a journey into your most creative, free, and powerful place ever— your imagination!

We become what we most think about. Your new possibilities and success can be created by you and only you. You will become what you think about every day.

Let's cut away all limiting thoughts, and rise above your fears to the place of freedom and creation.

Stand in your power! Success is your birthright! Move in this moment from optional to non-negotiable.

Every great leader, prophet, visionary, role model, and legend visualized their future *before* they took action.

Know that you have as much right to the joy, love, happiness, and abundance as any other living creature on this planet, and it's yours for the asking and creating.

You have *nothing* to lose and *everything* to gain.

Now . . .

Choose a quiet place. Turn off your phone. Clear your mind. Everything you need to do will be there waiting for you on the other side of this journey. Let it all go for now. Relax and release any physical tension. Become more committed to your inner images than to your physical presence.

Now, I want you to take a deep cleansing breath, filling your abdominal area full of breath. And as you exhale, gently feel your body sinking into a relaxed state.

To help you go into a deep level of mind, I will gently guide you through a relaxation of your physical body.

Feel your scalp relax. Feel this gentle feeling of relaxation flow down your forehead. Now to your eyes . . . Feel your eyelids relax. Feel that sensation of relaxation on your eyelids. Feel that slowly flowing throughout your body.

Move the soothing feeling to your face . . . and your throat . . . your neck . . . your shoulders. Feel them sink into deep relaxation.

Now your upper arms . . . your hands . . . your chest . . . your abdomen . . . your thighs . . . your knees . . . your calves . . . your feet.

And feel that feeling of relaxation flow all the way down to your toes.

Now . . .

VISUALIZATION SCRIPT FOR LIVING YOUR LIFE ASSIGNMENT

Pablo Picasso said, "Everything you can imagine is real." So true. Now, think about your life assignment—the most ideal career or passionate pursuit that will give you absolute satisfaction, great benefits, and more than enough money. Imagine a perfect day in just such a pursuit.

Breathe in deeply—and as you exhale—visualize yourself preparing to start your day. It's a new day. You're excited to meet your colleagues. They are supportive, friendly, and cheerful. You have no trouble communicating with your superiors. In fact, they understand you like the back of their hands. See yourself in complete harmony with everyone at work.

Your coworkers are so different. Yet they seem to be in love with the way you work. They love your ideas and they never stop surprising you with their support.

You are so creative and resourceful at work. You feel great. You feel alive. Feel the feeling of joy, satisfaction, and pride as you go through the events of the day. You're playful, fun to be around, alert—and productive.

Now, allow yourself to be extremely grateful for this work. Let the feeling of gratitude flow out like a river from your heart. Take a deep breath . . . hold it . . . and . . . while exhaling . . . let this feeling of gratitude emanate from you into the Universe as a payment for letting you have your dream career. Amplify that emotion. Fill yourself with it.

And now, think about the first step—a task you'll be doing that will help you secure this dream career of yours. Something that you could do today . . . or tomorrow. Once you know what that task is, picture yourself completing this task.

You now celebrate its accomplishment. You are so excited by the amazing possibilities. Feel the excitement in your heart. It's so real. Know that you can attract anything you want. Right now, you are powerfully attracting the conversations, the circumstances, and the people you need to make this manifestation come true. Give thanks. And carry with you this feeling of gratitude as you go through the rest of the day.

CLOSING DOWN THE VISUALIZATION PROCESS

Slowly begin to feel your back against the chair again. Feel your feet on the ground. Feel your breath again. Begin to come back into the room. When you are ready, very gradually start to bring yourself back into the now moment.

Now completely rejoin your physical body. Hear the sounds around you in your now environment. When you feel ready, you may open your eyes.

Welcome back! Go throughout your day thinking about and reciting positive affirmations that support and add great energy to this creative visualization.

Remember this in everything that you do: as was said in the Sermon on the Mount, "Ask and it will be given to you, seek and you will find, knock and the door will be opened to you. For everyone who asks receives, the one who seeks finds, and to the one who knocks the door will be opened."

Remember to be in radical *action* toward your goals. Ideas and visualizations are worthless without action.

Finally, accept that this visualization is so! This is your future, being shown to you like a motion picture with you as the star. All you need now is action, unwavering faith, and a purpose bigger than yourself.

I'm your sister in this journey, and I believe in you.

THE DRAIN GAME: HOW TO STAY INFUSED, ENTHUSED, AND INSPIRED

Although I've talked a lot about what to do if your job or business is an unfulfilling activity for you, what if you're in a career that excites you, that you planned for, and that you've been happy doing most of your working life?

I applaud you.

In fact, I'm delighted. Not only are you in your right livelihood, you're probably living your life assignment in this season. Now it's time to grow yourself as a career professional, as a practitioner, and as a subject-matter expert. This will help you stay enthused and inspired about the work you do all day. (Even if you have reframed your job as "your investor," there are many ways to stay enthusiastic and inspired, and you might even discover a new area of interest for yourself.)

Growth and skill-building is key.

STAY INSPIRED THROUGH CAREER GROWTH

If you're eager to move up the ladder and pursue an aggressive career path, set yourself on a trajectory. Identify the next career move for you—and identify what you must do to qualify for it. If you're a teacher and going back to school would enable you to get promoted and become a school administrator, wouldn't you move mountains to carve out the time, find the money, enlist your family's support, and do anything else necessary to earn your advanced degree? And if you were just starting out in your career with designs on a management or even (eventually) a more senior position, wouldn't you identify and approach a mentor at your company who's done exactly what you want to do?

I find that I personally stay enthusiastic whenever I'm improving, growing, taking on new challenges, or stepping up my game.

If you're a business owner like me, would becoming a member of the board at your trade association excite you? Would contributing to a major study, becoming a speaker, or adding book writing to your résumé make you feel inspired? Does being interviewed in the press keep you enthused?

Or what about starting a new division, creating or inventing a new product, or negotiating a major strategic alliance—all these could infuse you with newfound energy for your work. The key is to continually grow *yourself,* not just your portfolio, to become someone who attracts bigger and more exciting deals, exposure, and opportunity.

STAY INSPIRED BY CELEBRATING CAREER GOALS BOTH LARGE AND SMALL

When you give yourself bold goals, be sure to break them down into smaller "milestone" goals and targets to work toward. Then, every time you achieve a fraction of that goal or the goal in its entirety, celebrate yourself.

In our society today, we often find ourselves under-celebrated because we're waiting on someone else to celebrate us. A better approach—one that will keep you more enthusiastic—is to celebrate yourself for small, bite-sized, palatable achievements.

I recently met Bishop T.D. Jakes for the first time. He's been someone I looked to as a mentor and a teacher for years, but we'd never met in person. He's taught me so much over the years through his books, audio programs, and television programs. Years ago, I learned from him that sometimes you've got to bake your own cake, light your own candles, and throw yourself a party. That was a great lesson for me. It taught me that I'd been waiting on other people to celebrate me, and when they didn't, I didn't either. Sometimes months—even years—would go by without any celebration until I realized it's *my responsibility* to celebrate me.

When I started celebrating my smaller wins, it filled my tank for my bigger wins. I'd invite some girlfriends over and do our own version of Ladies' Night. Or I'd take Jelani to the movies or host my family for dinner and a ball game. No matter what I did, I would always share with my community why I was celebrating myself—then be uplifted as they joined me in acknowledging my win.

When I finally met Bishop Jakes in person, I looked him in the eyes and thanked him for that bake-a-cake-light-a-candle lesson. It warmed my heart to see him standing slightly offstage—watching me deliver my presentation. When he first galvanized me through his books and cassette tapes, I was still working out of my walk-in closet—striving to validate myself in the self-development industry. To look up and see him now, standing in front of the Jumbotron at Disney Dreamers Academy watching me speak—with his hand over his heart like a proud Papa Bear—just meant everything to me. I thought, *Yeah, I baked my cake, I lit my candles, I threw my own parties and celebrated myself*—and now I was at the point in my career where others started celebrating me, too.

I had to fight back tears of gratitude and reverence while standing onstage. Patting myself on the back later, I thought, *He taught me something 12 years ago, and I learned my lesson well.*

To make sure you're continually on track, set small goals that are believable and achievable, and that support larger achievements you want to accomplish. Whether you plan goals to achieve by the end of the week, month, year, or more, acknowledge your success in a way that makes you feel abundant.

STAY ENTHUSED BY BECOMING A CONSTANT
AND NEVER-ENDING LEARNER

Being a constant and never-ending learner is another way to stay enthusiastic about your work. Just the process of research, investigation, study, and learning new things keeps your career constantly new, fresh, and exciting.

I never want to "arrive" at optimum knowledge—wherever that place is—because the excitement for me is in the exploring. It's exciting to put on your construction hat with the headlamp on the front and navigate what's next for you. Where can you find this thrill of exploration? In books, podcasts, audio sessions, live trainings, and in webinars, summits, and other online events. Delve into someone else's mindset and see where that new insight takes your career or business. Being a continuous explorer is something that will keep you energized because learning something new awakens a part of you that wasn't awakened before. It shakes you out of complacency and jolts you into new thinking. For me, it's almost like a double-door opening to new possibility. I felt that jolt when I read *The Go-Giver* by Bob Burg and John David Mann, a book about being an integrity-based, wildly successful businessman who had mastered the art of giving at an entirely new level. After all these years of being a CEO, it inspired me to strive further.

I thought, *Okay, there's more to do. I still have time. How exciting. There's someone who's gone before me and mastered the art of serving. They've created a breathtaking life pouring into others.*

Every time I read something or hear something interesting—or anytime someone creates a new paradigm shift for me—I feel like there's a road I've been bypassing for years. Now I can travel down this road and be a learner. The best part about being a continual learner is that it has nothing to do with anyone else—it's you filling your own tank. It's you selfishly being willing to fill yourself just for your own benefit.

STAY INFUSED BY BECOMING THE GO-TO EXPERT AND PASSING ON YOUR KNOWLEDGE

Of course, as we continue to gain new knowledge, the fact that we are servant-leaders, givers, and providers dictates that we should pass it on. When you do that, you become an electrifying teacher and a recognized authority—whether in an informal circle, with your girlfriends or colleagues, or in more formalized settings as an author or public speaker.

When you share what you know, you become a more value-added friend or colleague. You bring a greater sense of contribution to any circle that you are part of. And you become recognized as an immediate authority in the area that you've studied the most. Don't be surprised when this benefits your career or your business. Let's say, for example, that you're an entrepreneur who has mastered online marketing. You may have created a complete online launch formula, mastered self-publishing a book online, or learned how to attract the attention of major publishers. That mastery allows you to advertise your services as a go-to expert. You might be an expert in the area of accounting or (one of my favorite needs) home and office organization. You, too, can grow a robust business or career around these skills.

WHAT PROBLEMS ARE YOU SOLVING? WHAT JOY CAN YOU BRING?

Work is an act of service that you are being paid to deliver for people. One final way to stay inspired and enthusiastic is by looking at what you're accomplishing for people—whether solving problems, taking away pain, bringing them joy, helping them accomplish their goals, or something else. Ask yourself, even if you're not working with the ultimate end user or customer, whether your work brings relief or joy. If so, you can thrill to the idea that you are closer to your life's calling.

Concentrating on the ultimate user allows you to move away from focusing on the mundane, tactical aspects of your job or business to focusing on the outcome instead. One client of mine, Zenovia Andrews, discovered this truth. Though she was already engaged full-time running someone else's company, she passionately wanted to start her own consulting firm where she could light a fire in other entrepreneurs. Though her time was divided, Zenovia jumped in full-force and built her own business in order to be able to work directly with the people who could benefit most from her expertise. She wrote a book for entrepreneurs titled *All Systems Go,* and now helps them establish systems that eliminate waste, inefficiency, and frustration.

AN ABUNDANCE OF OPPORTUNITY: THIS GOD WE SERVE IS OFF THE CHAIN

When you are living abundantly and blissfully engaged in your current life assignment, opportunities to expand your work, gain new knowledge, connect with higher-level thinkers, and simply have more fun will *also become more abundant.*

In fact, throughout your working life, opportunities to grow your career, expand your business, and live your life assignment will appear in the form of chance meetings, random conversations, and that intuitive tingling in your belly that doesn't go away. Your job is to listen, investigate—and act, if appropriate.

ATTRACT MORE OF WHAT YOU LIKE TO DO

When I think about creating or attracting new opportunity in my career, I know basically what I'm looking for: opportunities to expand the business, ways to impact more people, and connections that will bring me new markets and new sales leads. In your career, you have a mental wish list, too. If you don't, make one today. Some things come to you with comfort and ease and are just plain fun. My advice is to write them all down. Better yet, put them on a vision board. Build a wish list of opportunities that you want to come your way to excite you, intrigue you, challenge you—and that you want to bring into your work life or business.

Remember, too, that you're a magnet for what you focus your energy on. Discover first what you like to do most. Then, proactively look for opportunities to do more of what you like—not more of what you don't like.

> This God we serve, He off the chain!!!!
>
> —Steve Harvey, texting a message about the Abundance Now book
> project prior to pitch meetings with New York publishers

SPEND TIME DOING RESEARCH

Ask yourself, *What would I like to spend my days, evenings, and weekends doing?* This goes for not only your current "work," but every other activity, too. If you don't know what opportunities inspire you, start researching what you like to do. Go shopping in your mind and see what people do that intrigues you. Find those things that make you say, *Oh, I wish I could!*

If you're thinking of starting a business or a new employment path in one of these newly researched areas as part of your work toward abundance, kick your research into high gear, and don't give up your investor (your job) just yet.

In my entrepreneurial training programs, I encourage my students to allocate 4–6 hours of research a week for 30–45 days before making any move. Get a three-ring binder and fill it with the information and data your research reveals. Learn from the mistakes of others in this area. Learn their best practices. Then see if what you're investigating is a fit for you.

You may be surprised at what you find.

I once worked with a student who was really confused about

how he wanted to roll out his training business. Although I coached him for hours, he never really took off running toward his vision. Finally, I said, "Listen, just do your research. You haven't gotten around to that yet."

A short while later, he called me and was absolutely *on fire*. It turns out that in the first few hours of his research, he'd gone online and found a gentleman on the East Coast who was doing *exactly* what my student wanted to do on the West Coast. Suddenly, he could see himself in that other person's lifestyle—delivering the same kind of content in his own unique way.

To this day, he's never stopped running. He is constantly building his training company and expanding his vision. In fact, he's now positioned to serve over 10,000 people in the next year because of a few hours of research that allowed him to "see" his training company in action. Since then he's conducted many more hours of research—but this time on how to grow his business to previously unimaginable heights.

LOTS OF LITTLES ARE BETTER THAN ONE BIG BREAK

I think too many of us are waiting for our big break—that one idea or chance that will set us up for life—when lots of excellent (but smaller) opportunities for advancement wait, languishing for our attention. This is a particular dilemma for entrepreneurs. Because we're exposed to so many new ideas, trends, marketing schemes, and other opportunities—and because we're accustomed to aggressively pursuing new forms of revenue—we have the knowledge, drive, and support team to do almost anything we want.

But should we?

I contend that lots of smaller opportunities which steadily build upon what you're doing now are worth far more in the long run than one big break for which you have to disrupt all your other activity.

Abundance is your birthright. From the day you were
born, you were allocated an abundance of joy, love,
opportunity, and an abundance of prosperity, ideas,
and resources. It is your birthright merely because
you were born. Don't give away this blessing that was
allocated to you. Cash in on it and embrace it.

—Lisa Nichols

This lottery mentality goes for developing multiple streams of income if you're an employee, too. Be prudent about the secondary income activities that you get involved in. One area that's often *imprudent* are the many work-from-home scams that promise to purchase the output of items you assemble from home—after buying lots of supplies and assembly parts from the parent company. Other questionable opportunities for secondary income are activities where you simply don't have adequate knowledge, time, or money to fully exploit the opportunity. You make the initial investment, but ultimately you don't make money because it's outside your area of expertise, takes more time than you have to spare, or requires even further expenditure. It's easy to "invest" in a business opportunity, then spend tens of thousands of dollars more in inventory, travel, or services—only to see no profits. Not only will you have impacted your family's finances or time, you will have lowered your self-confidence for future opportunities.

Stay in your lane and look for smaller projects that you have adequate expertise, time, and money to pursue—for example, consulting in your field to smaller companies who can't afford a full-time employee, but who will pay you for occasional projects. Or subcontracting to a firm that already has clients but doesn't have the expertise to deliver a portion of a contract. You can even advertise your services for odd jobs you're good at such as organizing, home staging, writing, handling publicity, or making repairs—things that require virtually no investment and very little time. While smaller opportunities may not send the kids to college, together they could pay for some expenses so you can expand your lifestyle or add to your prosperity.

TO LAUNCH OR NOT TO LAUNCH: BUSINESS 101

Although I became a business owner (and though the upside for creating wealth is *generally* better with a business versus working for someone else), I want to be clear about one thing: not everyone should be a business owner. For many people (perhaps you), their highest form of contribution is actually supporting or partnering with someone else. Depending on your work style, your level of detail, and where you are in your career or personal development, you may work better as a team member versus a leader.

To be candid with you, there are many days when I've said, *God, if I had it to do over again tomorrow, I don't know if I would want to be at the top.*

Still, I believe being a CEO is in my blueprint, but that's not the case for everyone. Of course, this is not a measure of who is more important or smarter, because CEOs still need analysts and operations managers and technicians. Moreover, if everyone were a CEO, no one would be working in the trenches every day to move the business forward.

So, while not everyone wants or needs to be in the CEO role, I do think that owning your own business—with responsible planning and effective systems—can move you to a place of abundance and prosperity. I won't say it will move you better, quicker, or faster, however. It took me 20 years to get to a place where I could take my company public. And I can't say it's more freeing, either, because for many years I was tied to my business while my friends who were employees got to take vacation days. They didn't have to own the vision and build it, too.

> I believe, for the first time in history, entrepreneurship is
> now a viable career.
>
> —Eric Ries, *author of* The Lean Startup

Of course, if you *do decide* to start a business—or you already own one—here is some clear and important advice:

1. *Forecast your plans for growth.* Focus on the one thing that most business owners think is a waste of time but that actually is the best use of your time—navigating and forecasting plans for growth at least 18 months to 3 years out. Chart the path of where you're going, where you want to end up, and what would be considered a step or goal along the way. This way, you're not reacting to opportunities—but rather, you're creating opportunities in the direction of your plan.

2. *Start planning from the beginning, especially prior to start-up.* Most entrepreneurs are living off passion, and though that's very necessary, you also need to live off planning. From everything I've personally seen and experienced, it's virtually guaranteed that your business is going to cost you three times more than you thought it would—and take three times longer to develop. Preparation is key to reducing this time and cost. Research your industry, the market, and the competition. Understand your "USP," or Unique Service Proposition—that one thing you do better than anyone else in the marketplace. Understand pricing for your product type, and research what the market will bear.

   Understand who your ideal client or customer is—that person who will buy your products and services at a premium ticket. More to the point, what *solutions* will you offer them?

How will you sustain your business and keep your audience engaged?

There are so many questions that you need to answer and plan a strategy for, but here's why I love those questions: when you make a plan, all you have to do is work the plan. When you don't make a plan, you're forced to make it up as you go along.

3. *Get good at marketing.* Something business owners don't do enough of is marketing, marketing, marketing. Your company may offer amazing solutions, but if no one knows about them, your business isn't worth anything.

4. *Sell like your life depended on it.* No one can sell you better than you. Hone the sales scripts, offers, and sales tools you use to sell effectively, then train others to replicate what you've perfected.

5. *If you're going to build a business, build it on cement versus sinking sand.* Spend more time learning how to be an excellent CEO than you spend on your area of technical expertise. In the early days of my career, when I focused solely on building my skill set as a speaker, I discovered that I didn't own a business—I owned a job. As long as I was onstage, the business wasn't growing. I was constantly in survival mode. However, when I began to operate like a CEO and focus on building my business on cement (versus sinking sand), I began to focus on the marketing systems, finance, sales systems, and overall operations of my business. The result was that I began to generate multiple streams of revenue—making money when I was both on and off the stage. Not only did my annual revenue increase, my peace of mind and joy grew, too.

MULTIPLE STREAMS OF INCOME ARE THE
BEST ROUTE TO WEALTH

Be aware that owning a business is not the only route to wealth—or even the best route. Multiple streams of income are. And you don't have to own a business to have numerous, stable sources of income.

If you work for someone else, but you want to expand your lifestyle or live a life assignment that's not tied to your job, start seeking out other ways to bring in income and at the same time pursue your passion. These include short-term consulting contracts, a blog coupled with affiliate relationships to sell other people's products to your readers, or a specialized service company delivering something local businesses would rather farm out.

In her book *Instant Income,* Janet Switzer calls these multiple income streams "occasional entrepreneurship"—that is, one-time, hassle-free, low-commitment projects that can be found almost everywhere you look.* Even back when I still worked for other people, I served as an occasional consultant on local community-based projects where they needed an organizer—someone to be the voice of the project, plan events, conduct surveys, do marketing, or motivate local residents into action.

REASONS NOT TO BECOME AN ENTREPRENEUR

Understand that if the world was meant to only have entrepreneurs on the planet, there would be no corporate arena. And there would be a whole lot more chaos! Entrepreneurialism, by itself, is an unstable role to be in. In fact, the average entrepre-

---

* Janet's book not only gives criteria for ideal streams of income, but also includes marketing strategies and other ways to successfully launch an "occasional" enterprise. *Instant Income: Strategies That Bring in the Cash for Small Businesses, Innovative Employees, and Occasional Entrepreneurs,* McGraw-Hill Education, 2013.

neur has to be in that role for five to seven years before there's some form of stabilization.

If you're considering starting a business (or own one right now that's struggling), recognize that most successful entrepreneurs share a common thread. They're self-starters. They're also hungry for sales.

No one is going to sell your product and your business better than you, so you have to be great at sales or learn how to be great at sales. If you're adamant that you don't want to do sales, my advice is: don't start your own business. The theory "build it and they will come" is just that—a theory. No product or service acquires customers simply by virtue of its existence.

Unfortunately, in our culture, entrepreneurship has become seductive. We have a tendency to focus on the sexy part of entrepreneurialism—including the "freedom" that people talk about so much. *I'm my own boss,* they say. *I don't have to go to the office.*

But the flip side is, *I don't have benefits. I don't get vacation time. And I don't have a steady paycheck. Plus I'm working 18 hours a day.*

Owning your own business isn't a job. It is a lifestyle. If you aren't looking for that drastic a change, take a step back before you leap.

In my case, I was in business for 11 years before I felt comfortable securing business credit because I never knew what my income was going to be. I was in business 11 years before I was willing to purchase a piece of real estate. It's not that I couldn't afford the property before, but I didn't know how stable my career was. As an entrepreneur, there's a certain level of instability that you'll need to sign up for. Of course, you can minimize that by living off your savings, but I can't tell you how many people have come to me who are in that reality and are worried because the minute you start your business, the clock starts ticking on the depletion of your nest egg. Even a year's worth of living expenses in your savings account is far too little.

Lots of people go into entrepreneurship with the pie-in-the-sky attitude of *I'm going to build it, stabilize it, and start earning serious money from it—all in twelve months.* Although that can happen for some people, it's not the norm. In my experience, it takes two to three years of solid investing and building to create consistent growth and steady revenue.

If you don't have the entrepreneurial spirit, if you're not willing to put in a lot of time, if you're looking to slow down—these are all reasons not to become an entrepreneur.

Finally, you have to be a visionary. You have to be willing to walk alone. You have to be willing to be the only one who holds your vision for a while.

If all these realities are not for you, that's okay. There's no judgment here. Entrepreneurs are not any better than employees. In fact, I remember 15 years ago when we would mumble that we were business owners because being an entrepreneur was equated with being flaky, flighty, and too lazy to hold down a real job. Now, with so many successful entrepreneurs getting so much media coverage, this path is becoming more and more validated to the point where entrepreneurship courses are taught at most colleges and universities.

But don't feel that if you're not an entrepreneur, you're somehow not playing full out. That's not the case.

IS SUPPORTING OR PARTNERING BETTER FOR YOU?

Even if you never own a business, you can still pursue your passion and purpose in a supporting or partnering role. And if you've built your skill set steadily over time, you'll be in big demand by business owners who need the expertise you have to offer. This is where the consulting lifestyle becomes very lucrative and very freeing. You work only for people and projects you like, you earn good money, and you create a lifestyle and schedule that you dictate.

Just as I recommended that you become a constant and never-ending learner, my advice here is to acquire specialized knowledge that makes you more valued for roles where you can prosper substantially. To gain that knowledge, why not link up with someone who is already doing what you want to do?

I'm a big believer in the concept of "free training." That's why I sat in 35 meetings with Jim, the attorney from Chapter 3. I encourage people to volunteer as much as they can. In fact, we always have several hardworking people who volunteer at my events. Volunteering with us is so popular, in fact, that our team has names for the opportunity, everything from the Backstage Platinum Pass to World-Class Training in HD to the Diamond Field of Information. Our volunteers do everything from running errands to making copies to handling up to 75 wardrobe changes for on-site video shoots—just working really, really hard. But the training they get in exchange for that hard work is priceless.*

Volunteering is fun. You'll be immersed in the work and collaborating with people who are also passionate about that activity. You won't believe the impact it will have on your decisions in the future—simply supporting and learning from someone who's ahead of you in the field.

When you approach others to learn from them, by the way, don't ask, *Can you train me?* but rather, *Can I be free labor for you?* Don't impose more work. Offer up relief, and then become a sponge.

Finally, if you plan to excel at supporting and partnering, don't hide your light. Support, be a partner, but be the best in

---

* If you would like to learn the training and development business from the inside out—either by volunteering or by becoming a world-class speaker through my speaker-training program—please call my office at (760) 931-9400 or e-mail support@motivatingthe masses.com. Ask for our Customer Experience Concierge.

your field. Become a leading expert, even a media figure in your niche.*

BALANCE IS A MYTH, HARMONY IS A MUST

Regardless of whether you own a business or support and partner with someone else, it's important to give *all parts of your life* the time they deserve—and that's not necessarily equal time for all parts. One of the most powerful statements I've ever heard came from my good friend and mentor Ivan Misner, founder of BNI International.

He said, "Lisa, balance is a myth, but harmony is a must."

It's true.

In fact, for decades, life coaches and personal-growth trainers have urged us to strive for "work-life balance." But if you think about that idea, it's actually unrealistic.

Here's why. Let's say your career requires you to work from 8:00 A.M. to 6:00 P.M. in a typical day. That's ten hours or about 42% of your day. Add eight hours for sleep and that takes up another 33% of your day. Then there's the approximate three hours per day taken up by "tasks" such as commuting, running errands, and eating meals (13%)—and what's left is just 12% of your day for the "life" portion of work-life balance.

Only when you do the math can you see that work-life "balance" is a phenomenon that would *never* be achieved unless you worked, slept, and lived like this:

---

* For help developing your leading-expert career—to either support or partner with others—talk to one of my coaches about my Speak & Write to Make Millions program. Visit www.motivatingthemasses.com. If consulting is a better path for you, Janet Switzer makes available an entire series of free tutorials that will help you develop a successful consulting business—including a free tutorial on how to charge $500 to $1,000 per hour for your time. Visit www.JanetSwitzer.com.

6 hours	6 hours	6 hours	6 hours
work	sleep	tasks	downtime
25%	25%	25%	25%

A far better approach to keeping your life sane is to strive for the *harmony* my friend Ivan Misner recommends. Make sure that the 20% or 50% or 12% that you spend in any one area actually gives you what you need—whether it's 5% of your day spent in exercise and meditation, or 50% of your day spent in building your business, or 8% of your day spent in quality time with your spouse and children.

Build benchmarks, boundaries, policies, and systems into these times to ensure they deliver what you need during the hours (or minutes) actually spent. If you commute one hour per day, attend your own "drive-time university," studying the greatest names in leadership, innovation, self-development, or business via audiobooks or TED talks. If your family time is limited due to your career, hire a personal assistant three or four hours a week to handle your recordkeeping, grocery shopping, laundry, errands, or other tasks that would otherwise cut into this time with your family. And with your job or business, strive to reduce mundane tasks (this is where those volunteers can come in) so you can focus on your genius—which could ultimately lead to being able to work fewer hours while being more productive, too.

CREATE ABUNDANCE THROUGH YOUR WORK BEFORE MOVING ON TO THE FINAL STEP

Once you apply these newfound insights to *your* career or business, you too can begin living more abundantly—pursuing your current life assignment with joy, bliss, and enthusiasm. Of course, there's one more of the 4 Es that we've yet to explore: the Endowment approach to money.

CHAPTER 5

The Fourth E: Endowment for a Beautiful Future

With the assignment God has placed on our life, we
were also given the means and the intention to fulfill that
assignment. The Divine Plan on our lives comes bundled
with the resources required to deliver on it.

—Lisa Nichols

Oh, the sweet smell of success. A beautiful home. The luxury of
free time. Exciting travel. Blissful relationships. A healthy lifestyle.
And the pleasure of knowing we can easily take care of our family.

Wait a minute. Doesn't all that take . . . *money?*

While we've looked closely at shifting your mindset from scarcity to abundance in every other area of your life—focusing on
Enrichment of Self, Enchantment in Relationships, and Engagement in Work—I've left the most essential area until last.

Financial wealth and prosperity, or your Endowment.

Today, unfortunately, most people equate *money* and *prosperity*
with wads of cash and rich people who have enough to splurge
their way through life without a care—never thinking about how
their needs will be met, how they spend their time, how they conduct themselves with others, or whether they pay attention to the

concerns of . . . well, anyone. "The Wealthy"—society tells us—can afford to focus on themselves and ignore others. They can buy happiness while the rest of us struggle. They can demand loyalty where it isn't due, enjoy special treatment just because they have money, and spend like crazy consuming everything—literally anything—they lay their eyes on.

Of course, these descriptions aren't necessarily accurate. But with stereotypes like these, it's no wonder that a negative image of wealth and prosperity has taken shape over time in our culture. Perhaps it's even how money came to be seen as *evil* to the majority of our population.

DID YOU GROW UP WITH A NEGATIVE MONEY MINDSET?

Many of us learned from well-meaning parents that money is not readily available to us. Or that it's somehow accessible only to a small group of people who are smarter, prettier, better educated, better connected, or more worthy than we are.

You may have heard as a child:

- Money doesn't grow on trees.
- The rich will always get richer; the poor, poorer.
- Save your allowance because there's no more where that came from.
- Rich people get money by scamming the rest of us.
- If you're rich, you can't be conscious, spiritual, or ecologically aware.
- Life is hard and the "little guy" never gets a break.

If any of the above statements became your "money mantra" as a child, or if you've come to associate money with hardship, deception, something that's difficult to earn, or cruelty to others, let me help you reframe this negative mindset by asking a simple question: Have you ever wondered what "rich people" think about money?

RICH PEOPLE THINK DIFFERENTLY

In his book *How Rich People Think,* Steve Siebold—who has spent nearly three decades interviewing millionaires and reporting on what separates them from everyone else—describes a far different viewpoint from the traditional thinking. In his list of "21 Ways Rich People Think Differently," Steve illustrates that people who enjoy substantial financial wealth, material riches, time freedom, and other forms of prosperity have a far different mentality when it comes to getting rich and staying that way (a mindset that is usually fostered during childhood).*

Although I first reacted to these survey results by saying, *Ouch, I'm one of those "average people" he's describing,* I also know that whenever I want the result someone else has achieved, I strive to adopt their mindset—even if it's painful to hear or off-putting to my current thinking.

Here are just five ways, Steve says, rich people think differently:

1. *Average people have been brainwashed into thinking that MONEY is the root of all evil, while rich people believe POVERTY is the root of all evil.* While there's a certain amount of discredit in lower-income communities about "getting rich," he says, wealthy people know that money makes life easier and more enjoyable—and that there's no virtue in doing without.

2. *Middle-class people believe you have to DO something to get rich, while wealthy people believe you have to BE something to get rich.* Millionaires know their true goal is to become human success

---

* You can find Steve Siebold's list of "21 Ways Rich People Think Differently," as told to journalist Mandi Woodruff, at www.businessinsider.com/how-rich-people-think -differently-from-the-poor-2012-8?op=1.

machines that can produce outstanding results and substantial wealth whenever required.

3. *Average people live beyond their means, while rich people live below theirs.* It's a secret the wealthy have used for centuries, Steve says. They live below their means not because they're smarter than the rest of us, but because they've amassed enough wealth to live like royalty and still have money socked away for the future.

4. *Average people think they have to choose between raising a great family and being rich. Rich people know you can have it all.* The masses have been conditioned to believe it's an either-or equation, he writes, and that with riches comes a rejection of family. The rich know you can create anything you want with a mindset that's rooted in love and abundance.

5. *Average people teach their children how to survive. Rich people teach their kids how to get rich.* Children of the wealthy learn early in life to see the world objectively. They understand that some people will live an abundant life, while others simply won't. And if they can understand early what those differences in lifestyle mean, their parents believe—they'll be more likely to strive for financial wealth as adults.

While many of Siebold's realizations sounded harsh and judgmental to me at first, as I've told you, I am always committed to learning what I don't know. Sometimes, I simply have to be willing to hear painful lessons. In giving you these distinctions, my goal is to empower *you* to make a choice. This awareness is not meant to judge you—but rather to inspire you.

Of course, I didn't always have a "rich" mindset. When I was growing up in South Central Los Angeles—a largely African American neighborhood notorious for gang activity and the cramped households of the working poor—the lessons I learned about money created countless negative beliefs.

Back then, money was hard to make and difficult to keep. I witnessed my mother and father do their very best to provide for us. But my mother used to say that money was burning a hole in her pocket. I literally thought that money was hot, divisive, and something to be gotten rid of quickly. As a culture, the name of the game was "earn it, spend it." While my parents worked hard at steady jobs that were better than most in my neighborhood, they still had limited education about how to save money and manage their finances. Our basic needs were met, but not every bill could be paid. Some languished for months. There was always a bill that had to be negotiated. It was often called "robbing Peter to pay Paul" when we had to choose which bill would go unpaid. Financial lack and scarcity were a normal way of life, but neither I nor my extended family members even knew that we were poor because, to us, it was just normal.

Our family was love rich, memory wealthy, and family abundant, but in the face of these financial hardships, our household existed under an "either-or" mentality—we could either buy this or have that . . . but never both. Victory was simply getting to the next month. We never talked about building wealth—we only talked about surviving. To my mom and dad, wealth came from family experience. They invested all their energy into making sure their family was solid. No one ever talked about thriving. We never experienced financial abundance. All we knew was how to manage the struggle. And outside of my family, I heard the same conversations about struggle in my schools, community, and church.

But one day, after 25 years of internalizing and reinforcing these limiting beliefs and experiences around money, I picked up a copy of a book I've mentioned before: Stephen Covey's success classic, *The 7 Habits of Highly Effective People*.

Chapter by chapter, this book was a revelation. It felt like water in the midst of a drought and oxygen when I felt I was suffocating. Page after page, it seemed like Stephen Covey was throwing me a lifeline. In fact, I was blown away by the idea that acting a certain way—practicing certain habits and behaviors—could ultimately lead to a better life. More money. More happiness. Getting out of just another job I hated and finally having the means (and tools) to really enjoy living.

Although I had been raised with a certain money mindset that no longer served me, I learned I could choose to change it, and then actually make the change—for the better.

TO CREATE PROSPERITY, YOU MUST FIRST CREATE A NEW RELATIONSHIP WITH MONEY

Once I approached my relationship to money from a new angle, I began to see the purpose of money very differently. Money was no longer the root of all evil. Money was no longer about world domination.

I began to think of money as an instrument. Money as a tool. Money as a critical team member for achieving your dreams and desired lifestyle. While money can have a choke hold on you, it can equally be a source of freedom. Money is a change agent for our lives and for the lives of others.

When we shift our relationship to money—when we decide that money is good, money is available, money creates freedom, money creates memories, money cuts the ties that bind people in place, money provides possibility, and that money can be an instrument versus an all-consuming struggle—then money becomes a conversion tool in our lives. It becomes the thing that gives us access to transformation, access to social cause, and access to economic responsibility.

How were *you* raised to think about money? If you grew up

believing that somehow money is a struggle or that prosperity is outside your reach—know that you have the power within you to change this scarcity mindset into one of abundance.

IDENTIFYING YOUR MONEY BLUEPRINT

As you begin to focus on accumulating wealth, you may find that old ways of thinking, lifelong behaviors, and long-ago life experiences can't help you anymore. They haven't prepared you for substantial wealth—and, in fact, you're probably getting the feeling they're actually holding you back. How might this feeling initially manifest? It may appear as frustration, and resentment toward your life circumstances that planted such thinking, or perhaps as a sense of liberation and newfound freedom. It may even appear as excitement about this new way of thinking—as you realize that your old mindset no longer fits you and you replace it with a more solid belief system that you actually trust as your new truth.

In my trainings, we do a lot of work to redraw people's "money blueprint." A money blueprint is the unique combination of beliefs and actions that results from cultural, economic, and other life experiences you've encountered since childhood that today influences how you make money, what you think about money, how you spend it, and how you react when money flows into your life.

Now that you're older, your money blueprint is deep-rooted as a series of subconscious "triggers" that cause you to act and react in certain ways. You aren't always aware that the past is influencing the way you relate to money. But it is . . . in five distinct ways.

YOUR CULTURAL BACKGROUND AFFECTS
YOUR MONEY BLUEPRINT

When I began to earn serious money—as my company grew and I was able to draw more and more cash from the business to fund my personal financial goals—I discovered that I had a cultural bias against spending money on myself for fine foods, designer clothes, luxury travel, and other comforts of a wealthier lifestyle. For example, I grew up as an African American woman baking chicken and peach cobbler, eating cabbage and cornbread—the simple, delicious, economical comfort foods that were part of my culture. When I began to spend more on dining out, I learned to also love filet mignon, lamb chops, and salmon, but it still took time and lots of expanded life experiences for me to give myself permission to embrace and truly enjoy the luxuries that I did not grow up experiencing.

I discovered that this same cultural imprint affects all of us when it comes to money.

My cultural influences, for example, included a heavy emphasis on faith, God, and family. Those were our riches. In fact, we often heard the Bible scripture from the Sermon on the Mount, "Do not lay up for yourselves treasures on Earth, where moth and rust destroy and where thieves break in and steal; but lay up for yourselves treasures in Heaven . . ." (Matthew 6:19–20). This taught me that money wasn't something to be enjoyed here on Earth.

What have your cultural influences taught you?

Does your culture tell you to do more with less—to constantly stretch a dollar? Does it say that money gives you status and that more is always better? Was money a positive element of your culture? How does that affect your view of and interaction with money now?

If your culture growing up was one where most families experienced financial struggle or lack, we'll talk in just a moment about how to reprogram this thinking that "life is hard." If you grew up as a young woman in a culture that discouraged working outside the home, we'll change that, too. If your parents came from a culture that continually denied themselves (and you) small luxuries but never explained the reason for this frugality, you'll have to work extra hard to master the art of appropriately and benevolently spending accumulated wealth on yourself and your loved ones. And if you grew up in a comfortable home where lack of money was never an issue, but instead, your family's abundant wealth caused absentee workaholic parents, family fights, or even drug abuse and isolation at school—I'll help you take on a completely different viewpoint that will better serve you.

YOUR ECONOMIC BACKGROUND HELPS DRAW YOUR MONEY BLUEPRINT, TOO

It's probably no surprise that the amount of money your family had growing up—the economic situation you were in—has had a tremendous influence on your relationship with money. Was there always enough—or never enough? Were there frustrations or arguments about money in your home? Was money (or the lack of it) always a thing of worry? Did lots of money provide a comfortable lifestyle, but also keep your parents working day and night—so they never had time for you? Did limited money mean that your parents had to play favorites—that some of your siblings got what they wanted, but you didn't? Was money the reward for all things or was it the great divider of the family?

If money was divisive back then, realize that you may have a divisive relationship with money now. If there was never enough money growing up, then your current perception of money is probably rooted in scarcity. No matter how much money you eventually make, you may still believe you "never have enough." How can *that* show up later in life? A friend of mine was so poor growing up that he owned just two white shirts to wear to school. Every day, his mother would wash one of them for him to wear the next day. He grew up to be very successful and now has a closet with over 150 white shirts—just because of the scarcity he experienced as a child.

On the other hand, if your family had money, but was mainly focused on keeping up with the Joneses, then your relationship with money may be about competition.

And if money was a source of joy—the reason you got to take fun vacations or buy pretty things—then your blueprint will correctly categorize money as something that can help make you and others happy.

You need to be aware of what economic level your blueprint is helping you aspire to. In a study of blue-collar workers, for instance, researchers found that the highest economic strata most participants aspired to was upper middle class—earning slightly more than the rest of society. They did not want to be upper-class individuals living off substantial inherited wealth or invested capital—or part of the super-rich class who were billionaires. I find this fascinating, but not surprising. Whenever my team coaches clients to greater prosperity, one of the first hurdles we face is the mental "wealth ceiling" that prevents clients from seeing themselves as "wealthy."

GENDER HAS A SURPRISING INFLUENCE ON OUR RELATIONSHIP TO MONEY

If you're a woman, your ideas about substantial wealth and its creation might have been singularly influenced by what society or your family taught you. Depending on your generation, society may have told you to marry a man who earns lots of money—that if you can find someone who'll be a good provider, you'll be okay. Notice there's no room in that advice for creating a positive self-worth as a woman or for becoming a valued economic partner to your husband. Although lately we women have pushed back on that advice—saying, *We can make our own money*—the more dated view has been the norm in our society until recent years. Even today, women own just 20% of businesses making over $1 million.* And a recent Pew Research Center study said there still exists a sizable wage gap between men and women—with women

* See http://nawbo.org/section_103.cfm.

earning only about 84% of what men do.* Of course, if you're a man, the opposite may be true for you. Your manhood and self-worth may be attached to how much money you make or how well you're providing for your family. Society has been far more supportive of women who choose to stay home and take care of children than it has for men who choose to do the same when it makes more sense in their family dynamic.

So while you may not have chosen to follow the gender blueprint of society—or that of your family—these messages are still there in your subconscious waiting to be changed and challenged.

YOUR GEOGRAPHIC ORIGINS AFFECT YOUR MONEY MINDSET

What about your geographic origin—the place where you grew up? Your childhood community may have had a diversity of cultures and ethnicities, but there is still a geographic umbrella to everyone in that community. Growing up in South Central Los Angeles, as I did, we had a far different relationship to money than kids growing up in Beverly Hills. And if you grew up in a rural part of the country, you'll likely have a different relationship to money than if you were raised in an urban center. This goes for geographic regions *within* countries and also *between* countries.

As my coauthor, Janet Switzer, and I have traveled the world speaking to different audiences (in over forty countries), we've seen tremendous differences in how people perceive money—including what they'll do (or not do) to acquire it. One of Janet's biggest eye-openers occurred while shopping in Shanghai one Sunday afternoon between speaking engagements. Stopping by a leather shop to buy some gloves for her mom, Janet asked how late the shop stayed open so she could return and match another

---

* See www.pewresearch.org/fact-tank/2015/04/14/on-equal-pay-day-everything-you-need-to-know-about-the-gender-pay-gap/.

pair of gloves to an elaborate shawl she also wanted to buy. In perfect English, the owner replied, "We're open every day until 10:00 P.M. We wouldn't make any money if we closed early like they do in America." Geographically, he had developed a much different mindset from shop owners in America, he had acquired the necessary language skills to sell his goods to almost anyone who walked in—and he displayed the same urgency to make money as other entrepreneurs Janet has encountered in China. When you look at *your* geography, what has it taught you about your relationship to money? Did it give you a mindset of ease and abundance or tightness and scarcity? Look at your existing or previous community and simply take inventory of the prevailing mindset and how it may have influenced you.

YOUR SPIRITUAL UPBRINGING CAN BE A HELP OR A HINDRANCE

Finally there is the spiritual influence on your money blueprint. Your faith—or the religion in which you were raised—can tremendously impact your feelings around money, regardless of whether that faith is still part of your life or not. In some spiritual backgrounds, for instance, money and prosperity is an indication of godliness. In others, it's the root of all evil. In still others, you should aspire to earn only what you need—then give any excess to the church and charity.

Tithing a full 10% of your earnings is also common with many faiths.

How was I raised? Well, I grew up in Baptist churches. I can still remember one of my early role models, Sister Brown, who—next to my Grandmother Bernice—was the most godly woman I knew during my younger years. She was an angel on Earth. She served people. She found food for the homeless. She volunteered to help others.

But Sister Brown was also broke.

While she always had some kind of charitable project going—a fish fry or a food drive—she had to raise the necessary money to make it happen. Unfortunately, the unspoken message I absorbed from that relationship—a subconscious conversation that became part of my own money blueprint—was that, to be really faithful, I had to be broke. I needed to be able to do good works on no money . . . so that I could be as godly as Sister Brown.

For years, this unspoken message had a big influence on me. I volunteered a lot. And for the first three years of my speaking career, I spent much of my time speaking to women's shelters and rehab facilities for free—just trying to serve. I spoke 42 times for free before I started getting paid. At first I was paid $50, then $300, then more and more. But after delivering powerful speeches on living your dreams or designing a life that you love—after serving hundreds of willing listeners with my words—I would come home from that standing ovation experience only to find that my lights were cut off.

And what I noticed was that, as I began to make more money as a speaker, I also began to question whether I was being true to my calling to serve, my calling to do God's work.

While I was undoubtedly serving others—in more places and more often—I still questioned it *because I was making money doing it.* I still held this image of Sister Brown in my head—a godly woman doing everything for free until she went to heaven. And if she did it for free, I reasoned, then why am I asking to be paid for my gift?

This was a major struggle for me—all based on spiritual input to my money blueprint.

YOUR BLUEPRINT ISN'T RIGHT OR WRONG

Of course, none of these cultural, economic, or spiritual influences make your blueprint right or wrong. They simply make up your foundational mindset. Your blueprint was created mostly before you were aware—and long before you were able to make any decisions about money yourself. So don't discount the mindset of your old money blueprint because that is what got you here.

It is what it is.

But it also gives you a starting point for reforming your blueprint into one that will better support your ultimate financial goals. You get to choose a new money mindset starting now. You get to redesign your money blueprint—create a new one—to fit the breathtaking new reality you are creating for your future.

What parts of your cultural, economic, gender, geographic, and spiritual blueprint can you love and embrace—and which do you need to release because they no longer support who you are today?

WHAT GOT YOU HERE WON'T GET YOU THERE

Following is an exercise I use in my trainings to help people release past influences we know won't support future financial goals—those childhood lessons and unspoken messages that can't possibly help you because they're simply incompatible with where you're headed.

To begin the process of eliminating any negative money beliefs, let's go back through the five areas that influenced you in the first place: cultural, economic, gender, geographic, and spiritual. Take out a piece of paper and begin thinking back. What was happening in your household around money during childhood? How did your parents react to financial stressors? What did they do with their money? How did they spend it? How did they talk to you about money? Were you granted your requests for money or was there "never enough" for your needs? Were they "responsible" or "irresponsible" with their money?

And when you started earning an allowance or generating a small income from odd jobs, babysitting, or a paper route, what did you do with *your* money? Were your parents in agreement with your money decisions—or did they disagree with your actions?

Jot down your remembrances about money growing up—grouping your memories into the preceding five categories. Your list might look like this:

CULTURAL

- Virtually everyone on my street in South Chicago was African American.
- Most fathers worked in nearby steel mills, while most moms stayed home to care for family.
- Our community was a tremendous support structure with neighbors helping neighbors.
- We ate traditional comfort foods that were economical, but delicious and filling.
- No one I knew owned a business. A business was something complicated and difficult.

ECONOMIC

- We lived in an older house that needed repair but was in a safe neighborhood.
- My mom would deposit my dad's weekly paycheck, then pay the bills and take out 25 cents for each of us kids as our allowance for doing chores.
- We were considered the working poor, but I never knew that because our neighbors lived about the same way we did.
- I earned money doing odd jobs for other people. It wasn't a lot, but I always had pocket money to buy something pretty or get new clothes.
- My parents had a checking account, a small savings account, but no investments. I never knew

what the stock market was or how other people invested their money.

GENDER

- My grandmother lived with us once Grandpa Joe passed on. She and my mom ran the household.
- I was very good at creating relationships with other girls, my teachers, and my neighbors.
- When I was a teenager, lots of employers offered jobs that were ideal for girls.
- My brothers teased me for getting As in math and science. *Girls aren't smart,* they said.
- No woman in my family ever went to college. Some never graduated from high school but got married instead.

GEOGRAPHIC

- Because we lived in a distressed part of town, we were friends with neighbor kids who had our same standard of living and shared our mindset around money.
- We shopped at local stores and rarely compared prices from businesses that were farther away.
- When I started a paper route to earn enough money to buy a bike, customers were slow to pay, so I learned that making money was hard.

SPIRITUAL

- Our church actively helped the poor in our neighborhood with food and clothing.
- My minister urged parishioners to tithe a portion of their paychecks every week.
- Once, when a neighbor was too ill to work, our church members paid his rent for three months.

- Once, when I mentioned I wanted to own a hair salon one day, my Sunday school teacher said girls should become mothers, not business owners.

Next, circle or highlight on your list the one or two circumstances that have been the biggest driving force in your current relationship to money. Which have largely influenced your current actions and thinking around money?

In my household, for instance, small amounts received from our grandparents for birthdays or Christmas were spent as quickly as possible. As soon as we got the money, it was shopping time—and we didn't stop until the money was all gone. I bought chili cheese dogs at the local car wash, bubble gum, candy, costume jewelry, sandals—anything fun. I'd even treat my friends to fast food, buying them all lunch. Broke was level set. We were like lottery winners who not only spend all the money, but who are heavily in debt within a few years of receiving their winnings. I followed that pattern.

Later, I had to work hard to overcome this powerful driver.

CHANGE YOUR BEHAVIORS THROUGH AFFIRMATIONS

When you have *your* list written and highlighted, begin writing affirmation statements—thoughts and images that paint clear pictures of your new behaviors—to neutralize the old drivers and develop more positive ones. (Review the section "Use Affirmations and Begin Living the 'Rich Life' in Your Mind" in Chapter 2.) Create one affirmation for each highlighted or circled "driver" on your list that you want to release.

As you write each affirmation, remember to start with the words "I am"—two powerful words that your subconscious mind interprets as a command, a directive to make it happen. Write each affirmation in the present tense as if you're already conducting yourself or responding with the new behavior. Be sure to write how you *do want* to act, not how you don't.

Make it specific. For example:

IF YOU CIRCLED: *No one I knew owned a business.*

AFFIRMATION: *I am confidently and joyfully running a $7 million business selling organic, custom-formulated cosmetics through dozens of retail outlets.*

INCORRECT: *I want to start a business so I can earn substantial money.*

IF YOU CIRCLED: *No woman in my family ever went to college.*

AFFIRMATION: *I am so proud that I'm attending Northwestern University Law School on a full scholarship.*

INCORRECT: *I want to go to college and become a lawyer.*

Finally, use emotional words that create a feeling of the joyfulness, gratitude, happiness, pride, or confidence you *would be feeling* if you were already displaying the new behavior. By far, this is the most powerful aspect of using affirmations to change your thoughts around money. When you begin affirming, seeing, and feeling yourself acting with confidence, able to solve problems within minutes, powerful, knowledgeable, relaxed, secure—your subconscious mind will move heaven and earth to bring about those circumstances *for real* in your life.

DIAGNOSE THE PROBLEM, RESOLVE IT, AND MOVE ON TO YOUR ABUNDANT NEW LIFE

As you strive to strengthen your relationship with money and change your money blueprint, you may have to walk through a painful reality. You may get uncomfortable. You may become soberly aware that the cycle you are in financially happened because you had a subconscious commitment to it.

You have to be committed to fixing it, even if it gets painful. You have to be committed to your own breakthrough so you can move on and work toward something more positive—your exciting and abundant new life.

When I was jet-skiing with my family a few years ago, I fell and broke my leg in three places (yes, I'm that talented person who can actually break bones on the water). I remember going to the emergency room with my ankle turned sideways and my leg in excruciating pain.

The doctor took one look at it and said, "Lisa, we can heal this, but it is going to hurt. I have to crack it back into place." *Can we all say OUCH together!*

Just as I had to do with my broken leg, you're going to have to crack a few of *your* broken places back into alignment. It takes that discomfort, that temporary pain, to set you up to heal—so you can have a more vibrant, healthier relationship with money, get to the next level, and begin enjoying the financial prosperity that has been your birthright from the beginning.

What are some of the painful moments *you* might have to heal from? Perhaps it's a divorce due to money problems, a job loss that led to the loss of your home, or a failed business deal that depleted your life savings.

Moving your money blueprint from the subconscious to the conscious—and examining it—may be challenging, but it's worth it. Then you can create a new one.

FEELINGS OF REMORSE, ANGER, AND BETRAYAL ARE NORMAL WHEN YOU LOOK AT YOUR PAST

One thing I will caution you about. As you catalog your childhood memories and begin to write affirmations to change them, feelings of hurt and anger will likely surface. You may feel that what your parents "did to you" has kept you from the life of abundance you deserve. While you may love your parents—who, by the way, did the best they could with the knowledge and upbringing *they* had—you may also feel betrayed.

You may also feel remorse or anger *at yourself* that you haven't yet created the life you want (a feeling that seems to be the most common among my students). You may be angry that you don't yet have the skills or knowledge to be rich. Perhaps you feel you wasted your peak earning years or simply weren't focused enough in your early career. You may find yourself stuck in debt that you can't overcome. Whatever the reason, you're not where you want to be.

This exercise will uncover where you really are in your journey toward financial prosperity—and frankly it can be uncomfortable for a lot of people. When I began to deep-dive into my own financial mindset, it was sobering and unsettling, and—to be honest—I felt embarrassed. In some respects, I began to feel like a fraud. I had built my career as a motivational speaker, and yet I was uncovering my own limiting, toxic thinking around prosperity.

For instance, I used to believe that if I were born into limited prosperity, I would always live with limited prosperity. I believed that wealth isn't for people who look like me or who came from my background. I believed that I couldn't have financial abundance because I didn't have a degree or the proper certification. I even believed that if I created too much financial abundance, then love would be difficult. What can you do when those uncomfortable feelings come up for *you*? My heartfelt advice is to honor those feelings, but move on. Don't dwell on them. You need to be focused on your future, not your past.

Just know that the conversation you're having with yourself—the exercise we just went through—is necessary to being able to shift your mindset *and your outcomes* with money. While many people want to simply talk about how to make more money or save more money or multiply their money, few people ever have the conversation that we're having right now—which is a critical prerequisite for changing your relationship with money.

Of course, once you're ready to have a new relationship with money—to create a new era of abundance in your life—let's talk about what financial prosperity really is . . . and what it means to you.

CREATE A NEW DEFINITION OF FINANCIAL SUCCESS

Have you ever attended Harvard University? I haven't. In fact, most people I know haven't. But my colleagues and I have still learned a lot from Harvard's approach to money. In fact, because of the caliber of student the university has turned out over the years, Harvard has experienced a wealth of major donations from alumni that, accumulated, now surpasses $30 billion (yes, that's *billion* with a B). Their "good works" have helped create an *endowment fund*—an amalgamation of cash and other assets that, when invested, generates an ongoing flow of earnings and dividends that fund virtually anything that Harvard wants to do.

The endowment's administrators can fund student scholarships for disadvantaged but promising youth. They can finance a wide variety of professorships across a vast array of academic fields. They can fund groundbreaking scientific and medical discoveries.

And they do so extensively.

Well, what if *you* treated your own financial life like a Harvard University endowment? The good work that you do—through your career, your business, your smart investments, and your contribution to others—would come back to you in the form of earnings, benefits, and other enrichments that could be used to build for the future. As you move more fully into financial abundance, like Harvard, you should begin to think of the broader web of your work and personal activities as a portfolio of wealth that goes beyond the normal cash, expenditures, assets, and liabilities you manage for the living of daily life. This unique portfolio can be a powerful source for building new capacity to create new opportunities in the future, well beyond your own lifetime.

I've made that my goal. I believe everyone should hold this as their own financial goal, too. But let's be clear: building, investing, and then managing this kind of financial portfolio takes a specific skill set that we *all can learn*—so don't buy into the myth that this type of lifestyle isn't meant for all of us, and only some are born into such privileges. It's time to cash in on your birthright.

Of course, this Harvard-style endowment would also include *karmic investments*—unique non-monetary "assets" that enter your life *to enrich your life* more than money ever could. I'm reminded of the story of Nulu Naluyombya, a 28-year-old Ugandan woman who's the founder and executive director of Success Chapter, a nonprofit organization that focuses on leadership, entrepreneurial training, and personal development for young women in her country.

As a young girl who often worked doing laundry and cleaning houses to earn money for school fees, getting an education was difficult. Her parents never finished high school and the family's irregular income could never ensure that Nulu's school fees would be paid regularly. Still, Nulu persevered and eventually graduated from college and even earned an MBA.

Along the way, Nulu recognized the challenges confronting other young girls in Uganda. For one thing, the country has the highest youth unemployment rate in Africa—as high as 83%, suggests the African Development Bank.* Not only that, but Uganda has one of the highest teen pregnancy rates in sub-Saharan

---

* As quoted in *The Guardian:* www.theguardian.com/global-development/2014/jan/16/uganda-unemployed-graduates-held-back-skills-gap.

Africa—1 out of every 4 teenage girls becomes pregnant and some are forced into early marriages by their parents for money.

Before Nulu had even finished her MBA at Makerere University, she launched Success Chapter and began working with local schools to inspire young girls to stay in school and avoid pregnancy. By 2013, Nulu and her small team had trained over 1,000 girls in life skills, self-esteem, sexual reproductive health, career guidance, and other topics.

As her program's success grew, people started to talk about her work. As a result, Nulu was selected for participation in Generation Change—a program established by former Secretary of State Hillary Clinton—which not only brought Nulu together with other young change leaders in Uganda to network and compare best practices, but also helped Nulu build capacity for her programs by providing training in financial management, leadership, project management, and other organizational skills. Generation Change also provided small "seed grants" for projects from the United States Embassy in Uganda.

As Success Chapter grew and increased the number of schools it worked with, Nulu recognized she would need other trainers to join her if she wanted to expand nationally. She envisioned training girls who could return home to their local schools and mentor their classmates. Nulu launched the Girls Leadership Academy, which has so far trained 50 young women with leadership potential to start clubs and programs throughout Uganda that pass on the life skills and personal development curriculum learned at the Academy.

When Nulu discovered that President Barack Obama planned to invest in the future of Africa through his Young African Leaders Initiative, Nulu quickly applied for its highly competitive flagship program, the Mandela Washington Fellowship. She was stunned when she was one of just 500 people selected from over 50,000 applicants throughout Africa. Her *karmic investment* was paying off big-time.

Traveling to the United States, Nulu received her first leadership training at Tulane University in New Orleans before joining Fellows from 40 other African countries in meeting President Barack Obama and U.S. government officials at the President's Summit in Washington, D.C. While there Nulu was selected as one of just 100 Fellows invited to stay in the United States for a 14-week internship to gain further networking opportunities, leadership skills, and management training.

It was a life-changing experience. Her work had started to pay off.

In fact, the experience eventually allowed Nulu to reach a broader audience with her message about the needs of young women in Africa and the obstacles hindering African girls from accessing education. She was even one of 40 young leaders selected to meet with First Lady Michelle Obama in a private discussion on challenges affecting girls in Africa.

On her way to Washington, D.C.—her first trip to the United States—Nulu participated in my Speak and Write to Make Millions conference and eventually went on to write her first book, *Go Girl: Success Principles for Women.* My team instantly fell in love with Nulu, and Susie advocated that she be able to tell her story of what she has persevered through to get to the United States. There wasn't a dry eye in the room as Nulu shared vivid details of both what she was subjected to and what she was committed to. We are now Auntie Susie and Auntie Lisa. Our community instantly embraced Nulu, with many people in the room running up and handing her money, personal notes with homes she can stay in, and access to even more blessings. Susie took Nulu to the beach. It was her first time at any beach. I've even adopted Nulu into my team of event volunteers to give her hands-on experience in managing world-class events.

Today, Nulu is busy creating partnerships with other Mandela Washington Fellows to expand her programs to other African countries. She is clearly one of Africa's best and brightest. And though she may not be making millions personally, her needs are being met and her work is being advanced through the riches that others bring to the mix—because of the *karmic endowment* she has built over time.

Similarly, Lewis Pugh of Great Britain—a maritime lawyer—is the only person to have completed a long-distance swim in every ocean of the world. Over a period of 27 years he has pioneered swims in the most hostile waters on earth including those in the Antarctic, the North Pole, and the Himalayas—developing an understanding of the beauty and fragility of life and its many ecosystems. Millions have viewed his talks at TEDGlobal, and he campaigns tirelessly for the creation of Marine Protected Areas and changes to the legal framework governing oceans. In 2013, the United Nations appointed him *Patron of the Oceans.* And he recently embarked on a lengthy expedition to the remotest part of the Antarctic Ocean to further his work. Clearly Lewis has built an endowment of good works, financial support, and opportunity that makes it possible to pursue his passions and advance his cause.

But perhaps my favorite story about making *karmic investments* that, in turn, bring about the resources that allow you to do good works is the story of my close friend Lynne Twist.

For nearly 25 years, Lynne worked committedly on hunger and poverty issues as an executive with The Hunger Project—traveling nonstop between countries like Ethiopia, Gambia, Guinea-Bissau, India, and Nepal. She eventually managed operations in 47 countries, working with people like Mother Teresa, and oversaw more than 10,000 staff and volunteers. Not only that, but she secured funding from many of the most respected philanthropists of our time. She came to revere the people she served—people who were rich in wisdom, courage, resilience, and love, but simply poor in circumstances.

By 1994, Lynne was completely dedicated and fulfilled in the role of working to end world hunger until one day, John Perkins, a close friend from a partner organization, asked Lynne—as a favor—to spend two weeks co-leading a study trip to Guatemala for 44 of their donors. With little time in her schedule to spare, Lynne decided to do the trip.

That trip literally changed the direction of her life.

"While visiting the foundation's projects for the Mayan people in the mountains near Totonicapan," Lynne recounts, "we had the opportunity to do an all-night ceremony with a Mayan shaman." During that ceremony, Lynne had a crystal clear vision of indigenous people in a remote area of the Amazon rain forest—calling for contact with people from the modern world.

Startled by this vision, Lynne shared it with her friend John—who had just returned from working in the Amazon. He told Lynne about the Achuar people who lived in a remote region of the Ecuadorian rain forest—people who had almost no contact with the outside world. They had become aware through their dreams and visions that danger would eventually come to their territory. They wanted to reach out and create modern-world friends who would educate them, be their contacts with the outside world, and act as allies in navigating the modern world's greed for oil and other minerals beneath their forests.

Though Lynne was moved by her vision—and by John's urgency that they respond to the call of the indigenous people—she had no intention of becoming the messenger the Achuar people were asking for. Still, she began to be troubled by continuing and vivid dreams of plaintive faces crying out from the rain forest. Over the next two years, Lynne repeatedly saw the faces in meetings, on airplanes—with her eyes open—and while she was driving.

She was haunted and terrified by these visions.

Not only that, but her friend John—who'd been with Lynne and the shaman on that fateful day in Totonicapan—had experienced similar visions and eventually traveled to meet with the reclusive Achuar people who pleaded with him, *Come now.*

Bring 12 people from the modern world, they said—people with open hearts, who have a global voice, people who know that the rain forest is critical to the future of life and who understand that indigenous wisdom may be critical to the survival of the human race.

Reluctantly, Lynne traveled to meet with the Achuar and finally comprehended the profound message they had to share. In 1996, Lynne and her husband, Bill, cofounded The Pachamama Alliance—a nonprofit organization whose mission is not only to empower indigenous people of the Amazon rain forest in preserving their lands and culture, but also to use insights gained from that work to educate people in developed countries in fostering a thriving, just, and sustainable world.

Because of the *karmic investments* Lynne has made throughout her career, the opportunities, resources, and connections she needs to carry out her mission simply appear. She consults with many of the most notable companies and institutions in the world, including the Red Cross, Amnesty International, the Sierra Club, Microsoft, Procter & Gamble, Charles Schwab, the Stanford Business School, the MIT Sloan School of Management, and Harvard University.

Additionally, she's received countless opportunities to work as an adviser and presenter to prestigious organizations, including the Desmond Tutu Foundation, the United Nations Beijing Women's Conference, the Alliance for a New Humanity Conference with Deepak Chopra, and the Nobel Women's Initiative—an initiative of six women Nobel peace laureates who work together to end violence against women and girls.

I am constantly in awe of Lynne's service to humanity. Each time I chat with her or share a meal, then dance the night away with her, just being in her presence inspires me to want to do more, to be more, and to become a better citizen of the world.

What about *you*?

What career, passionate pursuits, charitable works, or valuable connections could *you* add to your financial nest

egg to create a Harvard-style endowment that supported anything that you wanted to do?

If you've been waiting for someone to define a lifestyle like this for you, you and I are probably speaking the same language. But if you find the idea hard to believe, difficult to digest, and a stretch to imagine in your life, realize that we've been placed in each other's lives for a reason, and discovering this new way of thinking (and living) just might be it.

IF "WEALTH" IS SO MUCH MORE THAN MONEY, HOW DO YOU KNOW WHEN YOUR NEST EGG IS ENOUGH?

In a recent survey, UCLA professor Lynn Vavreck[*] asked people how much annual income would make them feel "rich." While some people answered as low as $10,000 and others answered "millions of dollars," the average amount respondents cited was somewhere between $293,000 and $501,000 a year (with their answers largely depending on how much they were already making).

If I asked you the same question, would you be able to answer—thoughtfully—how much you need every year in order to feel you've "arrived"? Have you researched, for example, the cost of buying and maintaining your dream home, enjoying extensive travel, making cash gifts or offering other help to your family, enthusiastically pursuing your hobby, improving your health, doing meaningful philanthropic work, enjoying a career or starting a business you love, and experiencing other things you want to do?

My experience is that this kind of rich and rewarding lifestyle requires a lot more income than $501,000 a year. And while it saddened me that most respondents in Professor Vavreck's survey were so conservative in their responses (I would have answered $2 million or more), the saddest outcome of the survey report

---

[*] As reported online in the *New York Times*. See http://www.nytimes.com/2014/06/17/upshot/definition-of-rich-changes-with-income.html?_r=0&abt=0002&abg=0.

was that almost three-fourths of the people believed they would *never become rich.*

Another study—one I cite in my trainings—reports that 80% of individuals *will never be financially free.* This is an incredibly damaging mindset to hold on to. Because our future life experience begins *first* in our minds, it hurts my heart to know that every single one of those people are correct. They will never be financially free because they've already declared it to be so—*in the words they've spoken.*

Don't let a fatalistic mindset, conservative outlook, or group destiny be your fate. To start the process of becoming financially prosperous, accumulating a nest egg, and building a safety net, let's look at how much is enough for you.

MONEY IS NECESSARY TO LIVE A PROSPEROUS LIFE. BUT HOW MUCH?

When creating a plan for funding your abundant new life, have you considered what it will cost? It always surprises me when people claim to want expensive possessions or luxury homes or five-star travel, but they have no idea what's involved in acquiring that, using it, or maintaining it. Don't get me wrong. I'm not asking you to go without, but rather, I'm asking you to be smart about it and *first* research whether your pending purchases or lifestyle changes make sense in light of your other financial goals. For instance, if you'd like to own a boat, have you investigated:

- The cost of a boat—new or used?
- The monthly rate for a boat slip at the local marina?
- What kind of license or safety certificate you need?
- The average cost of yearly maintenance, including winter storage?

- The current interest rate on boat loans if you plan to finance it?
- How often you could use the boat with your current number of vacation days?

If you don't know this information, don't move forward until you have it. And even after you do, determine how it will fit into your overall goals before you make the financial commitment. Will it keep you from paying off your other debt and becoming debt free? Will it prevent you from sending your children to private school? Will it keep you from investing for your retirement?

It may be that you can rent a boat instead for the few dozen days a year when you will *really* be out on the water—or perhaps you could more economically go on day trips with a sport fishing outfitter where you would be treated like royalty and get to fish in the best waters.

Of course, the Millennial Generation has learned this "rent instead of buy" lesson better than any of us. I know. My son, Jelani, is now 20 and rarely purchases anything, unless he's *really* going to use it long term. In fact, one of the business models I really admire is Rent the Runway—a company that rents expensive designer gowns and accessories for a night out or a weekend. They're now a $50 million company and poised to become one of America's biggest shippers, as well as the country's largest dry cleaner.

An abundant life consists of (in addition to great service to others) nice things, great experiences, exciting travel, and an inviting home. And there's no question you need money to do (and own) all that. But just how much?

When I was much younger, I wrote my first annual budget— and I've produced one every year since, both for my business and my household. I recommend you do the same using two columns—one for your absolute current expenses and one for your dream life.

To quickly determine the amount of money you'll need, start with your basic expenses. Make a list of everything you spend money on every month—the mortgage or rent, your car payment, utilities, credit cards, your gym membership, health care, your mobile phone, and so on. Next to each item, jot down the monthly amount you pay or an average amount if the charges vary. Continue writing your list with those things you pay for *only once or twice a year,* such as insurance, property taxes, or tuition. If you were to spread these costs over 12 months, what would the monthly cost be? Jot that number down next to each of these periodic expenses. Add up all the line items and you now have your base monthly cost of living—costs you *must pay* just to survive, meet local laws, and live with a modest level of comfort.* If your current income covers these expenses (and then some), great. If it doesn't, we'll be talking in a moment about how to bring in more cash.

But first, the fun part. Envisioning your abundant life.

Remember the section in Chapter 1 called "You Can't Hit a Moving Target: Get Crystal Clear About What You Want"? This is where you did a little dreaming and put some serious thought into what your ultimate life would look like. Of course, some dreams cost virtually nothing—like the time you invest in great relationships or the cost of a gym membership to achieve a healthier body. But if you planned for a lot of possessions or rich experiences or a nonworking lifestyle, you're going to have some costs—potentially a lot of them. Now it's time to do the research.

One of the things that I'm constantly asked—particularly since I was in the movie *The Secret*—is, "Why should I save money for something big. Won't it just show up in my life? Can't I just

---

*For more elaborate budgeting tools, you can search online for templates using the search term *free household budget worksheet.*

manifest it with my focused intentions, constant prayer, and meditation?"

I call this belief the "lottery mentality" since the Law of Attraction says you must *first* ask, then believe and receive. While I am a profound believer in the Law of Attraction and the act of setting clear intentions, constant prayer, and engaging in meditation as a way to get clear and strong energy out to strengthen your request and to get God, the Universe, the Divine (whatever you call your source) to operate on your behalf, you *must must must* add turbo fuel to your request with action. You only win by taking action. When you're in action—doing research, talking to sources, finding out what things cost—you are taking action *because you believe that new possession or new experience will come into your life.* This sends a powerful signal to the Universe that you *expect and anticipate* owning that item or enjoying that experience. After all, you wouldn't be doing the research if you didn't expect to own it someday, would you?

Start doing the research not only for this reason, but also to assure yourself that you actually want that item. Your research may provide new information you didn't know before. Or you may discover that, as part of your work, because of a new acquaintance or due to a unique circumstance, that item you want is actually easier (and cheaper) than ever to obtain. Only your research will tell you.

Even now, I go through the same fact-finding work (or my staff does) whenever I want to make a purchase or add an experience to my life. For many years purchasing a car was both exciting and very painful for me. I would feel confused and overwhelmed by the options and bombarded and bullied by the salesperson. I always begged my dad to go with me as my advocate. When I began to adopt the practices that I am teaching you here, my car-buying experience became a lot more pleasurable for me and maybe a bit more painful for the salesperson.

Recently, I purchased an Audi A8 after my nephew and I spent hours researching different luxury cars. I researched mileage, features, depreciation rates, and lease options. By the time I walked into the Audi dealer, I was so crystal clear on what I wanted and how much I was willing to pay that it startled the salesperson. After I viewed the car I knew that I wanted, I slid him the pre-written dollar amount that I was expecting him to sell it to me for. Astonished, he replied, "I could never authorize selling you this car for that amount." I replied calmly, "Then you are not the person that I should be speaking to." I drove off the lot with my new car for the exact price I offered. I called my dad and celebrated!

Once you've done the research, exhausted your list, and know the annual cost of doing, being, and having every material thing and experience you want, this becomes your Goal Yearly Income Level. Now you're ready to start pursuing that income level with passion and laser-beam focus.

> My grandmother says that convenience and conviction
> don't live on the same block. Your convictions will require
> you to be inconvenienced.
>
> —Lisa Nichols

NOW THAT YOU KNOW HOW MUCH YOU NEED, ARE YOU PREPARED TO GO THERE?

As you move into earning, building, and acquiring the things you want, you're going to have to amplify your game. You're going to have to become a smart, confident, forward-thinking, and financially savvy individual.

Are you ready for that?

When I conduct my trainings, Chief Operating Officer Susie Carder and I work personally with people (as do my coaches) to make sure they're prepared to get to the next level. It isn't just a prosperous mindset that's needed here, but an underlying financial infrastructure that is ready to help you manage your new life. Without it, earning a lot of money is like taking a drink from a fire hose—it's too much to handle. Both Susie and I have seen what happens when massive money starts flowing without safeguards—or even basic financial understanding—in place.

One example from my training program really stands out in my mind. A student of mine designed a phenomenal marketing campaign that earned her six figures in an eight-week period. She immediately went out and leased a luxury car, then promptly moved into a larger home. Six months later, she was struggling to pay her bills and keep her head above water. In fact, she was so mired in financial struggle that she could no longer focus on the creativity needed to earn additional revenue for her business.

For this reason, Susie and I created the Financial Readiness Assessment tool in the next section. Take some time going through this exercise, then depending on your score, make the changes needed or put the necessary infrastructure in place to handle your financial future.

FINANCIAL READINESS ASSESSMENT

In completing the Financial Readiness Assessment, you'll likely have to answer some questions in a way that might make you feel negligent—meaning, *I don't really have that together* or *I haven't done that yet.*

Don't beat yourself up. Don't have a pity party. Don't start feeling sorry for yourself. And don't fudge the truth in order to "save face." It's simply an indicator of where you are now. It does *not* mean this is where you'll be in the future. In fact, simply doing this assessment will make you more cognizant of where you want to be.

You'll be rating yourself on a scale of 1 to 10—with "1" being *I'm not really good at that, don't know how to use it,* or *have never even heard that* while "5" means *I understand it, but I'm mediocre.* Or *I'm lazy about it and I know I need to do more work.*

The "10" designation means *I got it handled. It works for me. I understand it, and I'm utilizing it all the time.*

You could be anywhere on the scale. But relax and don't worry about your score. In the twenty years Susie has been using the assessment tool with upwardly mobile individuals, no one has ever scored 100%.

Not even me.

So don't shortchange *yourself* by being less than brutally honest. Go through the questions and give yourself a truthful rating score on a scale of 1 to 10.

QUESTION 1:
"I HAVE A CLEAR, WRITTEN, WORKING BUSINESS PLAN OR PERSONAL LIFE PLAN."

If you have a new business, you need a full comprehensive business plan that looks at your vision, your mission, your strategy, your marketing and sales, your operations, your finances, your organizational development, and so on. I've been in business 15 years, so my business plan is less comprehensive because many of these things are already in place. I already know my vision, my mission, and my organization—these days, I'm working on strategy, marketing goals, partnerships, and so on. Every year, I rewrite a new business plan.

If, on the other hand, your "business" is your life—a great career, solid personal finances, stable relationships, good health, and so on—your "business plan" would contain information like *Where do I want to be in one year? Three years? Five years? Ten years?*

What does your spiritual life look like? What does your retirement or investment or debt-reduction strategy look like? What relationships do you want to have in your life and how do you want to make them better? What's your health regimen?

Your personal plan should also include details about your financial goals, of course, and these should always be *written down*.

Rate yourself on a scale of 1–10 with 1 meaning, *Oops, I haven't done a plan yet*, while 10 means, *Got it handled and I follow it*. Don't judge yourself. This is just an assessment of where you are and how far you need to go.

QUESTION 2:
"I USE A FINANCIAL TRACKING SYSTEM SUCH AS QUICKBOOKS FOR MY BUSINESS OR QUICKEN/MINT ONLINE FOR MY PERSONAL FINANCES."

If you're in business, there are several different software programs you can use to manage your sales, payroll, expenses, and other business transactions. The same applies to personal finance software that tracks your personal, household, and medical expenses, taxes, and more.

Not only can this tracking software help you see where you're overspending, it can help you find extra money you didn't even know was available to you. If simple financial tasks like balancing your checkbook or getting ready to file your taxes frustrate you, a software program will give you more peace of mind and help you easily control your money. If you're not technologically inclined, hire a professional for an hour to load the software and set it up for your business or household (some software programs are available as online versions you can share over the Internet with your bookkeeper or accountant).

For now however, rate yourself. A score of 1 means *I don't balance my checkbook now* or *I don't even wanna know what's goin' on!*—while a 10 means *I look at my financials every month, balance my checkbook every month, and know the week-by-week specifics of my financial life.*

"I HAVE AND FOLLOW CLEAR FINANCIAL GOALS—DAILY, WEEKLY, MONTHLY, AND YEARLY."

This is not just about having an *idea* of where you want to go financially; it's about having a set of clearly defined daily, weekly, monthly, and annual financial goals that you hone, refine, and follow. Although you may not hit your goals all the time, if you at least know what they are, you can break down each goal into actionable steps—then do the things necessary to get there.

For example, if you have a goal to earn $180,000 a year in personal income, what do you need to do in order to accomplish that? Do you need to sell $2 million worth of products and services for your employer because you're a salesperson earning 9% commission? If you're a web designer or graphic artist with very few costs beyond marketing yourself, you might have to sell only $200,000 worth of services to bring home $180,000 after your telephone costs, Internet connection, office supplies, and outside services are paid. If you want to grow your business beyond selling just your own services, what must be done to generate greater revenue that will support other people who must also earn *their* living?

My company coaches a lot of small-business owners who want to grow their revenues to $1 million or more, yet you'd be surprised how many of them don't want to discuss setting financial goals because they don't want to put pressure on themselves or their staff—or they don't want to feel like a failure if they don't hit the mark. But goals are important—not only for driving what you work on each day, but for a much more important reason: they're something positive to focus on. They're something you work *toward,* versus a negative financial past that you may be *running away from.*

This difference in mindset is empowering.

But be sure to set *realistic* goals. Goals that set you up to win. Goals for the next 12 months, 3 years, 5 years, and 10 years. Goals that stretch you, but that are also achievable in the near term.

When you set goals that are too large, you are primed for defeat. In fact, many people dread financial planning and goal setting simply because, at one time, they set stratospheric goals that could never have been achieved in the short time window they specified. Instead, these days, they rely on that *lottery mentality* I mentioned before. They may want to bring home a substantially higher income, but they don't have the necessary activities or resources in place to earn these stratospheric amounts. The only way to meet their goal is to win "the lottery."

Think about your current situation for a moment and then rate yourself on how well *you* have set financial goals that are attainable and intentional. A score of 1 means *I don't have any,* while 10 means *You bet! I've got my goals written down, they are realistic,* and *I have a written plan of how to achieve them.*

QUESTION 4:
"I KNOW HOW MUCH MONEY I NEED TO SAVE AND INVEST TO ACHIEVE FINANCIAL ABUNDANCE."

You know how much money you currently need to live on. But do you know how much your desired *future* lifestyle costs? Do you know how much you'll need to save and invest to pay for that lifestyle?

When my goddaughter was eight years old, she talked constantly about where she wanted to live, the kind of car she wanted to drive, the places she would visit, and the exciting things she would do when she "got bigger."

Her mom wisely sat her down and calculated—at eight years old!—what these necessities would cost and how much she'd need to have invested to afford them year after year. They discovered she "only" needed $8,000 a month to live her dream—a sum that, I can tell you, is easily attainable. Since then she and her mom have planned how much in investments she'll need to generate that $8,000 every month without working.

When you're really clear about how much money you need to live your dream (not just survive), building the finances required to quickly get there becomes fun, exciting, and inspiring. And when your investments reach the point that you no longer need to work to survive—when your money does all the work and earns all the money for you—*that's real prosperity and abundance.*

It's the freedom that lets you pursue the exciting Harvard-style "endowment" of a life I talked about earlier. Janet Switzer calls this investment-funded lifestyle "living on invested capital." You don't touch your nest egg—you spend only the interest, dividends, and earnings your nest egg produces. And while every financial planner uses a different formula, most agree that a conservative annual income from your invested capital—an income you can really count on year after year—is about 8% of your invested money. That means $1 million in investments would earn you $80,000 a year before income taxes. If you can't live on $80,000, do what's needed to invest *more than $1 million.*

But don't worry that a million dollars or more is beyond your reach.

With a starting investment of just $25,000—an amount that is easily amassed as I'll reveal in a moment—plus adding $250 per month consistently, the power of compound interest brings you to $1 million in about 30 years. Invest even more every month and your $1 million goal will arrive much, much sooner.

Of course, the earlier you start, the better off you'll be. If you're 20 years old today, do everything you can to start a small nest egg—then be diligent about adding to it regularly. While friends are spending $250 a month on clothes, eating out, and the latest electronics, you'll be building an enviable financial

future. Create multiple income streams to boost these investments, and you could retire well before your peers, as well.

But don't get me wrong. I'm not recommending that you live
a frugal life for 30 years before you really get to live. But I do
want to illustrate the financial transaction that's needed to build
a nest egg that supports you. A little later in this chapter, I'll talk
about ways to earn a substantially larger *current* income that not
only funds a great lifestyle *today* but also lets you invest heavily *for
your future.*

For now, spend some fun time calculating exactly how many
years and dollars are required to amass your "financial abundance fund" by using the online calculators at Bankrate.com.
They let you create different investment scenarios by inputting
your starting investment, monthly contribution, number of years,
and more.*

Of course the real fun begins when you start planning your
abundant future lifestyle—and determine what that will cost.
What will your rent or house payment be? What would you have
to pay for your dream car? What kind of travel budget would
you need to live your desired lifestyle? Although some people
want to "check out" and head for the nearest beach shack on
a tropical island someday, most of us want the luxury lifestyle
we feel we deserve. After decades of hard work, we want "the
rich life." Well, the rich life costs money—so reread the section about getting crystal clear on what you want in Chapter 1
to determine what an abundant lifestyle means *to you,* then
research what it will cost, and how much you need to have
invested to pay for it.

If you haven't determined your Financial Abundance
Goal—that amount of invested capital you need to support
your dream lifestyle—you're at a 1 on our rating scale. If your

---

* Of the many investment, loan, and other calculators at this website, our favorite is the
"How Long Until You're a Millionaire?" calculator at www.bankrate.com/calculators
/savings/saving-million-dollars.aspx.

goal is so vague that your only "dream" is to pay your rent this month, you're also at a 1. Scoring 10 on the rating scale, on the other hand, means that you have financial goals, they're measurable—and you know the milestones you must reach to amass your financial abundance fund. A 10 means *I've got a plan and I'm working it.*

QUESTION 5:

"I KNOW MY MONTHLY BUDGET AND I STICK TO IT."

I talked earlier in this chapter about creating a budget for your future abundant life. But what about today? Do you have a written budget of what you *must* spend, how much you *must* invest, and how much is available for optional purchases? If you have this kind of budget, do you stick to it? Do you hold yourself financially accountable to your budget?

Here a score of 10 means *Yes!,* 5 means *Sometimes,* and 1 means *No, never.*

Of course, many people—perhaps you—are unclear about what a budget really is. Perhaps you think it means *putting yourself on a budget*—that is, limiting your ability to spend on the things you want. Perhaps you're thinking, *No one should be the boss of me* or *No one can tell me how much I can spend.* Rest assured that a budget is a tool like everything else I've recommended. It's something that gives me peace of mind. It moves my financial picture out of the realm of ambiguity and gives me clarity.

In business, a budget lets you also look at the percentages of revenue being spent on certain activities to see whether that spending is out of line for your industry. It helps you pinpoint costs that could be reduced through smart buying or even eliminated by pursuing alternative solutions. It is a useful and smart means to an end.

QUESTION 6:

"I TRACK MY PRODUCTIVITY AND EITHER RAISE
MY PRICES BASED ON MY ABILITY TO PRODUCE—
OR HAVE ASKED FOR A PROMOTION AND RAISE
AT WORK BASED ON MY INCREASED SKILL SET
AND HIGH PRODUCTIVITY."

Are you actively working to increase your skill set and your knowledge? Are you striving to make yourself more and more valuable to the world?

As I've said, I've made it a policy in my life to always be learning, growing, and improving. And while I certainly conduct plenty of my own seminars and deliver tons of keynotes at industry events, I also attend *other people's trainings as a participant, student, and learner.* Not only has this constant and never-ending improvement enabled me to build my own business, but it's given me a much broader repertoire of knowledge and results to access when it comes to advising my private clients. I've increased my own value as a consultant through many years of learning and then applying and testing what I've learned.

If you own a business, you too should be keeping track of the results you're creating for customers and clients—then raise your prices based upon your own ever-greater ability to produce. I also recommend that you proactively survey customers about their outcomes, then ask for testimonials that demonstrate these results.

Similarly, if you work for a corporation, have you researched what you need to do to move to the next income level? Are you aggressively conquering that new skill set? Or are you passively waiting for someone to recognize your new talents and grace you with a paltry 3% cost-of-living adjustment for your "efforts"?

If you're responsible for your own financial well-being and responsible for your own productivity, then you have the right to ask for a raise. Today, raises aren't given because you've been at the company for 15 years. Raises are given based on results. So shift your mindset from an entitled view—*I'm entitled to a raise because I've been here a long time*—to a results-driven mindset: *I deserve a raise because I produce more than other employees or now have a unique skill set that's profitable to my employer.*

I don't have a college degree. I didn't start out with specialized professional skills. But I looked at how start-up companies "bootstrap" their way into business, then replicated that to start my own. Since then I've continued to pursue knowledge on my path to phenomenal business success.

Along the way, this knowledge became a valuable resource to *other* business owners, including my students, clients, and marketing partners.

How well are you tracking your productivity and value to others, constantly improving it and quantifying those results, and then *communicating this improvement* to your customers, employer, or other people who are partners in your financial success? If the answer is *Not very well* or *Wow, that seems really egotistical,* give yourself a 1 on our rating scale. A 10 means *I'm avidly measuring my success and talking to whomever I need to in order to improve my financial picture.*

QUESTION 7:
"I AM COMFORTABLE WITH THE AMOUNT OF DEBT I HAVE."

Do you know month to month whether you can manage your debt—or does your debt manage you? Does your level of debt cause you to make financial decisions that would be made differently (or benefit you greater) if that debt didn't exist?

While a lot of people say *I'm comfortable with my debt,* what they really mean is *I make the minimum payment every month, so my debt is easy to manage and doesn't impact me.* These people are making the minimum payments because they can't afford to pay more.

If this describes your comfort level, you actually have too much debt. And it's likely to become an unconscious burden weighing you down as you try to build your financial future.

Of course, this question may not apply to you. You may have no consumer debt at all, or you may pay your credit card balance in full every month. And if you're the cash-and-carry type who doesn't buy until you have the money to do it with, great job! You are managing your debt appropriately.

Plus, not all debt is bad. With the right kind of debt, you can buy a home or fund your education. Plus, you need a certain amount of manageable debt repayment to establish good credit.

If you're confident that you use debt appropriately, that you've limited your debt to specific purchases, and that you're on track to pay off the debt in a timely way—give yourself a 10 on our rating scale. If, however, your debt is out of control with no end in sight—or worse, if it's impacting the financial decisions you make about your future—give yourself a 5 or lower.

QUESTION 8:
"I CARRY NO HIGH-INTEREST DEBT."

Using high-interest credit cards to make purchases, then carrying a balance on those cards from month to month, will keep you in a cycle of amazing discomfort.

Look at the interest rate you're paying on each of your credit cards—then look at the number of cards you have (and use) every month. Decide what you need to do to eventually eliminate that high-interest debt and manage your credit card balances every month (including using debit cards in the future). Not only will it give you greater peace of mind, but you'll also be on the road to financial freedom much sooner.

If you carry no high-interest debt or you comfortably pay off your cards every month, give yourself a 10 on our rating scale. If you need to pay off and eliminate those cards, give yourself a 1.

QUESTION 9:
"I UNDERSTAND THE DIFFERENCE BETWEEN GOOD DEBT AND BAD DEBT."

The first time I came across this question on our assessment, my answer was 1. Frankly, I had no idea there was a difference in quality of debt, and it never occurred to me that debt could be "bad." Like many people, debt was just a reality. Debt meant that I could purchase things I couldn't pay for yet.

Eventually I learned the difference.

"Good debt" is anything that's going to pull you forward into the next financial bracket. A home mortgage that lets you buy a house and benefit from growth in equity over the years is one example. If you've created a product that costs $10,000 to produce but will earn you $100,000 in revenue, borrowing to pay manufacturing costs would be another example of good debt. And bringing in smart investors to help fund the growth of your company—as I did—is yet another example of "good debt" that's designed to build something of value or bring useful products and services to the world.

"Bad debt" on the other hand is using that credit card in your purse—on which you already owe $10,000—for things you can't recall buying or doing.

For now, rate yourself on a scale of 1–10 with 10 being *Yes, I know the difference and I only use "good debt."*

QUESTION 10:
"I KNOW THE DOLLAR AMOUNT NEEDED TO MEET MY MONTHLY BUDGET, AND I'VE GOT A 'COMMUNITY' THAT HELPS ME ACHIEVE THAT."

Does it ever seem like the more you make, the more you spend—*and the less you have left over*? You might even have some help in creating this problem from your family, employees, and friends.

If your spending is out of control and the people you've surrounded yourself with are sabotaging your financial future, rate yourself between 1 and 10 on this assessment question.

The reality is that following a budget that lists your minimum monthly expenses—but that also includes your savings, retirement investments, debt reduction, and other contributions to your personal financial goals, plus a little extra for rewards and celebrations—is virtually the only way to become financially abundant. In fact, when I do this, something magical happens: I actually hit those numbers and attain those goals.

In addition, a budget gives you an income target—the amount *you must earn* to meet your goals. Not only is this imperative for self-employed people, it's a good exercise for anyone. If you don't make enough to meet those *necessary* items listed in your budget, you'll be less likely to spend on nonbudgeted "impulse" items that don't contribute to your future.

Of course, the people around us can support (or hinder) us in meeting our goals. In fact, our "community" members not only set up our mindset by imposing their own belief systems on us, but their prosperity (or lack of it) also becomes something we tend to mirror over time. Our lives tend to imitate the people we hang out with the most—both in our beliefs *and in our income level.* Surround yourself with powerful people who inspire you to achieve significant financial goals—whether it's earning a substantially greater income, becoming 100% debt free, or building your company through an impressive new revenue source.

Who's in your circle of influence? What energy are they surrounding you with? If you're the big fish in a little pond, there won't be a lot of people challenging and motivating you. And if they all earn significantly less than you do or frequently have money problems themselves, why would you want their financial influence in your life? In the same way, our immediate family can affect how we spend and invest money. If your spouse and children disregard the household budget or aren't on board with paying down debt, you'll have a difficult time achieving these financial goals on your own.

But the sabotage can also be a lot more subtle than that. If you have an opportunity to take on an outside consulting project, for instance, that will quickly generate several thousand dollars to eliminate your last remaining debt, do family and friends urge you instead to take the day off and go shopping with them? Do your employees know your limits for specific costs, yet continually overspend? Leonard Lauder, the former chief executive of the Estée Lauder Companies—net worth $8.1 billion—once said, "You are only as successful as the people who work for you want you to be." Wow.

Don't get me wrong: you don't have to replace your circle (and you certainly don't have to replace your family!), but you should be expanding your circle to include people who will amplify everything you do.

What is your community helping you achieve?

WHAT WAS YOUR SCORE ON THE FINANCIAL READINESS ASSESSMENT?

If you scored above 5 on each of the questions, congratulations! You still have some work to do, but you're at a great starting place. Choose one financial challenge each month and conquer it. If debt is your challenge, create a plan to become debt free using the many financial advice books available today. If tracking your budget is an issue for you, fire up your software, get current with the data entry, and make it a new habit to start running regular reports.

Similarly, if you scored below 5 on any (or all) of the Financial Readiness Assessment questions, you've got some work to do on your way to managing the abundance that's about to happen for you. Get advice from a small-business consultant, personal financial planner, financial coach, or debt counselor—so you can feel more confident and self-assured, one of the true hallmarks of abundance.*

ONCE YOU'VE TAKEN THE ASSESSMENT, IT'S TIME TO START BRINGING IN THE CASH

When I was in my twenties, I made a commitment to become free from financial worry. As a service coordinator at the Los Angeles Unified School District's Healthy Start Family Resource Center, I made just enough money to pay the bills and set aside a small amount. *Why not become the first investor in my dream?* I thought. So I started with the only tools I had at the time—a paycheck and a basic checking account.

For over three years, I wrote a check to myself and sent it deposit-by-mail to the bank—starting with a check for $110. Each time I wrote a check, I would increase the amount by 5%. And always in the memo line I would write, *funding my dream.*

Little by little, my bank account grew. Within a year, it was growing by even bigger numbers. And within two years, I got a second job so I could accelerate my savings by sending the entire amount of that paycheck to the bank—continuing to write the check to myself with the same message in the memo line: *funding my dream.*

One day—three and a half years later—I went to the bank to make a deposit in person. As the bank teller recognized my name, she called the rest of the operations staff over to meet me and congratulate me. They had been watching the checks come in—one by one—and wanted to meet the woman who was so committed

---

* To work with an Abundance Now coach on planning your prosperous financial life, go to www.AbundanceNowOnline.com and click on "Work With a Coach." If you're a business owner (or want to develop a second income), download Janet Switzer's free revenue-boosting tools at www.JanetSwitzer.com. Her *Instant Income 10-Day Turnaround Program* tells you what to do every day for ten days to bring emergency cash into your bank account.

to her own financial future that she sent regular checks to her own account and wrote in the memo line, *funding my dream.*

With great excitement and anticipation, the bank teller asked me the question everyone wanted to know: "Miss Nichols, what's the dream that you're funding?"

I chuckled a bit and responded, "I'm not completely sure yet, but I want to focus on inspiring people to reach new levels in their lives. I'm pretty sure that's gonna cost me, so that's why I'm saving."

Of course, what I didn't know at the time was how much I'd actually accumulated. For years, I'd simply mailed in the checks on a regular basis. So when I asked for my total balance and she pushed the printout toward me, the number I saw was more than $62,000! I immediately confirmed my Social Security number on the account to make certain the balance *actually* belonged to me.

Surely, I thought, this is someone else's account.

Up until that time, I hadn't known *anyone* in my family to have even $10,000 in the bank—let alone $62,000. But when the teller enthusiastically confirmed this was indeed my account, I began to cry. She began to cry. Then others behind the teller line—and even the manager—got teary eyed over the sheer joy of someone like me who, little by little, had funded her own dream.

What's *your* dream? What's the dream that's so important to you that you would take every penny you have over your basic expenses and write yourself a check?

For most people, struggling to survive doesn't leave a lot of extra cash. But if you knew with certainty that tens of thousands of dollars would be available to you to fund your future, would you get your financial house in order, bring in extra money, and begin to strategically find ways to make your money grow? The formula for getting rich isn't rocket science—and if I had a magic drink, I'd serve it to you. But the tried-and-true formula for amassing substantial wealth over time is simple and doable by everyone. Here it is:

1. *Write a budget that tells you every month where your money should be spent.* Include savings and investments—in any amount— as just another expense you pay along with your groceries, rent, and electric bill.

2. *Get out of debt.* Pay off your smallest debt first, then apply that now-available debt payment toward paying off larger debts. Keep going until you have zero debt—except for your mortgage (and many people pay that off, too). Get rid of excessive credit cards except one that you use for necessary online purchases or emergencies (or one business card if you own a small business).

3. *Find an additional revenue stream* specifically *so you can put that money toward a saving, investing, or debt-reduction purpose.* If your additional revenue stream is a second job, take that job with the intent of staying and earning *only as long as you need* to get your finances in order. Invest your second paycheck 100% into your financial goal (as I did) or use it to pay off old debt. Don't beat yourself up. Don't play with the extra money. Get in, get out—and get your future financial prosperity under way.

Aside from a second job, you can also pursue limited-time projects four or five times a year, provided they pay well and allow you to invest the proceeds. Start by identifying a skill set that you have—and that other people need—where you can hire out periodically for a fee. If you're an administrative person and have good organizational skills, you can print a flyer and offer your services to local businesses four or five times a year—doing one-time updates to their databases or organizing their filing systems or helping them get ready for a move. If you know how to use social media to promote a business, why not offer to manage the social media accounts of local businesses for $200 to $300 a month? And if you're a good writer, why not offer to write press releases or brochures for local businesses, churches, or nonprofits? You would be surprised by all of the small to medium businesses that are waiting on someone to come and assist them. They are just too busy to go find those people they need consultant help from.

Janet Switzer wrote a book I love called *Instant Income* that walks small-business owners through dozens of strategies that bring in cash quickly—plus the strategies that also work if you have a steady job but want to make money on the side. Janet has 13 criteria of what to look for in a short-term, minimum-commitment, hassle-free project.* Things like:

- Potential buyers can be easily identified and located—through local clubs or business networking groups, for example.
- Advertising opportunities are inexpensive and accessible—such as flyers at the local crafts store if you do quilting or business cards at the local pro shop if you're a golf instructor.
- Deadlines and other market forces cause people to buy now—especially at tax time, Christmas time, back-to-school, and so on.
- Expenses can be paid as you make sales or take deposits—if you ran an occasional catering business or a handyman service, for example.

Whatever additional revenue stream you decide to pursue, do it with a specific purpose in mind. Abundance doesn't include working three jobs, but you may have to do that to

---

* Janet's book is *Instant Income: Strategies That Bring in the Cash for Small Businesses, Innovative Employees, and Occasional Entrepreneurs.*

reach your goals. Do what you have to do—then start saving for your prosperous future.

4. *Begin to strategically find ways for your money to multiply itself.* There are three basic ways for money to multiply—and some don't require your oversight. The first is to simply open an investment account that uses mutual funds to invest your money in stocks and bonds (along with the money of thousands of other small investors). If you routinely send the investment firm checks to add to your account, you'll be surprised how fast it grows. Second, you can develop a product or service of your own and start a business to sell it. Third, you can invest your money in other people's businesses after carefully investigating the company, analyzing its history, and assessing its future. This is somewhat riskier unless you are familiar with the industry, the company, and its product and potential.

Now that you have the strategies above to help you create financial abundance for yourself and your loved ones, it's time to activate the entire formula—weaving together your own self-development, those Rocket Booster relationships, a life assignment that inspires you, and exciting financial prosperity that, just like a Harvard endowment fund, makes possible everything that you want to do.

It's time to activate abundance . . . now.

Only when you take action and start living inside this abundant new mindset can you truly set your feet on the path to privileged circumstances and a breathtaking future.

I'm so excited for you!

But there's just one more step to go. In our final chapter together, I'll reveal how to begin creating a *legacy of abundance*—including your work, wisdom, wealth, and life experience—that you can live now, but also pass on to others.

CHAPTER 6

Activating Future Abundance in the Present Moment

Every dream you have begins with the understanding that you woke up this morning ENOUGH. You are smart enough, talented enough, hungry enough, humble enough, and worthy enough for this dream to become your reality.

—Lisa Nichols

When you immerse yourself in the process of amplifying your game, you'll realize that *planning* for self-enrichment, better relationships, exciting work, and financial wealth is only part of the equation. At some point, you have to stop planning for these changes and start living them.

So how can you begin activating and enjoying abundance in your life *today* while still building the breathtaking future life of your dreams? Let's take a look.

LIFE IS NOT SHORT: THERE'S NO SUCH THING AS INSTANT SUCCESS

Nobody is an overnight success. I've sat with many of the most successful people in the world, and the stories they tell of their journeys to "success" are proof positive that slow and steady is how most truly successful people get that way.

When I was little, my grandmother would tell me the story of how a cactus grows underground for five months before ever sprouting above the surface. But once it's sprouted, that cactus would grow five feet *in one year* because it first took the time to grow a stable foundation.

Similarly, when I was in my freshman year of college, I learned in my psychology class about *relative deprivation*—the idea of wanting in your life right now what someone else has, without putting forth the 20 years of effort required to develop it.* I don't think more than 30% of that psych class at age 19 stayed with me, but this idea certainly did. Things simply require nurturing. The best things—those things that are steady and sustainable, that will stay with you—are going to require time. You can't Google-download a breathtaking future, nor can you microwave it. Those delicious desserts my grandmother made—sweet potato pie or a peach cobbler—were never made in the microwave.

I've remembered the concept of relative deprivation as I've spent time with my mentors over the years. As I would sit across from Jack Canfield or beside Oprah Winfrey or study Nelson Mandela, I had to remember that I could want what they have, but I *have to be willing to put in the time* to get it. I had to have constant discipline. As I looked at the examples of who I could become and what I could have in my life, I always reminded myself to develop my lifestyle and career on cement—not sinking sand.

In fact, there's a risk if you get to that advanced point and you're not prepared. We see this often when celebrities rise to fame too fast, and they just don't have the maturity to handle it. They're simply too young. They've amassed way too much money without enough awareness and life experience to know

---

* From Wikipedia: *Relative deprivation* is the individual experience of discontent when being deprived of something to which one believes oneself to be entitled.

what to do with that level of success. It requires them to make big decisions based on wisdom that they don't have yet. When you rise too fast, there's a risk of limited sustainability, and access to lifestyles and privileges that you haven't learned about or can't process. And there's a risk to your future branding. The mistakes and decisions you make now—some you will be remembered for.

So build slower and steadier. Be willing to work for it and, at the same time, gain the wisdom, knowingness, and sustainability to deal with it. This path reduces the chance that you can lose it because you don't know how to manage it. There's only one thing worse than never having the lifestyle you really want, and that's having it, but losing it, because you didn't know how to manage it. If you're going to introduce abundant experiences into your life and into the lives of your family, be responsible enough to build it on a firm foundation.

LIVE IN THE NOW WHILE BUILDING YOUR FUTURE

So many of us today are future paced and future focused. We're not happy now, but we will be when our ideal life shows up. We can't make the time today to look into that new opportunity or create that new friendship or call someone back for that 60-minute chat, because we're so focused on what's around the corner. We're busy. We're keeping our options open. We can't get tied down.

This mindset is often driven by dissatisfaction with our present circumstances, but the truth is that these "now" opportunities to connect and grow are actually what make our bright and compelling future come about. It's these baby steps that the Universe puts in front of us upon which the breathtaking future we want will be built.

When I appeared on *The Oprah Winfrey Show,* I said, "We look at 'better' as if something's wrong with 'now.'"

While that was back in 2007, I think that observation is even truer today. Too often, we reach out for things we *think* will make us happy, while we ignore opportunities to be happy *today.* If you sat down and took inventory of what you could be enjoying right now—this moment—I'll bet your list would go on for pages. Remember the Morning Gratitude Exercise I discussed in Chapter 1? Spend ten minutes before you leap out of bed to *be grateful* for what's in your life right now, and you would find hundreds of things, people, circumstances, possessions, and other situations to be grateful for.

> Gratitude is the magnet for everything good
> and empowering. Fear and lack lose their power in
> the space of gratitude.
>
> —*Lisa Nichols*

Of course, another risk with constantly dreaming of the future is that we're *not present* to what might come up today. We miss the opportunities, friendships, joys, and experiences that could make our lives a rich and rewarding adventure. We miss the chances to connect with enjoyable, sophisticated people. We miss the opportunities to explore new undertakings—including career opportunities and unexpected involvements with special projects—when we're overly focused on some ideal scenario in future time.

We also miss the opportunity for personal development, expansion, and learning, which is *what we actually need* in order to grow into our future self.

So how can you live in the now—taking in life's lessons and opportunities—so that you advance steadily toward the life you want?

1. *Do your Morning Gratitude Exercise.* Spend ten minutes before you get out of bed being grateful for what's in your life. Even if it's simply for the bed you just slept in and the food you're about to eat for breakfast, be grateful that you have those available to you. Be grateful for the positive relationships in your life. Be grateful for the fact that you're healthy enough to pursue an exciting future. Be grateful that opportunity exists in the world for anyone (including you) to take advantage of. Gratitude draws to you more of what you want. If we spend our energy being grateful for more of what we have now, then we create space for more to come. I really have lived by this belief, and it has brought me two major benefits. First, it really did bring me more of what I wanted, but before those things showed up, being truly grateful gave me greater peace of mind about where I was that day *on my way to that next great level.* As I mentioned in Chapter 1, find as many things as you can to be grateful for that don't cost money. Be grateful for the small things, and the spectacular things will show up. And you will soon see how spectacular these things that you referred to as *small* really are.

2. *Practice mindfulness.* An essential element of Buddhist philosophy for centuries, *mindfulness* is intentionally focusing your attention on emotions, thoughts, and sensations occurring in the present moment—then accepting these impressions without judgment of yourself or others or the situation being observed. It's as if you're watching a movie, observing what's happening without criticism or condemnation. Instead of watching life pass you by, mindfulness means you tune in to what you are experiencing now. In other words, don't just go through the motions of your day, but instead strive to observe, absorb, and be more aware of what you encounter. *Mindfulness* improves your well-

being by keeping you rooted in the present versus worrying about the future or reliving and regretting the past. It even improves your physical health by relieving stress, improving sleep, reducing chronic pain, and lowering blood pressure. And mindfulness meditation has become an important component in the treatment of mental health conditions, such as depression, anxiety, and eating disorders.[*]

3. *Plan your day with opportunities to be present.* As you make your plans for the day, also schedule time to connect with an old friend, go outside, leave the office early, take an exercise class, or meditate—all of which will help you focus on the simple pleasures life has to offer now.

4. *Edify others.* Find others' gifts and talents and then lift them up. When you edify others, you actually lift the entire room. It says, *I see who you are now, and I celebrate who you're being in this moment. And I celebrate everything you had to do and overcome and create up until this moment.* Edification never speaks to the future. It's about reaching back and celebrating someone's journey to their now. When you do that, you pour fuel into them. Plus, when I edify people, it breathes into you a sense of grace and ease in that moment.

> When you take a stand for someone and lovingly
> hold them accountable to the man or the woman
> they say they want to become, you are giving
> them the gift of possibility.
>
> —Lisa Nichols

Live in the "now" while building your future. Don't keep talking about what you say you're going to do someday. You can't

---

[*] Adapted from *Positive Psychology: Harnessing the Power of Happiness, Mindfulness, and Inner Strength,* from Harvard Health Publications, 2013.

circle "someday" on the calendar—*Someday I'll find that relationship. Someday I'll get hired for my dream job. Someday I'll start my own business. Someday I'll lose the weight.*

Someday I'll be happy.

Do what you need to do *now* to enjoy the life experiences you want. Don't wait until the recession stops, the mortgage is paid, the kids are out of school, or you get a raise. Don't wait until you get a better job, lose weight, handle your personal relationship, or life is perfect.

It never will be.

Right now—in this moment—you are smart enough, experienced enough, pretty enough, and rich enough. Focus on the present and stop waiting. Book that cruise. Sign up for that class. Call that contact. Move every other option off the table. Understand that it's *in your imperfection* that you are perfect for this journey. Give yourself permission to start today.

ACT AS IF YOU'VE ALREADY ACHIEVED TOTAL PROSPERITY

Throughout this book, I've introduced you to *visualization*—a tool that helps you "see" your future life *as if* you've already accomplished it. We know that the mind can't tell the difference between circumstances that are actually occurring in the present moment and circumstances you are merely imagining. As we've already discussed, the brain creates a state of *cognitive dissonance* in order to resolve what you see in your mind's eye versus what's actually happening in your everyday life.

In this final chapter of *Abundance Now,* I want to help you *act as if* you've already achieved total abundance by giving you a visualization script that will put those pictures in your mind.

As always, to use this script effectively, record it in your own voice (or have a friend record it), then replay the recording to guide you through the visualization session. Be sure to conduct your visualization sessions in a quiet and uninterrupted place. (It's not a process for listening during gym time or driving time, for instance.) Give your daily visualizations the time and space *you* deserve.

RELAXING INTO THE VISUALIZATION PROCESS

Let's use the power of your mind to create your ideal life. Your future experiences will start in your mind first, so let's take a journey into your most creative, free, and powerful place ever—your imagination!

We become what we most think about. Your new possibilities and success can be created by you and only you. You will become what you think about every day.

Let's cut away all limiting thoughts, and rise above your fears to the place of freedom and creation.

Stand in your power! Success is your birthright! Move in this moment from optional to non-negotiable.

Every great leader, prophet, visionary, role model, and legend visualized their future *before* they took action.

Know that you have as much right to the joy, love, happiness, and abundance as any other living creature on this planet, and it's yours for the asking and creating.

You have *nothing* to lose and *everything* to gain.

Now . . .

Choose a quiet place. Turn off your phone. Clear your mind. Everything you need to do will be there waiting for you on the other side of this journey. Let it all go for now. Relax and release any physical tension. Become more committed to your inner images than to your physical presence.

Now, I want you to take a deep cleansing breath, filling your abdominal area full of breath. And as you exhale, gently feel your body sinking into a relaxed state.

To help you go into a deep level of mind, I will gently guide you through a relaxation of your physical body.

Feel your scalp relax. Feel this gentle feeling of relaxation flow down your forehead. Now to your eyes . . . Feel your eyelids relax. Feel that sensation of relaxation on your eyelids. Feel that slowly flowing throughout your body.

Move the soothing feeling to your face . . . and your throat . . . your neck . . . your shoulders. Feel them sink into deep relaxation.

Now your upper arms . . . your hands . . . your chest . . . your abdomen . . . your thighs . . . your knees . . . your calves . . . your feet.

And feel that feeling of relaxation flow all the way down to your toes.

Now . . .

VISUALIZATION SCRIPT FOR MANIFESTING YOUR FUTURE LIFE

Your mind is like a blank canvas of possibility, waiting to paint whatever picture that you are willing to create.

Whatever you truly believe to be possible for your life, you are the author of your autobiography, the sculptor of your life masterpiece. You are the designer of your destiny. Visualize yourself as a powerful force of nature that can command your future experiences into existence simply with your intentions. You have the power of your thoughts, the power of your tongue, and the power of your actions. Feel that power and excitement. You are an initiator of great love . . . relationships . . . an architect of great wealth creation . . . an engineer of boundless fun . . . infinite joy and limitless laughter.

You make the world a better place because *you* are here manifesting great things. See yourself as always manifesting the very thing that you need or desire. You manifest small things like getting the very best parking space, having the friendliest cashier when you're checking out at the store, traffic lights turning green for you, people smiling at you more often, children enjoying your company, or simply choosing that absolute best book at the perfect time you need such inspiration. Visualize yourself manifesting big things with your infinite power of creation, spoken word, and radical action.

You manifest healthy, transparent, fulfilling love with your family with harmony and peace. See yourself manifesting the most perfect communication to help you to navigate through the rough terrain with grace and ease. Feel the joy in your heart when you finally realize that *you* can make it through *anything* in this relationship together, because you've manifested the skills to keep harmony and love in the forefront of your important relationships!

Visualize yourself experiencing an intense, passionate, romantic love affair. See yourself drawing it to you, your partner celebrating you, acknowledging your contribution to his or her life, and adorning you with love, adoration, and appreciation.

Visualize yourself manifesting the business success that you desire. Look at the things around you in your job or business, your team or coworkers, your sales, the money you have made.

You spoke your intentions to anyone who would listen and you jumped into radical action to race toward your goals becoming your reality. And now you are seeing each and every thing that you focused on, meditated about, or set an intention around coming slowly to fruition.

See yourself traveling around the world, enjoying your life and also helping others. You are sitting with families who have far less than you, who are inspired by who you are. You share your soul with them. You open up and pour into each one of them, and in return they pour back into you, and you are filled with a sacred, speechless kind of love.

You have manifested your local and international impact. See yourself in your local community, as well as globally directing the project of your choice. People are being served. Their joy is evident, their gratitude is humbling. You are there to see what you dreamed. It's now serving others.

Your mind is like a blank canvas of possibility, waiting to paint whatever picture you are willing to create, whatever you truly believe to be possible for your life. You are the author of your autobiography, the sculptor of your life masterpiece. You are the designer of your destiny.

Visualize yourself as a powerful force of nature who can command your future experiences into existence simply with your intentions. You have the power of your thoughts, the power of your tongue, and the power of your actions.

CLOSING DOWN THE VISUALIZATION PROCESS

Slowly begin to feel your back against the chair again. Feel your feet on the ground. Feel your breath again. Begin to come back into the room. When you are ready, very gradually start to bring yourself back into the now moment.

Now completely rejoin your physical body. Hear the sounds around you in your now environment. When you feel ready, you may open your eyes.

Welcome back! Go throughout your day thinking about and reciting positive affirmations that support and add great energy to this creative visualization.

Remember this in everything that you do: as was said in the Sermon on the Mount, "Ask and it will be given to you, seek and you will find, knock and the door will be opened to you. For everyone who asks receives, the one who seeks finds, and to the one who knocks the door will be opened."

Remember to be in radical *action* toward your goals. Ideas and visualizations are worthless without action.

Finally, accept that this visualization is so! This is your future, being shown to you like a motion picture with you as the star. All you need now is action, unwavering faith, and a purpose bigger than yourself.

I'm your sister in this journey, and I believe in you.

MANIFEST PROSPERITY WITH
THE LAW OF ATTRACTION

In 2006, the documentary movie and book I mentioned before—*The Secret*—captivated the world and introduced more than 20 million people in over 50 languages* to the age-old principle of deliberately manifesting what you want: The Law of Attraction.

The Law of Attraction says: *What you think about, talk about, believe strongly about, and feel intensely about, you will bring about.*† Your life is a physical manifestation of your thoughts and your energy. You shape your life experience in your mind *first* by what you think, then in your mouth by what you say, and finally in your actions by what you follow through on. Your life experience doesn't just pop up. It takes shape in your mind first.

I remember discussing The Law of Attraction on *The Oprah Winfrey Show* and explaining that everything you think about your life—and say about your life—is true. You will live in alignment with what you believe. You will call forth your truth because that is what you believe.

Your job is to decide what you want to believe, because that is your life taking shape. For example, if you walk into a restaurant and order chicken and broccoli, you would fully expect the waiter to bring chicken and broccoli. You don't worry if salmon and spinach is going to come, and—as a matter of fact—if chicken

---

* According to the movie's official website TheSecret.tv.
† Excerpted from *The Success Principles: How to Get From Where You Are to Where You Want to Be,* by Jack Canfield with Janet Switzer. HarperCollins, 2015.

and broccoli don't come, you would send it back and say, "That's not what I ordered."

It's the same way with the Universe. If you say, *I claim joy and happiness in my relationships,* you expect joy and happiness to show up in your relationships. But if something else shows up, you would take action to go get what you were claiming. By the same token, if you say, *I'm always tired, I never have enough money, I'll never find a good man, I can't trust women,* then that's going to show up in your life. Your life is happening in your thoughts and in your words long before it ever unfolds. And it unfolds according to your command.

You've probably seen The Law of Attraction at work in your own life in simple ways.

For instance, have you ever thought about someone, only to have them suddenly call you? Have you ever wanted to visit a specific place, only to have circumstances line up perfectly to go there? Have you ever had a thought in your head and before you could say it, someone said exactly what you were thinking?

That's The Law of Attraction responding to your thoughts and intentions.

You've probably seen this at work in subtler ways, too, like landing the last available hotel room on a busy holiday weekend, finding a prime parking space at the mall, or being able to purchase the exact item you want at just the time you want it.

Unfortunately, The Law of Attraction also works for negative thoughts. If you've ever worried for days over a potential outcome or failure or criticism, for example, only to see it come about *exactly as you'd envisioned it,* that was The Law of Attraction at work, too. Regardless of whether the thoughts you offer are positive or negative, you receive what you broadcast to the Universe. I'm not implying that it is ALL your thoughts creating this outcome, but I will say that energy grows where energy goes.

So how can you become more deliberate about the thoughts you offer and the outcomes you want?

Truly I tell you, if you have faith as small as a mustard
seed, you can say to this mountain, "Move from
here to there," and it will move. Nothing will
be impossible for you.

—*Matthew 17:20*, The Bible
(New International Version)

Remember the *affirmations* I taught you to use. They are one way of setting your intention, focusing on your desired outcomes, and offering deliberate thoughts. The visualization processes I've given you are another way. When you focus on mental pictures of what you want—in vivid detail, with brilliant color, attaching positive feelings to the images of you enjoying your desired result— you transmit powerful energy to the Universe and begin the process of stimulating an answering call by people, situations, and opportunities who also want to connect with their desired outcomes—for which *you* could be the ideal answer.

Meeting Oprah Winfrey is something I attracted.

In fact, I pasted her picture on my vision board, but I didn't just declare, *Lisa appears on* Oprah. I added the words, *Lisa tells all on* Oprah.

To this day, I have no idea why I articulated it quite that way. But nine months later, I got a call from Harpo Inc. and, while I wasn't shocked that Oprah's people had called (I was actually awestruck and grateful), what did shock me was that, after sharing my breakthrough story with producers, they said, "We'd like to send a film crew to South Central Los Angeles and capture your backstory."

Over an entire day, they filmed at my cousin's house, they filmed at my middle school, they captured my childhood pictures—they even filmed my vision board. While producers had expected the interview to be about three and a half hours long, it lasted over seven hours. We literally talked all day. When the show finally aired, Oprah spent virtually the entire third segment on my story. She put my vision board up on the big screen and pointed out that I'd actually pasted the words *Lisa tells all on* Oprah—*nine months before her producers had contacted me and expanded their original segment*!

Be mindful about what you say you want because The Law of Attraction delivers. Specificity matters.

> The moment you make a command to the Universe
> for something that serves your highest good—
> and then you get into action creating it—the Universe
> aligns with your request and begins to move that
> very desire in your direction.
>
> —Lisa Nichols

The simplest explanation is that connecting your thoughts to Source Energy—through deliberately and intensely focusing on what you want—allows you to submit your requests and have them connected to other thoughts, circumstances, and situations that are a match.

There's a three-step process to activating this power and using The Law of Attraction: Ask. Believe. Receive.

STEP 1: ASK

To ask effectively, you have to *first* be clear about what you want. The exercise in Chapter 1 will help you get crystal clear on this.*

Then, using the same guidelines I gave you for writing affirmations, focus on what you *do* want, not on what you *don't* want. Instead of affirming, *I need to make money because I can't pay my bills,* change your language to a more positive thought, such as: *I am easily and confidently earning more than enough money to meet my needs.*

---

* See page 21, "You Can't Hit a Moving Target: Get Crystal Clear About What You Want."

Focus frequently on these thoughts each time you repeat your affirmations. Add color, sound, emotions, and other sensory impressions to the pictures you see in your mind. What would you be seeing, hearing, doing, and feeling as you are living your desired outcome?

If your dream is to inspire millions via mass media, for example, see yourself walking onstage amid the bright lights of the studio. Hear your audience welcoming you. Visualize yourself wearing the latest fashions, interviewing intriguing guests, then working with your production team afterward, preparing for the next show. Focus frequently on these images throughout the day so you repeatedly transmit your desires to the Universe.

But don't focus on *how* your goal will show up. Let the Universe do the heavy lifting and align the necessary people, resources, and circumstances for you. Remember I said in Chapter 1 to have 100% intention, but 0% concern about the mechanism? That rule allows The Law of Attraction to do its work. Also remember that as the *how* shows up, you then must get in action.

But be aware of your other thoughts, too. Given that your thoughts provide the "ask," be careful how you talk about your *current* circumstances. Complaining or bemoaning your current situation—repeatedly and with great emotion—will just deliver more of what you have right now. Use positive language and speak of future possibility instead.

STEP 2: BELIEVE

What's the easiest way to increase your belief that your fondest desires are on their way?

Take action.

When you take action, you convey the *expectation* that what you want is on its way. After all, you wouldn't be in motion on a goal unless you had some expectation that it would happen, would you? Doing those things necessary to achieve your goal is the fastest way—energetically—to confirm your belief in its inevitability.

STEP 3: RECEIVE

Once you've asked for your desire to be delivered to you, then practice steadfast belief by taking the actions necessary. The last step in The Law of Attraction formula is to receive.

This requires you to recognize an opportunity when it appears, then quickly move forward on that opportunity—a response that seems difficult for most people. Why? Because instead of trusting our intuition that this is an opportunity the Universe has brought about for our benefit, we often analyze and dither until the opportunity fades away.

By jumping in with enthusiasm, investigating further, and making a start instead, you not only take steps to *receive* your desire, you also verify whether this is the answer you've been waiting for.

> If you do only one thing with the knowledge of The Secret,
> use gratitude until it becomes your way of life.
>
> —*Rhonda Byrne, author of* The Secret
> *and producer of* The Secret *film*

Of course, the quickest and most effective way to receive what you want is to maintain a state of gratitude for what you have *already received*. When you are grateful—and actively transmit that gratitude to Source Energy—it recognizes that you'll be grateful for the next gift, and the next. But more important, it keeps you focused on the gratitude you *will be feeling* when your stated desire enters your life—which is just one more way of attracting it in the first place.

STEP BY STEP: ACTIVATE ABUNDANCE TODAY

In combination with The Law of Attraction, intention and action is also the best way to activate overall abundance in the present moment.

If you could do one exercise a day—in addition to your Morning Gratitude Exercise—that would set your intention and activate prosperity for you, it should be planning and accomplishing micro wins in each of the four areas covered in this book: Self, Relationships, Work, and Money.

ACTIVATING FUTURE ABUNDANCE IN THE PRESENT MOMENT

Remember from Chapter 1 that a micro win is something that's easily doable and quickly achievable. It doesn't have to take all day—maybe just an hour or less. But accomplishing lots of little micro wins in your day not only brings you a great sense of joy and excitement, it eventually brings about the major macro wins you want in your life.

Let's look at examples of the micro wins *you* might accomplish in the next 24 hours to activate prosperity today:

> **Self**—*If you're focused on your health and fitness these days, why not set the intention to create micro wins in that area? For instance, could you do 30 minutes of stretching, breathing, or Pilates? Similarly, if your goal is to upgrade your physical environment, could you clear out the clutter in your closet and organize your shoes? If your macro win is to lead a jet-setter lifestyle, could you plan an amazing, breathtaking trip a year from now, then deposit your first $100 in a new savings account for that goal. Could you work on your vision board one hour a day until complete—including*

creating focused boards for specific categories such as your career or business, your love life, or your lifestyle? Could you nourish yourself through a really great book on spirituality or leadership? Could you take 30 minutes for a "spa moment" such as a facial mask, manicure, or sitting with your feet in your foot massager? How could you honor, celebrate, and love yourself?

Relationships—*With the time that you have, why not make a list of five people who you haven't reached out to for a while—then text random love notes to them or make random phone calls to catch up? Could you write love notes (I write these to my mom)? Could you spend 30 minutes finding like-minded groups to join in order to expand your social circle? Could you write a love letter filled with just love and gratitude to your children, partner, sibling, or parent?*

Work—*What micro wins could you create in your career or your business? One I recommend is creating a work environment that inspires you, so why not spend an hour each day creating organization, putting systems in place, or framing and hanging photos of you in successful situations? If you're a business owner, you could take time to invest in relationships with your team. Or you could set goals that drive you—even if no one else will ever know about them (they're your goals, after all!).*

Money—*Why not write a budget, organize your bills, file your documents, or take an hour to identify additional revenue streams? An hour spent three days a week creating a bigger income for yourself would go a long way toward the macro win of an upgraded lifestyle, if that is your goal.*

MOVE PAST WHERE YOU NORMALLY WOULD STOP

There's another benefit to creating micro wins every day. They keep you in motion—sweeping you past where you normally would stop.

In fact, they're imperative to overcoming our brain's natural inclination to stop us whenever we approach circumstances it *thinks* might be "harmful." Scientists now know that our unconscious mind is the storehouse for our emotions, habits, and memories—both positive and negative. It remembers failures, sufferings, and humiliations, plus a multitude of other negative events, then uses that history to protect us from the same thing happening again. Our unconscious mind is not focused on making sure our life is enjoyable or awe-inspiring. Its job is survival. So it creates its own protection mechanism—thoughts, fears, justifications—to keep us from moving forward in areas that are entirely new or where we've tried before and failed.

Creating micro wins can help you overcome the power of the unconscious mind in order to move past where you normally would stop.

What else can you do to keep moving?

Be accountable to your intentions. Set the intention to accomplish your goal—no matter what—then establish an accountability mechanism to make sure you create micro wins every day. Check in regularly with a Rocket Booster friend. Set deadlines on the calendar. Clear your schedule of conflicting projects. Do what you need to be accountable to the intention you've set.

Additionally, recognize and welcome fear-storms as opportunities for growth.*

In my case, I was pretty savvy about running a small, privately held company. But the day I initiated the process of going public, that knowledge went right out the window—and a whole lot of

---

* On page 107 of Chapter 2, see "Do It Afraid: Navigate Your Way Through Fear-Storms" for details on how to reduce fear that arises when you try something new.

unknowns replaced it. The idea of being traded on Wall Street, the idea of opening my financials to the world, even the idea of being required to report my numbers—there simply hasn't been anything more monumental or more frightening in my life to date. From the moment I filed the paperwork with the SEC and the tedious process of being approved began, there were so many fears to deal with. The fear of being approved. The fear of being rejected. The potential of being told mine is not a viable business (even though I know it's a viable business). So many fears. Many times—more than I can count—I just wanted to say, "Let's stop."

What I soon realized was that these fear-storms were there for a reason: to move me past where I would normally stop.

I recognized that fear is designed to keep you on your A-game. Remember when I told you about speaking at Disney Dreamers Academy and I met Bishop T.D. Jakes, the great evangelist and role model of mine? There he said, "Fear comes into your life to keep you studying, to keep you on your A-game, to remind you to practice. Fear comes in to keep you awake."

Fear doesn't come around to stop you. Fear comes in so that you can tap into your humility, and to make sure you do what you need to do to win. Fear is a welcome experience if it reminds you about the further work you must do.

Going public—and the fear-storms it brought about—has kept me studying, improving, and on top of my game. The minute I filed with the SEC, I was all in. Now I want to play a bigger game, be an even better company, and become a leader on par with my fellow CEOs on Wall Street in my own unique way.

Fear-storms will do that to you. If you're not afraid, you're not playing big enough.

Make it a habit to move past *your* stopping points. It's how we grow as people—readying ourselves to take on ever more complicated responsibilities and pursue ever more exciting opportunities. Moving past where you normally would stop actually prepares you for when opportunity comes knocking.

Monalisa Johnson—a video and animation producer in New York who's studied with me over the years—found lots of places she could have stopped before launching her own business in the highly competitive entertainment industry. As a vivacious and spontaneous young woman, she dreamed of working on both sides of the camera. But while Monalisa's family encouraged her to become an actress, her father reproached her, saying, "Get your head out of the clouds and think about getting a real job. Women don't do well in that business, and you need a real paycheck to make a living."

His words hurt. And they could have stopped her. But Monalisa's resolve to follow her passion into the television production and animation business only grew. She worked harder than ever to prove him wrong.

Of course, there were very few women active on the production side of films and commercials when she got started in 1993. It was a man's world. Not only that, but Monalisa was from the Deep South, a place where women of color were respected for little else than being assistants in that industry and many others. How could she—with little experience—ever be taken seriously by her peers or clients? Quitting seemed to be the easiest option.

But still, her dreams would not be denied.

In less than six months, despite the challenges, Monalisa wrote her business plan, got funding from a bank, quit her job, and opened for business. Her first clients came through referrals from her husband, a radio personality in New Orleans. But once he and Monalisa divorced, they fought over the future of the business. Without him, it seemed her dream of running a successful production house—which was now growing by leaps and bounds—might fold. Moving past yet another stopping point, Monalisa hired the necessary team and took over marketing her services in earnest—eventually replacing her husband's referrals, business ideas, and creative input. This strong woman illustrates my point that, despite the odds and no matter how big the fear-storm, being in action will move you past where you normally would stop.

Today, Monalisa continually moves past where she would normally stop. After being a giver her entire life—with little return from those she's blessed with her attention—Monalisa got clear about expecting more from her circle of friends. She put boundaries in place to attract more supportive and giving relationships. And she's moving past her stopping points in her romantic relationships, too. While she used to put the skids on relationships whenever she encountered less-than-perfect behavior from her man, today she's married to an amazing husband whom she loves, and she's working on her relationship skills to process any challenges that arise.

Additionally, she decided to begin creating her own television programming instead of waiting for the networks to give her shows to work on. Monalisa now has her very first show in development, *Prison Moms*. She's also founded an educational organization to help the parents and families of prison inmates.

What could you accomplish in your life if you moved past where you normally would stop?

ACTIVATE YOUR LEGACY STARTING NOW

By the time you've worked 40 years in a career or life calling, you will have spent more than 350,000 hours creating, learning, connecting, producing, earning, and serving—all while building a legacy that is uniquely yours.

But a legacy of what?

For centuries, our society has narrowly defined the idea of "legacy" as something few people get to achieve. If you're fortunate enough to leave a legacy, you probably made a lot of money, donated it to a prestigious institution, and got your name chiseled on the side of a building somewhere. That's a rather limiting definition of legacy, I'd say. So, as long as we're thinking of ways to create greater abundance in your life, why not rethink this conventional concept of legacy, too, and consider *instead* what you'll do—right now, today—with the knowledge, activity, and resources you're accumulating day by day?

How will you live every day, and how will you impact people for the better—improving the world for others who'll (hopefully) take up your work when you are compelled to pass the torch?

For me, legacy means living every day being worthy of the story that's going to be told about me one day. My intention is to live a life that inspires people to say, "Lisa was a woman who exampled to us how to work diligently with what God has given us, how to love across cultural, religious, and economic boundaries to build bridges committed to our life of service, and believed we should have fun while pursuing our life's calling."

For me, legacy means living my life every day being worthy of this story—and man, that's huge.

LIVE YOUR ABUNDANCE EVERY DAY, THEN LEAVE IT BEHIND AS A LEGACY FOR OTHERS

Creating a business, career, or additional revenue stream that brings you financial wealth is only part of living a rich and abundant life. Remember the Harvard endowment fund I talked about earlier—a legacy of cash and other assets that supports anything that Harvard wants to do?

You, too, must begin assembling *all* the assets required to "live your legacy" every day—plus leave it behind for others when you complete this life.

What does it mean to live your legacy? It requires amassing financial wealth, of course. But it also suggests that you should fill your life with a passionate career, rewarding experiences, nurturing relationships, supportive friendships, a beautiful home where you and family can renew and restore, hobbies and shared opportunities that bring you together with evolved and aware people, philanthropies and charities that you establish or support, traditions that you start—the sum total of a rich and rewarding lifestyle that you enjoy and that provides countless opportunities to bring others along with you.

When you complete this life, how will people view the mission, the activities, and the connections that you pursued? How will those you've carried along with you *use* these assets after you are gone to further your work and adopt your dreams as their own? Have you ever thought about it?

What, if anything, is holding you back from doing so?

When I was younger, I wanted to be just like my grandmother and Sister Brown—women who served others, who were loved by all, and who were seen as good by everyone they knew. They were pillars of their church, Good Samaritans who were always ready with a loaf of bread or a casserole, and the source of authority and wisdom in our neighborhood. They were incredible role models and a true inspiration for me—except for their lack of money.

This created a major struggle for me because, although I wanted to do good works, "broke" was something I did not want to be. However, as I began to make money and build a multimillion-dollar company, I realized the struggle was unnecessary. I could still serve *and* enjoy abundance by a simple change in my approach and mindset. I gave myself permission to pursue a life of service and contribution *and* enjoy a life of prosperity. One did not have to exist without the other. I had made *service* and *abundance* an either-do-this-or-have-that conversation.

When you are extremely successful at what you do—when you earn substantial money from your work—that result of "earning more" simply means that you are also creating a greater impact in the world. You can help more people. You can impact your community and the world around you. Not only is that outcome worthy of tremendous compensation, but there is also no shame or greed in it. You can't receive rewards yourself without expansion, activity, and benefit happening to the world.

When you consider it this way, suddenly paying attention to your bottom line allows you to serve in an ever-bigger way. In fact, this growing and expanding of your work *must be* a conscious thing, not something that happens by accident. I can accidentally inspire people all day long—simply because that's where my gift is. It's my service. Therefore, seeking to earn well from providing a service—including the process of selling—is a dignified conversation.

Could you build a legacy of honorable earnings, passionate work, a mission that inspires you, connections that empower you, rich experiences that renew you—and a plan for enrolling others who can continue this legacy once you're gone?

Of course you can.

> In my mind, an abundant life isn't just about shiny objects,
> an impressive address, or overflowing bank accounts.
> It's about creating a life of possibility and moving from
> scarcity and lack to prosperity and abundance in every
> area that matters to me.
>
> —Lisa Nichols

In my training events, we use a tool called the Living Legacy Planner. Although the classroom version is quite elaborate, I'd like to offer you a simplified version of this planning exercise in the next section.

LIVING LEGACY PLANNER: WHAT CAN YOU PASS ON TO YOUR "SUCCESSORS" STARTING TODAY?

There's a word used often in legal contracts that works perfectly when talking about legacy. The word is *successors,* and it means the individuals, organizations, businesses, and other entities who will take over your role, duties, and privileges after you're gone.

In legal agreements, these successors not only benefit from the money and other rewards memorialized in the contract but also are charged with continuing the work, goals, and intent of the agreement.

I like this idea.

Someone else—whom we have chosen, empowered, and inspired to carry on our work—will become the caretaker of something that's bigger than us, something important enough to make plans for.

Have you ever thought about what *you will do* in your life that's important enough to plan for its continuation? Do you know who you would choose to eventually take over your role or roles? Most important, *what can you do right now* to prepare these successors to take over your duties and enjoy your privileges—eventually passing them on to someone else? I'm not sure about your family situation, but until my generation it appears that the successors in my family were primarily given the training, inspiration, and empowered knowledge with the family history and stories, secret family recipes, and rich, priceless family customs.

Questions like these form the basis of the Living Legacy Planner. By answering these questions and taking a few simple steps in each of the five areas below, you can begin not only to live your legacy *but also to pass it on to your heirs today.*

Let's get started.

FINANCIAL WEALTH

Besides family culture, spiritual foundation, and healthy lifestyle norms, I believe the greatest financial legacy you can pass on to your successors is the right mindset around money. How can they earn money in their passionate livelihood? How will a budget help them manage their money? How can they use debt appropriately to build their futures? What's the best way to invest their regular contributions to a retirement fund or savings plan?

Fortunately, education is a legacy you can begin passing on today.

When you have conversations about money with your heirs or children, make sure these conversations are intentional, positive, and consistent in message. Instead of fighting with your teenagers about how they spend their money, turn the conversation to helping them envision an exciting future that can be funded through careful savings. Instead of complaining at the dinner table that bills are going unpaid, hold a family meeting to agree on a monthly budget. Instead of using victim language around money, educate yourself and talk with your heirs about how money, banking, investments, and credit actually work. Changing your own mindset and actions around money—more than anything else—will significantly impact the financial future of those with whom you share your legacy plans.

What are three things you can do to educate your successors about money?

1. *Include your successors as you educate yourself on managing finances and investing for the future.* As you conduct research, choose your financial planner, do your estate planning, and get your own financial house in order, involve your successors in these conversations and decisions—especially if they are teenagers.

2. *Talk to your successors about creating a substantial income pursuing something they're passionate about.* Most kids grow up with the belief that, to be financially successful, their goal should be to "get a good job." This surprises me when there are so many role models who've made a lot more money pursuing something they're passionate about—outside the traditional job market. One young man I admire, Dan Spring, was a major baseball talent in high school and college. Not only does he love baseball, he enjoys hanging out with people who love

baseball (and most other sports). Early in his 20s, Dan started a business called Spring Training Baseball Academy,* which offers private lessons year-round and weeklong baseball camps all summer and on breaks during the school year. It's now one of the most successful youth sports training companies of its kind—earning Dan a six-figure annual return on his "passionate" investment.

3. *Lead by example in the way you conduct your own finances.* Share with your successors the ways in which you are pursuing careful spending, maintaining a monthly budget, properly using credit cards, and regularly investing for your retirement.

RELATIONSHIPS AND CONNECTIONS

Earlier in this chapter, I talked about surrounding yourself with successful, inspiring, and empowering people who can help you amplify your financial wealth. In the same way, these relationships tend to expand *other areas* of your life, too, since financially savvy people tend to simply think bigger—about wealth, opportunity, lifestyle, and more.

Have you ever heard the claim *It's not what you know, but who you know?*

Financially successful people embrace this idea wholeheartedly and make connecting and collaborating a foundational principle in their lives. What relationships do you need to pursue to build a legacy and lifestyle that can be adopted later by your successors? Which of these connections would your successors benefit from?

Getting into relationship with people who can lift you up, then introducing your successors to them, is the best way to live your legacy today. It's one way you can take a major leadership

---

* You can find Spring Training Baseball Academy at STBaseball.com.

role in developing the future caretakers of your work—whether those custodians are your actual children, organizations, professionals, social-change leaders, or others.

1. *Include your successors in any planning meetings you conduct with key relationships.* The easiest way to introduce your successors to people who will educate them—and inspire them about major projects you're involved in—is to involve these future caretakers in the planning process of your business, charity work, and other professional matters today. Similarly, you should involve your legal heirs in meetings about estate planning, household finances, lifestyle decisions, and personal matters. Some of the best mentors young people can have are their parents' friends and colleagues.

2. *Help your successors identify, research, and approach mentors and advisers of their own.* Help them form their own "circle of influence" with key connections that will last year after year.

3. *Teach your successors the art of staying connected, bringing value, and being of service.* The best relationships are built on shared interests—but, more important, on shared support and value. No one likes to hear from you only when you need something. Teach your successors to seek out and cultivate healthy and mutually beneficial relationships.

SHARED OPPORTUNITIES, CHARITABLE PURSUITS, AND SOCIAL CHANGE

Even more valuable than your legacy of relationships will be those opportunities you create for your successors to collaborate on activities that interest them, but that also move your legacy forward. It's not uncommon, for instance, for super-successful parents to put their adult children in charge of the family's charitable foundation. And many authors ask their wives or colleagues to write companion books on how women, professionals, and other unique readers can use the author's advice. In my company, I've developed a team of world-class trainers who can coach and mentor clients on activities that I don't advise on but that are equally important to the client's success.

Not only do these shared opportunities groom successors to "take over the business" one day (if that's their wish), it helps them develop their own persona and platform as thought leaders in the marketplace—requiring skill building and relationship building of their own.

What can you do to involve your successors in shared opportunities, charitable pursuits, and social change today?

1. *Identify those aspects of your work, charitable pursuits, or lifestyle that should be continued or expanded—then ask your successors which of those areas interest them.* My office gets contacted regularly by companies (or potential "successors") who want to create strategic alliances related to specific aspects of my work. And many times, adult children will identify an opportunity in their parent's business that is underexploited, but that could be profitable and exciting. In 1969, a good friend of mine, Joe Dudley Sr., founded an extremely successful African American hair care and beauty product business. For nearly four decades, Joe built a wildly successful career as one of the first African Americans to found and run a multimillion-dollar business. *Black Enterprise* magazine ranked it 50th in the magazine's list of Top 100 Black Owned Businesses.

But Joe's daughter, Ursula Dudley Oglesby—who started in the business as a cashier at the tender age of seven and who went on to graduate from Harvard Law School—saw an even bigger opportunity for the business in adding cosmetics to the company's existing product lines. She recruited nationally known makeup artists, experienced chemists, and product developers to help her launch the line with its first fifty-seven products in 1992. Under her leadership, Dudley Cosmetics enjoyed double-digit growth and expanded to more than two hundred products. She eventually worked her way up in the parent company and, in 2008, became president of Dudley Beauty Corp LLC. Watching her passion and commitment to continue her parents' legacy—while growing the business as if it were her own—is inspiring to witness. Joe and I have talked often about his desire to leave a legacy for his children and grandchildren. He's been a great example of what I can achieve for Jelani and my grandchildren.

2. *Cultivate relationships with organizations—not just people—who can co-create or advance specific goals you can't pursue.* One way to ensure your social legacy lives on is to make it a part of someone else's vision, business, research, or life's work. Could yours become the project of choice for corporations who want to support social change? Could you align your work with a government agency or global NGO* that lacks your expertise? Once they begin assigning people and resources to your shared initiatives, chances are ideal that your work will live on and actually be expanded by future generations.

3. *Organize people around your work who have passion, time, and resources but who don't have the necessary expertise, connections, or systems.* By yourself, you can only do so much. But what if you could motivate thousands of people to take up your cause and do the work of bringing social change to a community,

---

* Nongovernmental organization: a not-for-profit, citizen-based group organized to achieve social, humanitarian, or political goals for a community, country, region, or international population of people. Examples include Amnesty International, Doctors Without Borders, World Wildlife Fund, and Oxfam.

industry, or country? Today, the Internet is the best place to reach people who share your vision and want to create change, but who don't know how to get started. From social media to crowdfunding, crowdsourcing, viral marketing campaigns, and more, you can recruit thousands of people worldwide—then identify the "stars" who have the abilities necessary to advance and carry on your work.

CAREER AND BUSINESS EXPERIENCE

It's common for small children to want to grow up and "do what Daddy does." But in reality, those children often end up in other careers or professions as adults. Even if you own a business, involving your kids at an early age is no guarantee they'll want to inherit it (whether or not you want them to).

Remember I wrote earlier that your vision, passion, and interests were *given to you*. They're unique to you—and the best you can hope for is that your successors take up your life's work and expand it in ways that are exciting and inspiring to them. Nothing can stay the same forever, so don't expect your legacy to look the same 30 years from now either.

That said, there are many ways to engage fully in your career now—and develop protégés who will continue your "work" (whatever it may be). Below are ways to stay forward focused—constantly expanding your professional legacy so that others will be inspired to eventually take it up and expand it on your behalf.

1. *Move to the cutting edge of your profession.* Because technology, research, and ideas are evolving at warp speed, you have to constantly pursue education just to stay even with your peers. But what if you identified an area of your industry that no one was thinking about yet—then educated yourself to the point you became known as a leading authority on the subject? Not only would you become much more

valuable to your employer or customers, you would attract others who are fascinated and motivated by the new ideas and methodologies you've discovered. Cultivate these followers—then identify the standouts who can collaborate with you on the exciting future you've identified for your industry.

2. *Create strategic alliances (or merge your company) to get the resources you need to grow.* If you own a business and have reached the point where you need operating capital, new equipment, talented people, or a new distribution channel in order to grow, why not start looking for another company that has those resources? Not only would a strategic alliance or merger help you expand your work or ideas, but it might take the pressure off you running the business so you can focus on what really inspires you.

Too many people put tremendous emphasis on the end goal of running their own company—when, in fact, that may not lead to victory at all. The ultimate win is to be able to do what you love and get paid for it. Needing to say that you own a business might be more about your ego than it is about the enjoyment of running a business. My coaches and I have often heard from business owners who say, if they had it to do over again, they would more likely choose to be a thought leader or top executive in an entrepreneurial company, not an owner. In fact, some of the best coaches and executives in my company are former CEOs of their own businesses. Susie Carder, CeCe Clark, and Jennifer Kem add something spectacular to my business and, in return, they get to touch more people—more than they were reaching on their own—impact more lives, and grow their revenue. I respect their brilliance, leadership, and guidance in "our" company to the point that I've made them shareholders in Motivating the Masses, Inc.

If you, too, could create a greater legacy by creating strategic alliances or negotiating an infusion of cash or talent, consult your legal counsel, accountant, and business adviser about adding partners, seeking venture capital, or taking your company public. You might end up playing a much bigger game and attracting successors who could take your work to a whole new level, years into the future.

3. *Form your own industry association.* Some of the most successful examples of people who moved their career from day-to-day employment to legacy status are the founders of industry advisory groups, marketing cooperatives, and trade associations. When you bring together your peers and provide an outlet for discussion, education, and sharing of best practices, you not only become a respected leader of your industry, you create a compelling reason for others to carry on your work. Countless examples abound, from Sunkist Growers (the marketing cooperative founded by California citrus farmers to pack and sell their fruit worldwide) to the Transformational Leadership Council (a group of the world's leading personal-development training companies) and even the Fantasy Sports Trade Association (a membership of North American companies serving some 41 million fantasy sports players).

LIFESTYLE AND HOBBIES

One of the greatest pleasures of an abundant life is the joy of involving your children, heirs, and family members in your rewarding lifestyle and hobbies. I'll never forget the day my son, Jelani, and I drove with our guide to the pinnacle of the nearby mountain range while traveling in Kenya. "Mom," he said with excitement, "look at me! I'm standing on top of one of the biggest mountains in Africa!" My non-negotiable pursuit of an abundant life created that once-in-a-lifetime moment for him. And I am very clear that my finances don't buy me *things* as much as they help me create the greatest memories possible.

You, too, can create a legacy of rich and rewarding life experiences—starting today—that your heirs will want to continue for the rest of *their* lives. Here are a few ideas.

1. *Create your own family traditions.* Whether it's a daily story at bedtime, vacationing at your lake house every summer, or pizza and a movie on Sunday nights, traditions teach family values, contribute to your children's well-being, and provide a sense of connection and safety. Why not begin your own traditions in addition to those handed down from your parents? Inexpensive traditions today can evolve into luxury traditions later—but often the most impactful traditions are free of charge.

   Jelani and I have a silly little tradition that I never thought would last this long. As a little boy, he would jump into my bed in the morning with a cute little grin—hankering to have his back scratched. He always purred like a kitten—something his grandpa always did—and even though Jelani is now over six feet tall and 220 pounds, he'll still snuggle close and purr as I scratch his back. And it's something both of us still grin about—something that keeps us close and connected. And even when he's much older and maybe even a father, he'll still be Mustard Man and I will be Garlic Girl.

   What are some other examples? If lifelong learning is an important legacy you want to pass down, you can have your children each tell something at the dinner table they learned that day—either at school or outside the classroom. If personal growth and achievement are part of your legacy, why not text your kids an inspiring message or TFTD (thought for the day) when they least expect it.* And if cultural her-

---

* To find short quotes for text messaging, search "success quotes" or "abundance quotes" online.

itage is a tradition you want to pass down, you can incorporate time-honored songs, prayers, or foods into regular events or special occasions.

2. *Plan a trip where you do good for others—together.* Whether it's a church mission trip, disaster relief, or building homes with Habitat for Humanity, these life-changing experiences create a sense of accomplishment, pride, and family bond that is unmatched. Not only do these trips instill the enjoyment of helping others, but they're off the beaten path of historical monuments, museums, and theme parks—and encourage a lifetime of adventure, learning, and doing for others. When their friends ask, "What did you do on your summer vacation?," you can rest assured the answer will be one they'll be proud to talk about. As a legacy you give to your kids, how cool is that?

3. *Turn your child's hobby into a legacy of learning and achievement.* For nearly 10 years, Janet Switzer's niece raised champion livestock and showed them at numerous county fairs and expos each season. When Janet wasn't consulting, writing, or speaking at international business conferences, you'd find her on the fairgrounds of countless small towns around the state—cheering, supporting, and coaching. Not only was it something enjoyable that Janet's family did together, but it instilled in her niece a legacy of confidence, problem solving, goal setting, hard work, and responsibility.

If you have a hobby of your own that your children want to pursue, so much the better—as long as you remember that skill building, confidence, and learning (not pressure and competition) is the goal. What can you and your children do that could become a family "legacy project" with your support and positive reinforcement?

NEXT STEPS NOW THAT YOU'VE COMPLETED
THE LIVING LEGACY PLANNER

As you complete this exercise, realize that the good news is you can live this legacy *every day* by pursuing things you are passionate about and enrolling others in the process through your example. You have it in your power to create new movements, new initiatives, new alliances, and new opportunities that you can enjoy now—and that others can continue someday. When you create a life that's worth living and work that is worth evolving, the likelihood is that your legacy will live well beyond your time on Earth.

Conclusion

Take action. It's the only thing separating
you from your dreams.

—Lisa Nichols

What is the most immediate thing you can do to start living abundantly, building your future, and establishing your legacy? Take action. Decide what you want, create a plan to pursue it, then *move forward*—regardless of your fear, your lack of experience or knowledge, your lack of resources, or *any other impediment*.

Just move.

In my lifetime and with the thousands of people I've personally worked with, there's one thing I've noticed that differentiates truly successful people from those who merely want to be.

Successful people have a bias for action.

They do it afraid, they have the crucial conversations, they step out of their comfort zones, and they spend the time and have the focus required to get a result.

"But where do I start?" you might be wondering.

I recommend that you turn back to Chapter 1 and begin by getting crystal clear about what you want in the 12 areas of your life. Determine the relationships you want, the career or work you want to do, the physical rewards you want to enjoy—all the hallmarks of your abundant life. Not only will you be surprised at your answers, but you may realize that you have a lot of those things present in your life *right now*.

Of course, once you make your list of wants, you can use the other skills you've learned in this book to break down each goal into baby steps, calculate the cost of each, research how to get it, and get into relationship with people who can help you. I've discovered that I've made the most progress when I systematically plot out the steps necessary to get to my goals—baby steps that I can accomplish with ease and celebrate when completed.

Once you decide what you want, it's time to pursue the 4 Es in earnest.

YOU DON'T HAVE TO MASTER EVERYTHING; YOU ARE "ENOUGH" RIGHT NOW . . . TODAY

Abundance is your birthright. When you practice **Enrichment** of your whole Self, not only will you be able to better pursue that abundance, but you'll enjoy it a lot more as you move into exciting new activities, directions, and opportunities.

Don't worry if you feel that you're not smart enough, connected enough, or "enough" in any other way. Remember that you don't have to master everything. Stay in your own lane. Master what *only you can do*—then reach out to the resources and people you need to help you accomplish the rest.

That brings us to the second of the 4 Es: **Enchantment** in your Relationships—the feeling of delight and magic you get from the people who surround you, support you, and encourage you. Who wouldn't want a host of Rocket Booster friends, colleagues, and mentors helping them succeed in areas that are important to them? Shake off the effects of the toxic people in your space and reach out for people who make you stand on your tippytoes. I want you to become intentional about the quality of your relationships—not just the current ones, but the new ones you want to form. I want you to become deliberate about the caliber of people you spend time with, learning how to seek out those people who inspire you to do better, create more, play bigger, and win more often (especially in your family relationships and romantic relationships).

Throughout the process of attracting and growing better relationships, be sure to use visualization and affirmations to get the Universe working on bringing those people into your life.

The third of the 4 Es we talked about is the **Engagement** you get from your Work, your business, or your career. I'm convinced that you have a calling in your life, a life assignment that commands your time, talent, and treasures. It's up to you to recognize whether you're in that calling now—or whether you need to shift into it, using your current "job" as an investor in your exciting and breathtaking future. There is so much opportunity out there to thrive—but at all times, strive to make it work for you. Strive to achieve harmony (but not balance) between the time you spend on your work and the time you dedicate to family, hobbies, and rest and renewal.

Just reframing your career and livelihood—just recognizing and beginning to live your life assignment—can make all the difference to how you feel about your journey.

But there's one more of the 4 Es to put into practice—the **Endowment** approach to your personal wealth and financial prosperity. If you need to work on eliminating those old "money mantras" you learned when you were younger, get going on this process in Chapter 5 so you can create a new relationship with Money. Then, start looking at what you need to do to bring more money into your life. Remember, too, that this journey of ours isn't just about financial wealth. When you treat your finances like a Harvard University endowment, the good works that you do—just like Nulu Naluyombya, Lewis Pugh, and Lynne Twist—will come back to you in the form of benefits and enrichments that can be used to further build your finances, opportunities, current impact, and future legacy.

DON'T WORRY *NOW* ABOUT HOW YOUR
GOALS WILL BE ACCOMPLISHED

When you know the "what," you can figure out the "how." When you become intentional about what you want—and you begin taking small baby steps of action—you can sit back and let the Universe provide the mechanism by which you'll achieve your goal.

Don't get so overwhelmed and immobilized by *how your goal will be accomplished* that you prevent the "what"—your actual goal—from gaining traction. Maintain 100% intention that your goal will be fulfilled. But, at the same time, have 0% concern about the *mechanism that will be used* to achieve it.

I also want you to become unshakable about achieving your most important goals. Become non-negotiable about them. Too many people today want an exciting future but aren't willing to put the time and effort into achieving it. The reality is that merely *wanting* to achieve a goal isn't enough. You have to act as if the accomplishment of that goal is non-negotiable. You must maintain the conviction that achieving it is necessary to your future.

When you move every other option off the table, the intention, passion, and determination you broadcast to the Universe will help to bring forth the resources and opportunities you need to fulfill your goal.

Merely "wanting" your goals is not enough.

> We look at "better" as if something's wrong with "now."
> —Lisa Nichols, *appearing on* The Oprah Winfrey Show

Of course, there's one thing we can't forget in the process of pursuing your goals for an abundant future: you're *already living* with a whole lotta abundance *right now.* You have good things going on in your life you can be happy about. That's why I recommend practicing the Morning Gratitude Exercise—to show you where you're living abundantly *today*.

The truth is that far too many of us are so focused on the future that we actually make ourselves unhappy. We're not happy now, but we will be when our ideal life shows up. We can't make the time today to answer that e-mail or support that friendship or pitch in on that charity project, because we're so focused on what's around the corner. We're too busy. We can't get tied down. But remember that these "now" opportunities to connect and grow are actually what make our breathtaking new future come about. It's these baby steps that the Universe puts in front of us that will bring about the abundance we so desperately want.

GRAB SOME FRIENDS AND GET STARTED LIVING IN ABUNDANCE TOGETHER

Because happiness throughout your journey is the secret sauce that makes it all worthwhile, I'd like to encourage you to share the information you just read with trusted friends as you're moving forward. Better yet, why not invite them on the journey with you by buying them a copy of this book and going through the exercises, planning tools—and life changes—together? It's the easiest and fastest way to start building Rocket Booster friendships that support you and celebrate you! Even better, get a group of colleagues or friends together in a monthly study group or mastermind circle where you can all work on your goals in a concerted way.

If you can't assemble a group just yet, there's another way to put your abundant new life on the fast track: make a commitment to put into daily practice the skills and strategies in this book—then *make yourself accountable* to someone other than yourself for your success. I often recommend that my students work with what's called an *accountability partner*—someone you can talk to at least once a week who won't judge you or advise you, but who will simply ask you whether you accomplished the goals you set for yourself that week. This is critically important if you're a solo entrepreneur without a team or anyone else who requires that you meet your deadlines. You can schedule a call with your accountability partner the same day and time every week—or every two weeks at most. You'd be surprised what you can accomplish when you know you have to "report in" on your weekly baby steps the next day.

I find that, too often, we go on this journey alone when we don't have to. There are support people out there—but also people who will get in your face a little if you don't move forward on your goals. I have an accountability partner in my COO, Susie Carder. And every client gets an accountability partner as part of their coaching program with us.

START COACHING WITH ME AND MY TEAM FOR EVEN FASTER RESULTS

If you were an Olympic athlete or an NFL football player or a celebrity actor, you wouldn't expect to succeed in your career alone. You would work with a coach who can guide you, correct your technique, identify areas for improvement, and give you positive feedback when you've accomplished a baby step that's critical. Many of the most successful people alive today have worked with career coaches to help them move forward—faster—toward their goals (including me).

One of the greatest privileges of my life is to have assembled a team of smart and supportive coaches who can help my readers identify new career opportunities, get their relationships right, build their businesses, start their authoring or speaking careers, and develop their legacy of philanthropic service. Some of our coaching programs start with an entire day of strategic planning where *I sit down with you personally* to work on your future. It's heady stuff. But it's something I enjoy more than the bright lights of the stage or the whirlwind of media appearances. Simply working with individuals to create abundant futures brings me immense joy.

To learn more about how you can be part of this coaching experience—including different levels of support that will meet you where you are in your life right now—contact my Customer Experience Concierge at (760) 931-9400. My team will get you the information you need and a coach who can put you on a whole new trajectory.

BONUS TOOLS YOU'LL WANT
TO DOWNLOAD *NOW*

Our time together and your journey doesn't stop with the pages of this book. My coauthor, Janet Switzer, and I have developed life-changing tools for you that will keep you focused, empowered, and enthusiastic as you implement what you've learned in this book. Before you jump into taking action on what you've read, do one more thing: turn the page now to read more about *Bonus Tools for Abundant Thinkers*.

They're free and downloadable at www.AbundanceNow Online.com.

FREE TOOLS FOR ABUNDANT THINKERS

Expand your abundant new life with these unique tools from Lisa Nichols!

Visit www.AbundanceNowOnline.com to download them FREE . . . then begin enjoying, expanding, and enhancing your abundant life—today!

Abundance Now FREE Live Training Event—See Lisa Nichols live and in person in a city near you! Enjoy a full day of inspiration, learning, and transformation as Lisa helps you define your best life, then gives you the steps and strategies for achieving it. Events are held in cities around the country, so visit www.AbundanceNow Online.com to register FREE as a reader of this book.

Abundance Now Newsletter—Stay inspired, informed, and empowered as Lisa Nichols brings you tools, tips, and strategies for creating an abundant life . . . *now.* Your very first issue includes Lisa's Personal Prosperity Assessment to help you plan your abundant new life!

"Abundant Life" Guided Visualization on Audio MP3—Sit back, relax, and begin manifesting your abundant life! Lisa Nichols will skillfully step you through this powerful visualization process, helping you "see" your abundant life as already achieved—a process that triggers the mind to take those actions and see those opportunities necessary to bring your abundant life to fruition. (Not for use while driving or operating equipment.)

"A New Definition of Abundance" Audio Course—More than just a conversation around privilege or finances, abundance is about your whole life and having it *all* more abundantly. In this unique audio course, Lisa Nichols gives you the tools to define abundance in every area of your life—on your own terms—plus she'll give you an action plan to go after the abundant, holistic life you define. She'll move you from feelings of lack, emptiness, and dissatisfaction— transforming your life into a meaningful journey that's the catalyst to live your life to the fullest. Listen in and fully flourish in the strength and power of *you*.

Register to see Lisa live, plus download your *free* tools at www .AbundanceNowOnline.com!

NO MATTER WHAT!
28 DAYS TO RESULTS!

In just 28 days, for a dollar a day, what would it mean to you to: Get Motivated, Shift Your Mindset, Achieve Results? This is perfect for anyone who wants to jumpstart their personal development journey and is excited to create a life full of abundance and joy - with a simple yet powerful goal-setting program.

It is designed with simplicity in mind, as too much too fast can simply overwhelm you and make you feel destined to not reach your goals.

As you go through the 28 days, you will receive targeted, actionable lessons and exercises curated to create momentum and new opportunities and to help you reach your specified goal. You can expect to not only challenge some of your current belief systems, but also to break through to a new level of awareness that will inspire you to continue to live this way.

It's time to start living and winning at this game called life!

iAM Motivated APP

Wake up motivated every day, with Lisa Nichols as your pocket coach, from the convenience of your mobile device!

How you start your day defines and sets the tone for the rest of your day's outcomes and productivity. The iAM Motivated app was designed by Lisa to help inspire and motivate you to have the best day ever, one of the easiest ways for you to nurture your life goals in less than 3 minutes a day!

Features of the iAM Motivated App:

- Schedule reminders that are automatically loaded up for you every day
- Ability to make "favorite" your top 5 tips from Lisa so you can go back and watch/listen anytime
- Full video of Lisa giving you your daily boost of motivation

It's the easiest and most convenient way to be coached by Lisa Nichols every day. Download to your mobile device now.

SPEAK & WRITE TO MAKE MILLIONS

Every year hundreds of aspiring and seasoned entrepreneurs from all around the world meet in sunny Southern California to attend the premier conference for speakers, authors, and business owners who want to build their brand to the next level.

At Speak & Write to Make Millions, the Motivating the Masses coaching team shares the step-by-step system Lisa used to grow her speaking business into a multimillion-dollar brand: From how Lisa became a featured teacher in the hit movie, "*The Secret*," to how she landed appearances on several high-profile media outlets and t.v. shows including the *Oprah Winfrey Show*, *Extra*, and *Larry King Live*, they hold nothing back.

WORLD CLASS SPEAKERS ALLIANCE

www.MotivatingtheMasses.com/wcsa

There are 2,000+ speaking engagements available every year. That means people around the world are looking for YOU - to inspire, empower, and move crowds with your amazing story. But to land those gigs, you need the FOUNDATION, TOOLS, TRAINING, ACCESS, and CONNECTIONS that will help you grow your speaking business to phenomenal levels.

So let's not waste another second.

This program is the most comprehensive training for Speakers available – using powerfully effective methods to help you seed, serve + sell to your audience, AND get you connected and on stages and/or in front of your ideal client NOW.

You will:

- Open yourself up to media notice, and create raving fans wherever you go
- Learn the steps to turn your fans into paying, in-it-for-the-long haul clients, buyers, or students
- Tell the stories that connect with your audience on the deepest level, so you can turn your amazing message into a transformational juggernaut
- Shift away from the old school approach to a successful speaking business (that may no longer be serving you)
- Shift into a never-before-shared speaking and marketing approach for the new school of this biz – where being different is just as crucial as being known

Decide to be a World Class Speaker today.

ABOUT THE AUTHORS

Lisa Nichols is one of the world's most-requested motivational speakers. She's a media personality and corporate CEO whose global platform has reached and served nearly 30 million people. Moving from a struggling single mom on public assistance to a millionaire entrepreneur, Lisa's courage and determination have inspired fans worldwide and helped untold audiences break through to discover their own untapped talents and limitless potential.

As Founder and Chief Executive Officer of Motivating The Masses, Inc.—one of the country's only publicly traded personal and business development training companies—Lisa has helped develop workshops and programs that have transformed the lives of men and women and altered the trajectory of businesses throughout the country and across the world.

Lisa is also a bestselling author of six books. Her seventh book, *Abundance Now*, from HarperCollins, was released in January 2016. *Abundance Now* continues Lisa's journey with her fans, providing a clear and practical blueprint for personal success direct from the life experiences of its beloved author. *Abundance Now* is the eagerly anticipated follow-up to Lisa's *New York Times* bestseller *No Matter What!*

Today, fans worldwide revere Lisa for her singular gift in teaching people how to master the accomplishment of unfathomable goals and to tap their limitless potential. Lisa has appeared on numerous television shows including *Oprah, The Today Show, The Steve Harvey Show,* and *Extra*— just to name a few. She's also celebrated for the impact she has made on the lives of teens. Through Lisa's nonprofit foundation, Motivating the

Teen Spirit, she has touched the lives of 211,650 teens, prevented over 3,800 teen suicides, supported 2,500 high school dropouts in returning to school, and has helped thousands of teens reunite with their families.

Among the prestigious awards and honors bestowed on Lisa for her extensive work are the Humanitarian Award from the Republic of South Africa, the Ambassador Award, and the Legoland Foundation's Heart of Learning Award. The City of Henderson, Nevada, named November 20 as Motivating the Teen Spirit Day and the City of Houston, Texas, named May 9 as Lisa Nichols Day for her dedication to service, philanthropy, and healing.

Lisa lives, plays, and works in the greater San Diego, California, area and on stages around the world—working alongside her world-class team committed to Motivating the Masses.

Janet Switzer exemplifies the personal achievement and professional accomplishment that come from applying these proven principles of success.

At age 19, she began her professional career as a campaign specialist for a member of the United States Congress, and by age 29 had built an international publishing venture with over $10 million in assets.

Today, she's the revenue strategist of choice for many of the world's top celebrity entrepreneurs. Her high-profile clients have included Jack Canfield, originator of the *Chicken Soup for the Soul* book series; motivational speaker Les Brown; underground business icon Jay Abraham; and tapping-therapy psychologist Dr. Roger Callahan, among many others.

She's the *New York Times* bestselling coauthor and marketing strategist behind *The Success Principles: How to Get from Where You Are to Where You Want to Be*—the #1 self-help classic written with Jack Canfield and published in 30 languages. Plus, she's the #1 bestselling author of *Instant Income: Strategies That Bring in the Cash for Small Businesses, Innovative Employees, and Occasional Entrepreneurs* from McGraw-Hill Publishers.

For over 25 years, Janet has also been at the forefront of helping business owners learn, grow, and profit. Her books, newsletters, and training courses are read and used by entrepreneurs in more than 80 countries. And her popular small-business column is syndicated to more than 220 media outlets worldwide. She's counseled thousands of companies and solo entrepreneurs on the systems and strategies that bring reliable, predictable cash flow.

Miss Switzer is a thought-provoking speaker at industry conferences around the world. She has traveled to nearly every continent speaking to entrepreneurs, independent sales professionals, corporate employees, and industry association members, and her training events are available throughout North America and Asia Pacific.

She has been a widely published journalist and is a former columnist with Nightingale-Conant's *AdvantEdge* magazine and *Training Magazine*. A popular media personality seen by more than 75 million viewers, she has been featured in the *Wall Street Journal, USA Today,* the *New York Times, Time Magazine, Entrepreneur Magazine, MSNBC, ABC Radio Network, Speaker Magazine,* and countless other publications and radio and television shows.

Miss Switzer's consulting division helps establish revenue-generation systems within small companies, while her publishing company offers tools and training courses that help business owners focus their operations and staff on bringing in the cash. Visit www.JanetSwitzer.com.

ACKNOWLEDGMENTS

This book, like everything else of great importance that I have created in my life, is the result of the dedicated efforts of many people. I extend my heartfelt thanks to:

Janet Switzer, whose expertise, guidance, and sheer ability to produce under incredible deadlines made this book possible. From introducing me to my literary agent to producing the book proposal to stepping me through the publishing process—and helping to create a book I'm so very proud of—you have been a true professional. Thank you, Janet, for your smart insights and long hours spent in the original conception and planning of this book; the easy-breezy interviews that captured my thoughts, stories, and training content; the writing of a manuscript that so eloquently presented my teachings; your work on AbundanceNowOnline.com and the book's marketing campaigns; and for keeping me always focused on serving the world. You are an amazing woman and I treasure you!

Steve Harvey, whose friendship and support in adding a foreword to this book made the message of abundance come alive for readers. You are a brilliant businessman and a talented orator. I admire your work ethic and your commitment to family. Thank you for reaching out to me so that I could be blessed by your friendship. I look forward to serving the world beside you.

Stephen Hanselman, my literary agent. You are more than an agent. You were involved with this book from start to finish with savvy advice, keen editorial insights, and superb guidance. Thank you for convincing me to broaden my message so more people could benefit, and for recommending a unique way to bring it to the world. Not only did you become a champion for my message, but you inspired me to serve the world in a much bigger way. I'm grateful for your dedication to educating and uplifting humanity. Thank you for joining me on this journey.

Carrie Thornton, my brilliant and supportive editor at Dey Street Books. Thank you for your enthusiasm and boundless energy for this project, for your uncanny attention to detail, and for smoothing the process of bringing *Abundance Now* to readers everywhere. Your thoughtful dedication to inspiring others through the written word has, in turn, inspired me. Thank you from the bottom of my heart for your partnership and for your friendship.

Michael Barrs, who oversaw the marketing of this book. I appreciate your unflagging efforts to expand the reach of this message through countless channels and markets. You are smart and insightful. Thank you. Lynn Grady, senior vice president and publisher of Dey Street Books, who championed *Abundance Now* at HarperCollins and who created rousing support for it with your amazing sales team. Thanks for the work you do to bring important educational and inspirational content to readers everywhere. I'm honored to refer to you as my partner in publishing.

Laurie McGee, who copyedited the manuscript. You have a keen eye and impressive attention to detail. Thanks for a fantastic job.

Amanda Kain, who designed the book cover and jacket. It's beautiful!

Zyaire Porter, who shot the cover photo. I had a blast in the studio. Thanks for a fun day and a superb set of photos! A very special thank you also goes out to my stylist Janelle Carothers, to makeup artist Tavia Gainer, to hair stylist Curtis Venters, and to Lakeisha Michelle. All of you worked tirelessly—with great energy and upbeat attitudes—to make the essence of me come alive in the studio. You truly are the bomb squad!

Heidi Richter, Kendra Newton, Shannon Plunkett, Andrea Molitor, Sean Newcott, and all the other professionals at HarperCollins who were instrumental in producing this book, the e-book, and the audio book—and getting them into the hands of readers everywhere. You are so good at what you do. I was delighted to work with you.

My son, Jelani Nichols, for being my gentle, calm reminder to breathe. In you, God me gave the most perfect child. Your grace, ease, and compassion toward others is inspiring to watch. I am truly grateful to have you in my life—not only as my child, but as my friend.

My mother, father, grandmother, and brother. You each serve as a fueling station for me. When I stop by and share either a quick moment or an all-out slumber party, I leave your presence feeling rejuvenated, inspired, grounded, and ready to serve the world again. You are my rocks. You give me far more than any words on paper can ever express. The world gets that best of me because I have a tribe like you.

Isiko Cooks, thank you for your friendship and inspiration. You and I have a beautiful son together and I appreciate how we have been intentional under our unique circumstances to parent as one voice. Thank you for working hard to maintain a place in Jelani's life and in my life. You are a good man.

Susie Carder, President and COO of Motivating the Masses, Inc., but most of all my sister-friend, for your vision of what this book could do for our community. You took up the torch and jumped in with enthusiasm. You are an awesome friend, an incredible coach, a visionary, and a force of nature. I'm constantly in awe of your wisdom, your tenacity, and your willingness to play big even when we are scared. Words simply cannot express my gratitude and appreciation for what you have done for me professionally and personally. I admire you.

Alex Henderson, thank you for your calm demeanor in the midst of my whirlwind life. You're a true gentleman.

Margaret Packer, my sister-friend, prayer partner, armor bearer, coach, and executive manager at Motivating the Masses, Inc., for your constant support as the company grew and our work expanded. You have constantly reminded me of the Divine assignment on my life to serve and heal. And you remain unwilling to allow me ever to think that the demand upon my life is greater than God's supply. For every time you have picked me up, dusted me off, and sent me out to serve the world again, I say thank you for trusting me. Our lives are both barely recognizable as a result. I love you, sis. To my MTM team: Tia Ross, Director of Motivating the Teen Spirit, for your tireless dedication and commitment to the most important aspect of my business—the children. Your caring and devoted advancement of my original work with hundreds of thousands of teens shows up in so many ways. You've not only been there from the beginning, but you've also kept the flame alive and expanded the program with grace, ease, and assurance. I appreciate you!

Jen Kem, MTM's Global Marketing and Brand Officer and my sister from another mister, your brilliance and excitement feeds my soul. Your creativity and vision for what's possible wakes me up early with great joy and anticipation. Nicole Roberts-Jones, Director of Development, for the commitment and passion you bring to every single project you touch. You are a Godsend who crossed my path twenty-plus years ago, and I knew then that we simply had to work together. Thank you for coming home. CeCe Clark, Director of Global Sales, for your unyielding tenacity and unwavering commitment to truly touch and serve the world. You are the sugar and the honey in the iced tea.

My ever-expanding team—including Shayna Rattler, Director of Corporate Development, and Sean Smith, Director of Coaching and Training—for instantly upleveling our game when you showed up to play. Your sense of excellence and work-integrity have been awesome to witness. Matt Gil, Community Fulfillment Specialist, Carla Rivas, Event Coordinator, and Virginia Andrade, Administrative Assistant, your demonstrable love and care for the work that we do, for our clients that trust us, and for the role that we play in so many lives. Your job is, in many cases, the most challenging of all because you have to be the MOST consistent in your daily representation of the brand, no matter what! Thank you for owning it like it's yours, because it is!

To my entire MTM team who supported the customers of Motivating the Masses, Inc., and kept the machine running while I was on the road and was involved with this book. I'm so proud of the professionalism and heart you bring to your work as you serve our community. You rock the world every day. Thank you.

And finally, thanks to the assisting teams and all the participants in my training events over the past two decades for sharing their dreams, struggles, and victories with me. Your passion to achieve and desire to change your lives is what continues to inspire me every day. Special thanks to my Global Leaders and friends for stepping out of your comfort zones and being role models the world can look up to. Your hearts and souls are woven throughout the pages of this book. This is *our* book. Thank you for believing in me—and believing in yourselves.

PERMISSIONS

Steve Harvey, Reprinted by permission.

Jelani Nichols, Reprinted with permission.

Kym Yancey, Reprinted by permission.

Sandra Yancey, Reprinted by permission.

Alyse McConnell, Reprinted with permission.

Susie Carder, Reprinted with permission.

Marilee Sprenger, Reprinted with permission.

TeeJ Mercer, Reprinted with permission.

Michael James, Reprinted with permission.

CeCe Clark, Interviewed by author.

Cynthia James, author/speaker. Reprinted with permission.

Ann Jaffe, Reprinted with permission.

Tia Ross, Reprinted with permission.

Nadia Vincent, Reprinted with permission.

Dr. Judy Hinojosa, Reprinted with permission.

Stacey Schufford, Reprinted with permission.

Margaret Packer, Reprinted with permission.

Pamela Loving, Reprinted with permission.

ABUNDANCE NOW LIVE
EVENT TICKET
A $597 Value

Lisa Nichols and Motivating the Masses invite you to attend
an Abundance Now Live event, as a complimentary participant.
To register and get more information, go to
www.AbundanceNowOnline.com/events and enter
information about your purchase.

This offer is open to anyone who purchases a new edition
of *Abundance Now* by Lisa Nichols and Janet Switzer from an
authorized retailer or directly from HarperCollins.com.
Original proof of purchase is required.

This offer is limited to the Abundance Now Live events only,
and your registration for the event is subject to availability
of space and/or changes to program schedule. A limited
number of complimentary tickets will be available for each
Abundance Now Live event, and will be distributed on a first-
come, first-served basis. This is a limited time offer and all
information about these events will be updated regularly at
www.AbundanceNowOnline.com/events and are subject to
cancellation or to end based on demand. The value of this free
admission is approximately $597 as of November 2015, based
on the cost of comparable Motivating the Masses courses.
While participants will be responsible for their travel and other
costs, participants are under no additional financial obligation
whatsoever to Motivating the Masses or Lisa Nichols. Motivating
the Masses reserves the right to refuse admission to anyone it
believes may disrupt the event, and to remove from the prem-